LATINO SMALL BUSINESSES
AND THE AMERICAN DREAM

LATINO
SMALL BUSINESSES
AND THE AMERICAN
DREAM

COMMUNITY SOCIAL WORK PRACTICE
& ECONOMIC AND SOCIAL DEVELOPMENT

MELVIN DELGADO

COLUMBIA UNIVERSITY PRESS
NEW YORK

COLUMBIA UNIVERSITY PRESS

Publishers Since 1893

New York   Chichester, West Sussex

Copyright © 2011 Columbia University Press

All rights reserved

Library of Congress Cataloging-in-Publication Data

Delgado, Melvin.

   Latino small businesses and the American dream : community social work practice and economic and social development / Melvin Delgado.

      p. cm.

   Includes bibliographical references and index.

   ISBN 978-0-231-15088-0 (cloth : alk. paper) — ISBN 978-0-231-15089-7 (pbk. : alk. paper) — ISBN 978-0-231-52178-9 (e-book)

   1. Hispanic American business enterprises.   2. Small business—United States.   3. Social service—United States.   I. Title.

   HD62.7.D455 2011

   338.6'4208968073—dc22

2011007619

References to Internet Web sites (URLs) were accurate at the time of writing. Neither the author nor Columbia University Press is responsible for URLs that may have expired or changed since the manuscript was prepared.

TO
**DENISE, LAURA,
& BARBARA**

CONTENTS

Preface xi

PART 1
SETTING THE CONTEXT FOR SMALL BUSINESSES IN THE UNITED STATES 1

1. INTRODUCTION 3

>   Social Work and Small Businesses 6
>   Urban Transformation (Place Making), Latino-Style 10
>   The Latino Community and Small Businesses 14
>   Definitions of Key Terms 22
>   Tensions Related to Small Business 25
>   Ambivalence of the Social Work Profession 26
>   Socially Responsible Corporations 28

2. LATINO DEMOGRAPHICS AND GEOGRAPHIC DISPERSAL 31

>   The Role of Demographics 33
>   Demographic Profiles of Three Cities 54

3. RACIAL AND ETHNIC SMALL BUSINESSES
IN THE UNITED STATES 64

Scholarly Attention to Ethnic Businesses 67
The Informal Economy 69
Theories on Ethnic and Racial Small Businesses 71
Community Economic Development: Business Profiles 77
Factors Facilitating and Hindering Business Creation 80
Typology of Small Businesses 88
A Life-Cycle Perspective 90

4. LATINO SMALL BUSINESSES AND COMMUNITY
ECONOMIC DEVELOPMENT 93

Latino Small Businesses 94
Latino Banks and Banking 99
Characteristics of Latino Small Businesses by Sector 102
Latino Newcomers and Small Businesses 110
Business Survival Rates 112
Profile of Latino Small Business Owners 113
Naming of Small Businesses 118
Social Interactions and Relationships 119
Community Service: Funerals 122
Income and Wealth 124
Acculturation 131
Marketing to Latinos 132
Community Development Perspectives 134
Latino Economic Development 136
Tourism 138
Latin American Businesses in the United States 140
Health Insurance Coverage 141
National Economic Vicissitudes 143

PART 2
COMMUNITY SOCIAL WORK VALUES AND ANALYTICAL FRAMEWORK 147

5. VALUES, PRINCIPLES, AND ANALYTICAL FRAMEWORK 149
Values 150
Practice Principles 153
Importance of an Analytical Framework 156

Analytical–Interactional Dimension   157
Stages   157

6. INDICATORS OF SUCCESS FOR LATINO SMALL BUSINESSES   163
    Social Indicators   164
    Framework and Indicators of Latino Small Business
        Success   169
    Need for Future Research   179

7. IMPLICATIONS FOR THE SOCIAL WORK PROFESSION   182
    Community Social Work Support   183

Epilogue   193
References   201
Index   261

PREFACE

WRITING A BOOK on Latino small businesses is similar to putting together a jigsaw puzzle that has hundreds of pieces without having the picture on the box as a guide. Although from the beginning I had a picture in my mind of what I wanted this book to look like, it was neither crystal clear nor highly detailed. Putting a puzzle together invariably involves both high expectations and an awareness of the difficult path that lies ahead. Similarly, in writing this book, with its wide-ranging subject matter, there were both ups and downs: I experienced moments of joy when I would stumble on a new piece of information that I had not imagined existed or would see a topic in a totally different light, but there were also times when I made little progress. Nevertheless, I always hoped that the next day I would uncover a key piece that would help me complete the puzzle.

Latinos have been the subject of numerous scholarly undertakings, but most studies have either ignored or only touched on the topic of Latino businesses. This book attempts to bridge the gap between knowledge of Latino small businesses and the field of economic and social development by illustrating how to identify and mobilize community resources to provide services to Latinos. Latino businesses can be supported in a manner that is culturally competent, thus opening up numerous possibilities for collaboration between the Latino community and community social workers and their sponsoring organizations. Cross-sector collaboration among public, private, and civic organizations and businesses takes on a critical dimension in urban communities of color, helping to increase the likelihood of a synergistic effect by encouraging creativity, learning, and innovation (Nowak 2007).

The importance of collaborative partnerships across conventional and unconventional spheres, as I advocate in this book, is summarized in the charge put forth regarding Latinos in California: "What now? California needs a plan to carry out the short-term goals, one that can help unleash the economic potential of Latinos. The reality is that no one institution by itself can achieve the long-term goal. Cooperation is needed from many different agencies and institutions. These institutions include, but are not limited to, churches, schools, universities, community colleges, mediums of communication, and philanthropic agencies" (Lopez, Ramirez, and Rochin 1999:40).

This book addresses six interrelated goals that merge theory, qualitative and quantitative data, history, and case illustrations to bring to life the critical role that Latino small businesses play in their community and how community social work can help to shape these institutions. These goals are:

- to ground the reader in the function of ethnic, urban-based enterprises;
- to explore the potential role of Latino businesses in providing a range of social, health-related, and economic support;
- to illustrate, through the use of examples, how community and economic techniques can be applied to business creation, sustenance and community social work practice;
- to provide an updated picture of the economic role that Latinos play in the United States and draw implications for how Latino businesses can continue to grow and influence social, economic, and political aspects of urban communities;
- to examine Latino demographic trends and their implications for community development; and
- to show, through review of the literature and use of case illustrations, how community social workers can interface with these establishments in ways that fulfill the mission of social work.

I am sure that some of these goals are more attractive to the reader than others. This is quite natural. My favorite analogy is that of a tool box. Community social workers work with many different tools. Some tools are preferred over others, and workers may be more adept at using particular ones.

Nevertheless, we never have the luxury of abandoning tools because that would severely limit our ability to start and complete a job. The same can be said for the goals listed above. These goals do not exist in isolation from one another or tap a set of values that are antithetical to one another. They are essentially a complete set that can and should be used in combination.

This book brings together many elements I have written about in the more than 125 peer-reviewed articles and chapters and 19 books I have published over the years, yet it is distinct in character. I often decide to write a book on a particular subject when the subject matter inspires me and I conclude that there is no other book on the subject. Mind you, it is not that I am afraid of competition. Instead, I believe that the subject matter is too important to have been overlooked from a book perspective. Despite an upsurge in Latino scholarship, there is little competition for this book from a business, social science, or social work perspective. This is both an opportunity and a sad commentary on the state of knowledge concerning this dimension of the Latino community in the United States.

This is not to say that there are no books on how to market to Latinos (Perkins 2004; Korzenny & Korzenny 2005; Sato 2006; Faura 2006). In fact, there seems to be an endless supply on how dominant-culture corporations can better understand the Latino market, with plenty of advice on how to analyze segments and surmount cultural barriers, and the best methods to advertise to this growing market. This book is not about those topics.

A clear vision of who should benefit from reading a book is often one of the initial considerations in writing it. I conceived of this book as a supplemental textbook for a variety of disciplines, with social work (planning and program development), rehabilitation, community psychology, education, urban planning, Latino/ethnic studies, and business-related courses standing out as the best homes for it. Community development centers and other institutions interested in racial and ethnic small businesses may find the book useful, as may the broader community. However, the primary audience will be community social work scholars and practitioners.

A word of caution is in order concerning the term "Latino" and the multiple groups and subgroups that comprise this construct. Montero-Sieburth (2007:82) raises an alert when addressing Mexicans in New England that also applies to this book: "the use of the monolithic term Mexican hides much of the variations that exist, the idiosyncrasies of each subgroup and the sense of survival, stability, and the advancements that Mexicans are experiencing. . . . It is the homogeneity and at the same time the heterogeneity of Mexicans that helps us understand their dual cultural and future citizenship existence."

I make every effort in this book to stress similarities and differences within the Latino community. Data gathered by governmental organizations rarely capture the intricacies found within the Latino community; in this book I discuss Latino groups individually whenever possible in the hope of doing justice to the achievements and challenges they face in the United States. Further, I strive to be as geographically inclusive as possible, although my East Coast background does wield considerable influence on the subject matter.

The practice of community social work continues the progressive evolution of the profession into new and exciting arenas. Community social work practice has historically been characterized by its embrace of social justice values and its desire to venture into uncharted areas. This book represents one of the latest efforts at carrying out this mission. Future generations of community social workers will venture into other uncharted territories to fulfill the promise of social work. Topics such as festivals, parades, naming of businesses, and the warmth and sincerity of Latino small business owners' relations with their customers and the broader community will emerge and take center stage.

In writing this book, I mulled over the desirability of devoting an entire chapter to one case study, as I customarily do, since doing so serves the valuable purpose of crystallizing for the reader central themes found in the literature and in my practice. In this book I decided not to do so because of my extensive use of case illustrations of Latino businesses throughout the United States. Eschewing an in-depth case study freed up valuable pages for theoretical and research content of great importance for better presenting and analyzing the material. I hope that this decision has not made it difficult for the reader to envision a role for social work in creating and fostering Latino small businesses.

Finally, I wish to acknowledge the assistance provided by Lisa Lofaso, BUSSW research assistant, and the insights and suggestions made by the anonymous external reviews of this book.

At the completion of a book, like a puzzle, it is necessary to sit back, marvel at the accomplishment, and enjoy the final picture. I sincerely hope that readers enjoy this book, although I admit that "marveling" may be a stretch.

LATINO SMALL BUSINESSES
AND THE AMERICAN DREAM

PART 1

▪▫▪▫▪▫▪▫▪▫▪▫▪▫▪▫▪▫▪▫▪▫▪▫▪▫▪▫▪▫▪▫▪▫▪▫▪▫▪▪

SETTING THE CONTEXT FOR
SMALL BUSINESSES IN THE UNITED STATES

On April 10, 2006, Latino immigrants and their allies took to the streets in more than 100 cities throughout the United States to advocate for comprehensive immigration reform.... Although the policy impact of this mobilization remains to be seen, one thing is perfectly clear: The cartographics of settlement for Latino and Latina immigrants have shifted in recent decades, and as Latinos filled the streets in protest, they mapped these shifts onto the landscapes of cities and towns throughout the United States.

—M. A. Vasquez, C. E. Seales, and M. F. Marquardt,
New Latino Destinations

1

INTRODUCTION

> The entrepreneurship literature appearing to date in social science and business journals has comprehensively described self-employment and small business ownership among African American and Asian immigrants. Surprisingly absent is a similarly comprehensive literature analyzing entrepreneurship among Hispanic Americans. Beyond sociological studies of Cuban self-employed in Miami, scholars have rarely explored this topic.
>
> —T. Bates, W. E. Jackson, and J. H. Johnson, *Advancing Research on Minority Entrepreneurship*

THIS BOOK SEEKS to fill an important gap in the scholarly literature on Latino small-business ownership in the United States and to do so from the perspective of community social work practice. It pays close attention to the interplay of social, economic, and political forces shaping small businesses and their relationships with the Latino community in urban centers. The current socioeconomic conditions and fate of urban communities are worthy of attention by national policy makers, as well as practitioners and academics, and the ultimate success of Latino-owned businesses is tied to the fate of the nation's cities given the high representation of such businesses in urban areas.

The nation's cities, and more specifically its inner-city communities, are at a critical crossroads. People of color—primarily Latinos, African Americans, and Asian Americans—are increasingly migrating to urban centers, which continue to attract both documented and undocumented newcomers to the United States. Unfortunately, the 2008 presidential campaign did little to highlight the importance of improving urban policies and understanding how these policies affect the well-being of urban residents.

Cities have historically played key roles in the social and economic development of the nation and in the process have absorbed millions of immigrants since the country's inception. It is no accident that the majority of immigrants have historically settled in urban areas and, with some notable exceptions, continue to do. Yet urban areas and the population groups attracted to them have generally not been part of the discourse on the nation's social and economic prosperity. This may in part be a result of the increased racial and ethnic composition of urban centers. I will address this topic in greater detail in chapter 2.

The emphasis placed on small businesses during the 2008 U.S. presidential campaign attests to the large role, both symbolic and actual, that these businesses play at the local and state levels (Shuman 2000, 2007; Audretsch 2002). In 2005 small businesses accounted for an estimated 80 percent of all inner-city jobs (McQueen, Weiser, and Burns 2007). In addition, they provide approximately 50 percent of the nation's gross domestic product (Conte 2008). Unfortunately, however, they have historically taken a backseat to big business: "From colonial times to the present, small business has been a dynamic force of American life. However, the dominance of big business has often overshadowed the significance of small business. Furthermore, our love affair with the entrepreneur as a self-reliant individual, epitomizing the American spirit, has sometimes obscured the complexity underlying small business success. The time for underestimating the importance of small business is over" (Alvarez 2009:72).

Conte's (2008:1) observations about America's fascination with small businesses highlights the integral part they play in the nation's economic fabric: "America has long revered small businesses for not only building the economy but also bolstering democracy. . . . Whether small businesses create a disproportionate number of jobs is not clear, but they clearly have influenced big businesses, which have adopted the flexible practices of small companies."

Small businesses are responsible for creating two-thirds to three-quarters of all jobs in the United States and furnish 44.5 percent of the private payroll (Michna and Bednarz 2006). Such enterprises represent 99 percent of inner-city businesses, generate 60–80 percent of new jobs annually, and provide half of all private payrolls in U.S. cities (Jones 2007–08). In essence, there is nothing "small" about small businesses in general and in urban communities of color in particular. However, the economic importance of small businesses often overshadows their social significance.

The relationship between community economic and social development has transformed the concept of entrepreneurship from an exclusive focus on economic value to include a spotlight on the profound social implications for communities and for previously undervalued subgroups. As I explain later in this book, the merger of social and economic interests has created a third perspective, that of Latino community social enterprises. Community social work practice provides social work with the requisite paradigms and opportunities to make important contributions in this area. Although this book is specific to Latinos, the implications extend beyond this one community to affect other communities of color as well.

The concept of entrepreneurship has also been broadened to encompass businesses that historically have not been considered in any serious discussion of the topic (Garcia 2004). Venkatesh (2006) typifies the expansion of this concept by vividly illustrating an urban underworld in Chicago that consists of informal, unregulated economic activity, largely unrecognized by the outside community. This economic activity taps into an entrepreneurial spirit that is vibrant and worthy of greater attention (Dickerson 2002).

The informal economy looms large in many urban communities of color, arguably no more so than in Latino communities. Jones (2007), for example, found that Latino-owned small businesses contribute significantly to the economy of the state of Washington. Jones estimates that unlicensed, informal Latino-owned businesses number between 10,774 and 12,826, with total employees ranging from 15,895 to 17,947, and annual sales from $1.62 billion to $1.94 billion. Nevertheless, gathering data on the Latino informal economy can be arduous: "A scarcity of data in researching many Latino self-employment activities such as babysitting, lawn service provider, day laborer, maid, and seasonal cultural food vendor presents a challenge for researchers. This may indicate there is a higher self-employment rate among Latinos than the official data suggest" (Robles 2006:244.) The field of social work is in an excellent position to help document the social and economic roles these establishments play in the Latino community.

Urban communities in the United States, including communities of color, with absent indigenous business owners have often been equated with colonialism (Chinyelu 1999). From this perspective, the selling of goods and services by owners from outside the community leads to prices and quality that reflect the subordinate status of the community. Nevertheless, the potential contribution of small businesses to economic development has been viewed rather narrowly, partly because economists have mostly overlooked such enterprises. The potential contribution of these businesses to community transformation goes far beyond economics, however, reaching well into the social and political spheres (Contreras 2004).

Many urban small businesses are unregulated, unreported, and untaxed, or simply off the books (Venkatesh 2006). However, their informal nature does not diminish the important economic and social roles that they play in the life of inner cities or their engagement of population groups that, because of their characteristics and life experiences, have been pushed to the margins (Losby et al. 2002; Alderslade, Talmage, and Freeman 2006). Small businesses, for example, have emerged as possible sources of employment for those with histories of criminal activity (Delgado, forthcoming).

Not surprisingly, the urban informal economy consists largely of people of color, including documented and undocumented newcomers, and as a result it plays an influential role in urban communities with a sizable concentration of these groups (Turnovsky 2004; Yamamoto 2006). The largely invisible qualities associated with informal economies make these businesses less well-known to the world outside the immediate community, but no less important to those owning and receiving services and products from these businesses. The informal economy is embedded in the fabric of a community and helps to fill a niche that would otherwise go unfilled. It is this embeddedness that gives life to such establishments. Lyons and Snoxell (2005) argue that marketplace social capital is a critical element of the informal economy.

SOCIAL WORK AND SMALL BUSINESSES

There are many ways to view ethnic and racial small businesses, but the social and health perspective is rarely employed. "Civic-minded capitalism" merges the importance of an economic bottom line with social values related to a community's well-being (Brush et al. 2007). Turcotte and Sika (2008:50) introduce the construct of social capital as a means of grounding a relationship between small businesses and the nonprofit sector, with direct implications for social work practice:

> Increasingly the notion of strengthening a community's economic base is being framed in terms of the language of social capital. Community development efforts increasingly adopted the language of social capital as a way to understand what communities must do to prosper. . . . Although disagreements remain about the exact nature of social capital, it is generally described as civic engagement, as formal and informal civic structures such as schools, neighborhood associations, and churches.

Estabrook et al. (2005), in a rare study of grocery stores and social capital, find that these neighborhood institutions often play important roles in fostering social capital, particularly when other forms of community assets are in limited supply. Similarly, de Haan and Zoomers (2005) advance the construct of "livelihoods" to capture conventional assets as well as social and human capital.

Developing small businesses and increasing business networks can also play prominent roles in advancing community social capital. Kay (2006) argues that social capital can be effective in uniting socioeconomic and community development. Westlund and Nilsson (2005), however, raise significant methodological challenges to measuring business investment in social capital, including differentiating between formal efforts (those officially sponsored by a company) and informal efforts (those undertaken by individuals who are part of a firm but do not officially represent it).

Viewing small businesses through a community social work lens opens up new avenues for the profession to serve the marginalized communities that social workers have historically viewed as part of their mission to address. For example, both Ferguson and Xie (2008) and Ferguson and Islam (2008) report on the feasibility of a social enterprise intervention involving homeless youth in which social and economic goals are met. Holguin, Gamboa, and Hoy (2007) find that Latino and African American entrepreneurs contribute more to society than do their white, non-Latino counterparts.

Valenzuela (2006) advances the notion that Latino community development necessitates a coalition of businesses, churches, government, and community-based nonprofit organizations coming together in search of common ground. Ethnic churches have traditionally not been considered potential economic engines supporting small businesses of color in the United States. However, it is estimated that the 50,000–75,000 African American churches in the country have $2.6 billion a year in bank deposits and 19 million members (Lacho, Parker, and Carter 2005). Approximately 10 percent of these churches underwrite small businesses, and 28 percent carry out some form of community economic development program. This is a prime area for the involvement of community social work practice.

The field of social work has enjoyed a long and distinguished history since its inception over a century ago in the nation's cities. One of the reasons the field has continued to expand, in both breadth and depth, has been its willingness to venture into new arenas. The redefinition of "social work" highlights the evolving nature of the profession. Other helping professions have also undergone their own evolution and expansion and have struggled with defining their primary mission.

Why should social work or any other helping profession enter the economic arena? The World Bank (2008) provides the primary reason: "The purpose of local economic development (LED) is to build up the economic capacity of a local area to improve its economic future and the quality of life for all. It is a process by which public, business and non-governmental sector partners work collectively to create better conditions for economic growth and employment generation." This book builds on this central purpose and taps into how community social workers and other helping professions can address society's undervalued communities in innovative ways by playing an active role in creating and sustaining small businesses.

Historically, community development centers have fostered neighborhood small business development, but social service organizations have not. That has now started to change as a greater awareness of the need to support community empowerment has emerged among nonprofit organizations (Baxamusa 2008). Local small businesses help economically marginalized communities keep the money they make and reinvest it in the community (Siles et al. 2006).

Rhode Island is a good example. In 2002 that state had 3,415 Latino businesses (Grimaldi 2009), representing 11 percent of all companies in the state (Kostrzewa 2008). Progresso Latino, a small, community-based social service agency in Central Falls, Rhode Island, typifies how community social workers can reach out to the Latino community and assist them in starting and maintaining small enterprises (Pina 2004). In 2006 Progresso Latino entered into a three-way partnership with Johnson and Wales University in Providence and the Rhode Island Small Business Development Center to assist the Latino community in creating small businesses. Progresso Latino now provides residents with training programs, startup technical assistance, and information on marketing and sales.

Because of the close association between the social and economic domains, other human service organizations across the country have also started to redefine their mission to include community economic development (Delgado and Zhou 2008). The expansion of nonprofits into Latino small business development is an emerging trend (Behnke 2008). However, regardless of the business–community partnership, each model of nonprofit involvement brings with it both advantages and disadvantages to small businesses and the communities they seek to serve (Reed and Reed 2009). Venturing into new frontiers for those without formal education or training in this arena is probably one of the greatest challenges facing human service organizations.

Robles (2006:241) advances the notion that Latino wealth is created through a collaborative community effort that encompasses "self-help housing, micro-businesses, and nontraditional family savings vehicles." Joint ventures that involve subsidized housing, local economic development, and provision of social services bring with them the potential for fostering small business development (Simon 2001; Whitehead, Landes, and Nembhard 2005). As one of their roles, community social workers can act as liaisons between the community and local government to facilitate social and economic development (Cordero-Guzman 2005).

Various non-Latino community-based institutions can also help foster development of Latino small businesses. Libraries, for example, can sponsor workshops and forums on developing small companies, offer on-site business advisory services, provide business-related videos and DVDs, make available Spanish-language materials, and even help sponsor fairs to attract potential entrepreneurs and government entities with interest in fostering small business development, such as the Small Business Administration (Cohn and McDonough 2007; Guerra 2007; Milam 2008). Partnerships between community social workers and librarians are an example of the possible types of interaction and collaboration.

These and other possible joint ventures, however, require new ways of looking at partnerships between various sectors of a community and the professionals that serve them. As Montero-Sieburth and Melendez (2007:xv) recommend: "The future research agenda for Latino scholars is likely to be shaped by the need to develop more appropriate conceptual frameworks. These should be developed from an understanding of the unique past historical period and with an unflinching look at the ways in which today's institutions can respond to the new challenges."

The quest for new viewpoints, frameworks, or paradigms is never easy. However, failure to do so will ultimately shortchange both the Latino community and the social work profession. The use of Latino businesses to deliver social and health services is certainly not new. More than twenty years ago, for example, Delapa and colleagues (1990) developed their "Project Salsa" initiative as a way of working with Latino community grocery stores to promote good health.

An ecological perspective on socioeconomic development that stresses community participation has the potential to address a variety of urban problems (Semenza, March, and Bontenpo 2006). Moore and Roux (2006), for example, note that low-income communities of color have twice as many grocery stores as do white, non-Latino communities. Howard and Fulfrost (2008) remark on the potential of geographic information systems (GIS) to help locate new fruit and vegetable markets in urban areas. In North Philadelphia's Progress Plaza, this collaboration has resulted in small business ventures that have increased neighborhood accessibility to fresh fruits and vegetables in local stores (Eckholm 2007). Pothukuchi (2005) presents a case study where partnerships resulted in attracting supermarkets to inner-city neighborhoods. Raja, Ma, and Yadav (2008) take a different perspective toward community development, emphasizing the need to support small, high-quality local grocery stores rather than attract supermarkets.

Inagarni et al. (2006), like other scholars, find that the lack of grocery stores with fresh fruits, vegetables, and other healthy foods in poor urban neighborhoods increases the likelihood of residents having a high body mass index and associated health problems. Lavin (2005) notes that access to a supermarket in New York's Harlem neighborhood increases the availability of healthy foods through the allocation of more space to nutritious products and lower prices.

The Hy-Vee grocery chain in the Midwest has hired dieticians in its Latino-focused stores to advise customers on eating healthier (Longo 2009). In San Bernardino, California, a certified smart farmers market, or "mercadito," has emerged to help meet pressing health issues in the community. One event organizer tells the following story:

> Rita, an 11-year veteran with the Community Action Partnership Food Bank of San Bernardino County, is the visionary and force behind the new market. "This is not your usual farmers market. We're trying to get people to change their eating habits and encourage a healthier lifestyle," says Rita, who, at 75, is something of an Energizer Bunny herself. "When people are healthy, family life is happier," she says. Fresh locally grown produce includes tomatoes, squash, corn, avocados, onions, chilies, watermelon, cantaloupe, pineapple and mangos. Fresh tortas and grilled greaseless carnitas, as well as fresh snacking fruit, also will be available." (Nolan 2009:2)

URBAN TRANSFORMATION (PLACE MAKING), LATINO-STYLE

The demographic changes that are taking place among Latinos have been well recognized in the academic and popular spheres. As Cisneros (2009:1) notes: "Simply put, the Law of Large Numbers means that quantitative changes invariably bring forth qualitative changes." The changes related to urban centers have multiple manifestations, including an upsurge in the establishment of small businesses that cater to community needs.

The academic and popular literature offers numerous definitions of "community," encompassing multiple elements and characteristics. However, one common element in most definitions is a commitment on the part of residents to a shared history and identity, and to similar values, norms, and symbolic meanings. Urban communities have the potential to integrate physical and cultural spaces in a manner that enhances community feelings and increases the connectivity among residents (Borer 2006; Ellin 2006).

Nowak (2007:1) offers a vision of community development, or place making, that captures this book's perspective with regard to Latino business development:

> I define community development as place-making. . . . Place-making involves business, households, government and civil institutions in efforts to increase economic opportunity, the quality of public amenities and flows of capital into the built environment. Place-making is a creative process that manages a range of practical tensions: between market and civic capacities and roles; physical design and social utility; and the need to integrate the old and the new. . . . There are natural place-makers who assume—in the course of making a living—a range of civic and entrepreneurial roles that require both collaboration and self-reliance.

Engagement in community economic development by supporting small business creation brings another dimension to urban social work practice: by helping to transform urban neighborhoods, Latino enterprises can offer potential new avenues for community social work interventions. "Latinization" of a neighborhood is a multifaceted process that includes a significant role for Latino small businesses.

Creating Latino business districts that incorporate and emphasize Latino themes, such as streetscapes that include community gardens, murals, and cultural designs on stores, serves to generate diverse services that enhance social and economic values in the community (Gross 2005; Schaller and Modan 2005; Wolf 2005). The painting of culturally influenced murals on commercial establishments is one way in which commerce and culture are united in Latino communities (Delgado and Barton 1998). Merchants who employ local Latino artists beautify a neighborhood and make their businesses stand out as they integrate into the social, economic, and cultural fabric of a community (Davila 2004a). The emergence of the "Latino urban" concept reflects the experiences of Latinos in urban settings in the United States.

In a study focusing on San Francisco, Corburn and Bhatia (2007) find that incorporating small businesses into community rezoning is just as important as creating open spaces and community centers in reducing health disparities among residents. Low's (2000) assessment of the role of the plaza in Latino culture and the interplay of space and culture illustrates the multifaceted dimensions of Latino communities. The plaza being developed in East Palo Alto, California, for example, includes structural settings such as a church, residential housing, businesses, and centers of government. To create a true Latino Plaza, however, strong relationships and a common social center must also be developed (Wildflower Institute 2003).

Estrada's (2006:7) vivid historical account of the Olvera Street Mexican marketplace in Los Angeles illustrates the merging of culture and business as critical components in creating a Latino community: "Whatever terms contemporary critics may use to describe this little street—'commercialized,' 'romanticized,' or 'tourist trap'—the fact remains that on no other street in Los Angeles are the layers of history and the stories of real people unveiled as they are on Olvera Street." Olvera Street's marketplace and plaza play both a social and an economic role by serving Latino community needs as well as annually drawing approximately one million tourists to the area.

The Latino preference for compact neighborhoods, large public spaces, and the sense of community that is fostered by plazas is highlighted in these remarks by an urban California Latino resident: "'I grew up in Mexico. We had a traditional urban square and plaza where everything is happening,' says Mario Chavez-Marquez, 31, who lives in one of downtown Santa Ana's new loft apartments. 'To me, it made sense to move back to the center, closer to my job. Now I can walk to a supermarket'" (quoted in El Nasser 2005:1). Marske's (2008) research on Atlanta's Plaza Fiesta shopping center reveals its influence in helping the Atlanta Latino community develop a cultural and geographic identity. Mendez (2005) argues that Latinos prefer lifestyles that support compact cities and will actively seek to transform existing urban neighborhoods to create these types of environments. Compact cities bring a built-in consumer base that facilitates economic enterprises. The Latinization of parks and public spaces further adds to the re-creation of urban communities. Compact cities also support the Latino preference for walking. Rojas (2006) notes that in California, Latinos account for 29 percent of the population but 46 percent of all pedestrian-related accidents.

Davis (2000) is one of the first scholars to systematically address both the physical and social transformation of urban communities by Latinos, which is different from that experienced during African American and European immigration to the nation's major urban centers. Stephens (2008) also raises an interesting point when commenting on how Latinos are transforming urban areas:

> Though no single detail is enough to qualify as an entire cultural tradition, Latino urbanism rests generally on an embrace of the public realm and more intense use of public space than anything common in Anglo neighborhoods. . . . Latino neighborhoods are adorned with murals, hand-painted

storefronts, and other "do-it-yourself design interventions" [according to James Rojas]. . . . "Latinos are going to continue to take advantage of any open space that's available. . . . We come from a cultural tradition of mercados and central plazas."

In chapters 4 and 6 I address the naming and decoration of small businesses, which support this observation.

Plazas serve as focal points for many of the key elements in Latino communities, such as open space, houses of worship, and commercial establishments. Along with plazas (Arreola 2004; Smith 2004; Vazquez 2007), community gardens (Saldivar-Tanaka and Krasny 2004; Shinew, Glover, and Parry 2004), public art (Delgado 2000; Yoder and La Perriere de Gutierrez 2004), and small businesses are integral and much needed institutions in Latino neighborhoods and other communities of color.

Broadening the concept of community well-being goes beyond individuals to encompass a variety of elements, including locally owned small businesses and the physical transformation of neighborhoods. Well-being as a construct is increasingly popular as a lens to view community social, economic, and cultural development. Jordan (2007), for example, advocates the use of well-being as a measure of social work's performance in carrying out its multifaceted mission related to undervalued population groups. The idea of well-being seeks to capture social and cultural aspects of community life in addition to economic dimensions, which coincides with the use of a socially responsible philosophy to shape how Latino small business owners view the success of their businesses.

Community social work can deploy many different social intervention methods in this new arena to integrate community economic development with systematic efforts to meet a wide range of social and health needs within the community (Twelvetrees 2008). The increased popularity of viewing community economic development from the perspective of assets facilitates social work involvement in this field (Delgado 2000; Green and Haines 2008). All segments of helping professions, not just social work, have the potential to contribute substantially to this bold venture, but those with a tradition of community practice (community organizing, management, and social planning or program development) may have the greatest potential contributions to make.

Community social work has gained prominence and importance in discussions of Latino communities and other communities of color in the United States. The systematic application of theory and techniques to increasing the cultural relevance of health and social services within these communities requires careful social planning and program development. Yet the benefits of community social work practice are not restricted to particular social arenas, issues, or problems; they can apply to what many in the field consider uncharted territory, such as urban small business development and criminal justice (Sonfield 2008). The emergence of a community capacity-enhancement paradigm, discussed in chapter 5, provides a conceptual foundation from which to address myriad community issues (Delgado 2000).

THE LATINO COMMUNITY AND SMALL BUSINESSES

The Latino presence in the United States is inescapable, regardless of one's social, political, or economic perspective (Delgado 2007; Yago, Zeidman, and Abuyuan 2007). As I will explore in subsequent chapters, Latinos as a population group can be seen throughout all sectors of the country, although they predominantly reside in major urban centers. In 2004 the Latino population in this country reached 41.3 million, accounting for almost half the national growth of 2.9 million between July 2003 and July 2004 (Cohn 2007). Latinos have become the largest group of color in the nation, surpassing African Americans.

The focus on Latinos in the United States—and the emphasis in health and human services on better meeting the needs of this growing population group—has generally overlooked a dimension that is not only increasing in significance but may ultimately be a key to how well this group does in the future (Diaz 2005; National Research Council 2006). Latino small businesses, as indicated in the quote that began this chapter, have not received their due attention (Queen 2008). Lofstrom and Wang (2007) find that Latino small businesses have fared quite poorly compared with their African American counterparts in terms of scholarly attention, but the literature on small businesses is starting to pay greater attention to the social roles these institutions play. Social responsibility can lead to short-term profitability, thus benefiting the business as well as the community (Luken and Stares 2005; Brugmann and Prahalad 2007).

The emerging concept of corporate social responsibility is not limited to large corporations. Some advocates of small businesses argue that such enterprises epitomize the concept (Jenkins 2006). Marquis, Glynn, and Davis (2007) advance the idea of "community isomorphism" as a means of capturing the influence communities have in shaping the nature and extent of corporate social action. Jenkins (2006) presents a four-part framework for better understanding corporate social responsibility: (1) the nature of activities;

(2) the motivation for engagement; (3) benefits to the owner and the community; and (4) challenges encountered by both. Assessment of these elements provides helping professionals with a clearer understanding of how communities and small businesses benefit from engaging in socially responsible roles. However, Lepoutre and Heene (2006) caution that assessing the impact of small businesses on socially responsible behavior is difficult because of the many nuances and factors involved in carrying out such responsibilities. The corporate responsibility exhibited by small businesses remains firmly lodged in the owner's largess and his or her views of the virtues and responsibilities of community involvement. The role of corporate responsibility must be carefully examined within the context of each small enterprise and the community within which it is located.

The social and economic roles of Latino-owned small businesses in communities throughout the United States have generally been overlooked by researchers and other observers and, as a result, are not well understood (Hayes-Bautista 2004a; Poole and Negri 2007; Robles and Cordero-Guzman 2007; Shinnar and Young 2008). More scholarship has been produced on small business owned by other groups of color, such as Chinese Americans.

Oberle (2006:14) makes an interesting observation in comparing Latino small businesses to the pioneer outposts of the nineteenth century:

> In the Old West, general stores were the center of economic and social activity. They not only sold foodstuff, tools, clothing, and other necessary items, but they also were a point of social contact. Pioneers could meet with other local residents, send letters to family members in distant cities, and receive news from relatives who were still overseas. In early America, the typical store was an Anglo outpost on the wilderness frontier. Now, in contemporary America, Hispanic-oriented businesses are increasingly Latino outposts on the Anglo suburban frontier.

Nevertheless, small businesses owned and operated by community residents still suffer from a lack of scholarly attention (Newell et al. 2008; Puryear et al. 2008). When they are addressed, there is a tendency to lump together ethnic and racial groups and businesses, effectively limiting our understanding of the uniqueness of each group and how racial, ethnic, gender, and migratory history motivates and influences small business development (Puryear et al. 2008). This research oversight has resulted in missed opportunities for community social workers and other professionals to contribute to the creation of healthy and vibrant urban communities anchored by social and economic institutions.

South Florida's Cuban community has often been held up as a model "minority" community in terms of economic success. Peterson and Roquebert (1993) identify six external factors that have shaped this success story: (1) accessibility of suppliers, customers, and new markets; (2) ethnic economic control of an ethnically saturated internal labor market; (3) capital availability and side investments; (4) land availability; (5) social networks and living conditions; and (6) government support. Galperin's (2007) analysis of the Cuban American community in Tampa, especially its Ybor City neighborhood, illustrates these key factors and the close relationship between small business and community social development. The introduction of Cuban cigars led to the designation of the area as the "Cigar Manufacturing Capital of the World." However, the 1930s and 1940s witnessed the decline of this industry, though it has since been developed as a tourist destination because of its rich architectural history and many restaurants and stores.

The potential for economic and social transformation by small business in communities of color is poorly understood, though some research has been done on this topic. One study, by Benioff (2008), explores UCLA's Center for Community Partnerships, which has created a project to support urban public markets as engines for urban revitalization. The study looked at several public markets: Los Angeles's Mercado La Paloma and El Mercado de Los Angeles; Oakland's Swan's Market and Fruitvale Public Market; and New York's Essex Street Market and Malcolm Shabazz Harlem Market. The findings were applied to the development of the Multiethnic Public Market of East Hollywood. These markets not only foster small business creation but also attract other businesses to the area, helping to reinforce cultural traditions that are important to these communities.

Sanchez-Korroll (1983) notes that in New York it is not uncommon for Puerto Rican small business owners to establish neighborhood centers, participate as community leaders, sponsor community sports teams (Price and Whitworth 2004), and contribute money or make loans to customers in need. In addition, a Latino small business association in Rhode Island, the Rhode Island Hispanic American Chamber of Commerce, has sponsored college scholarships and blood donation campaigns (Grimaldi 2009). In chapter 4 I describe numerous examples of the contributions of Latino small business owners to the economic and social fabric of their communities.

Levitt's study of Latino small businesses in Boston further highlights the multifaceted role these establishments play in the life of a Latino community:

> If someone dies in this community, the first place they come is over here. It is like in Puerto Rico, they come over here, we pick out a big can, we make a

collection. We start first with our own employees and sometimes we collect up to $500 for any burial in the community for anybody that dies. If you go to an American store, you can't tell them to do that. They won't do that. This store is like a community institution. We are always making contributions to the poor, to the city of Boston, to funerals. It is a pleasure to me. I even go to the funerals. (1997:151)

The role of Latino small businesses in funerals is addressed in chapter 4.

When small businesses are locally owned and operated, community empowerment results. Furthermore, small establishments bring a largely untapped potential for reaching and serving a population group that is growing in significance and will continue to do so well into the century. Latinos, for example, accounted for 81 percent of the population growth in the country's one hundred largest cities in the final decade of the twentieth century (United States Hispanic Leadership 2004). The increased diversity of the Latino community compounds an already challenging environment for understanding and meeting the wide range of health and human service needs in this community (Millard and Chapa 2001; Suarez-Orozco and Paez 2002; Smith 2006).

There is a need, however, to differentiate between Latino newcomers to this country and native-born Latino entrepreneurs: "Native and foreign-born Hispanics may have different motivations to enter self-employment; for example, native-born individuals typically do not have to overcome the challenges of migration, which often involves loss of human and social capital gained abroad, such as foreign-earned credentials and an individual 'network of contacts and other business associates'" (Shinnar and Young 2008:242). Brettell and Alstatt (2007) note that some Latino immigrants must hold a job while they try to save enough money to start a business that will allow them to develop a loyal consumer base of co-ethnics and eventually leave the labor market entirely to devote themselves to their business.

Native-born Latinos generally have more education and higher levels of English language proficiency, which provide them with distinct advantages over immigrants in the labor market (Hernandez 2002; Duncan, Hotz, and Trejo 2006; Reimers 2006; Delgado 2007; Robles 2009). Stone and McQuillan (2007) argue that it is important not to put all Latinos into a general category, instead advocating for a gender/ethnicity-specific perspective. In a study of Latino immigrants and U.S.-born Latinos, Georgarakas and Tatsiramos (2009) find that both groups enter into enterprise development from a position of unemployment and are more likely to exit to employment in the labor market, with small businesses serving as an intermediate step between unemployment and employment. Thus, Latino small businesses may represent a temporary way station rather than a goal, unlike the situation for many other newcomer groups in the United States.

The continued population growth of Latinos and other groups of color—fueled by migration (generally undocumented in the case of Latinos), high birthrates, and low mortality rates—has manifested itself in dramatic increases in the number of Latinos and other ethnic groups residing in urban areas; in fact, nearly 90 percent of Latinos live in urban areas (Delgado 2007). Many, just like their counterparts for whom English is not their primary language, are relegated to barrios, although there are signs of a growing dispersal to the suburbs (Davila 2004a; St. Clair 2005). Garcia (2003:23), notes that there are consequences for being Latino in this country, "in terms of opportunities, equity, access, and rights, that transcends any specific Latino subgroup."

Waldinger's (2000) observation that newcomers have transformed the profile of small business ownership in New York can also be applied to most major urban areas of the country, such as Los Angeles (Romney 1999). High-concentration geographical areas, or zones, which provide a built-in segmented audience, have proved fertile ground for businesses owned by Latinos or other ethnic and racial groups to emerge and thrive (Tienda and Raijman 2004).

The sociological term of "ethnic enclaves" is often used to describe these communities. Galbraith, Stiles, and Rodriguez (2003), for example, find that ethnic small businesses tend to rely on ethnic enclaves more than on other sources for labor input, and startup businesses do so to a greater degree than more established businesses. Greve and Salaff (2005) stress the merits of using a structural and cultural social networks perspective to better understand ethnic economies and how they link enclaves to the mainstream economy.

Toussaint-Comeau (2008) examines the role of ethnic enclave networks in promoting immigrant self-employment, concluding that these networks play a positive role in providing alternatives to wage employment. However, ethnic enclaves are also high-concentration areas for ex-inmates, former mental patients, recovering substance abusers, and other marginalized subgroups. Valenzuela argues that Latino community economic development is possible only if immigrant and marginalized workers are part of this effort: "Economic development is a viable tool to ameliorate working poverty among Latinos, but only if mainstream economic development strategies are reconsidered to account for the growing demographic that is immigrant and the workers on the margins in contingent jobs" (2006:142).

The dramatic increase in the Latino population is considered one of the primary reasons for the growth of Latino small businesses (SITEL 2003; Diaz-Briquets 2004; Hayes-Bautista 2004b; Landa 2007; Oh 2008). Zarrugh (2007) notes that the increase in Latino small business development is a direct outgrowth of population increases in the past decade. Some Latino small businesses supply more than one kind of service; for instance, it is not unusual to find self-service laundries that double as places from which to send remittances back home (Sacchetti 2008). These establishments seek to fill unmet needs within a community.

It is estimated that 550,000 new businesses are opened every month across the United States (Landa 2007). In California, Los Angeles and Orange County have a number of Asian enclaves, such as Chinatown, Little Tokyo, Koreatown, Little Saigon, Thai Town, and Filipinotown (*Economist* 2007). Small businesses in these communities flourished as the Asian community there grew by 15 percent (to 1.7 million) between 2000 and 2005. Asian Americans in Los Angeles recently formed their own chamber of commerce as a means of giving voice to some twenty thousand small businesses (Watanabe 2008).

This does not mean, however, that tensions have not resulted from these increases. For example, the *Los Angeles Times* reports on an effort that is under way to create a "Little Bangladesh" within Koreatown:

> The proposal has angered longtime residents who have worked hard to promote the district as a Korean cultural destination and economic hub. City officials, meanwhile, worry that neither side is taking into account the full diversity of an area that is also home to many Latinos and Thai Americans, among others. More than a name is at stake. Although largely symbolic, the recognition afforded by a special district designation can help establish a community within the cultural mosaic of Southern California. . . . When noted on maps and street signs, it can also attract visitors and help local businesses. (Zavis and Knoll 2009:A8)

Koreatown is similar to Miami's Little Havana in that the composition of these two communities is not completely Korean or Cuban. Koreatown is more than 50 percent Latino (Yu et al. 2004), and the majority of Little Havana's Latino community originated in countries outside of Cuba.

Latinos are opening up businesses at a rate that is three times the national average (Williams and Kang 2006). The U.S. Hispanic Chamber of Commerce (2007) estimates that there are two million Latino-owned businesses in the

United States, generating a combined $300 billion in annual gross receipts. One example is the Latino food concession stand at Yankee Stadium, opened in 2007 (Fernandez 2007a). "Salsa on the Go," serving products by Goya (the nation's largest Latino-owned business), represents a deliberate attempt to tap the growing Latino consumer base attending professional baseball games.

Roberson and Smith raise concerns that the category termed as "minority-owned" businesses may be too broad to understand the role of small businesses in communities of color. For example, businesses owned by women of color on average had lower revenues than those owned by their male counterparts or white, non-Latinas: "Clearly, at the performance level, there are significant differences between firms owned by minority men and minority women and between firms owned by minority women and non-minority women" (2006:276). Although data were not disaggregated according to ethnic and racial subgroup, there are undoubtedly differences between and within these groups (Burke 2002). Thus, the statistics on Latina-owned businesses may mask significant disparities in performance between such business and those owned by other racial and ethnic subgroups.

It is estimated that Latino small businesses will grow at an annual compounded rate of 9 percent and reach 4.3 million by 2012 (Wozniacka 2009). Latinos are opening businesses with minimal financial and technical assistance, making their achievement even more impressive. One study finds that 79 percent of Latino adolescents want to start their own businesses (compared with 69 percent for white, non-Latino adolescents), which bodes well for the future of this community (*ResearchWikis* 2008). The youthfulness of the Latino community opens avenues for recruiting and preparing Latino youth to enter into small business development. Hernandez and Newman (2006), for example, have developed a "service-learning" model of entrepreneurship education focused on Latino youth. Delgado (2004) studies youth entrepreneurship and identifies numerous school- and community-based efforts to teach business principles while young people of color serve their communities in various types of social enterprises.

Grey (2006) cautions against underestimating the economic impact of Latino small businesses within the community and in the country. Along with the population increase and the segmentation of this group, there has been a corresponding increase in Latino economic purchasing power. Cohn (2007) also points to the challenges in arriving at a clear picture of the Latino marketplace because of complications resulting from the characteristics differing generations, of native-born residents versus newcomers, and of geographical dispersal.

Kilgannon (2007) chronicles the emergence of small businesses catering to auto repairs in the New York neighborhood known as the Iron Triangle (between Corona and Flushing, Queens), which has approximately two hundred auto repair and parts shops. These forms of street-level commerce, which draw customers from both local neighborhoods and throughout the city, are known for their aggressive outreach to and bargaining with customers. These social interactions are often as important as the final price paid for a service: the human dimension they bring to the exchange takes on even greater significance when the seller and the buyer come from cultures where bargaining is integral to their way of life.

Pawnshops are another type of small business that seems to be ubiquitous in poor and working-class urban communities across the United States (Rossin 2003). For example, the Bronx has 65 of New York City's 162 licensed pawnshops (Fernandez 2007b). All but a handful of these establishments are located in the poorest congressional district in the United States. But pawnshops are not unique to New York: it is estimated that there are now about 12,000 such businesses across the country, representing an increase from 4,800 in 1986 (Fernandez 2007b). Caskey (1994) coined the term "fringe banking" to capture such enterprises as check-cashing outlets, pawnshops, and other establishments that cater to the urban poor in this country.

Social work and other helping professions that seek to deliver health and social services targeting Latino communities face numerous challenges, such as creating effective outreach and community education campaigns and locating and supporting Latino leadership for involvement in agency boards, advisory committees, and task forces. However, using a different lens to view the role of helping professionals in assisting communities of color to establish small businesses, as well as to focus on the partnering and collaborative process between practitioners and agencies in providing the necessary assistance, opens up new ways of reaching and aiding Latino communities.

The entrepreneurial spirit that is alive and well in these ventures is not often discussed in this country or in media coverage of this population group. For example, a greater understanding of what motivates Latinos and other groups of color to establish businesses, and what factors facilitate and hinder their success, is critical to the advancement of these communities and the nation. Social work cannot overlook businesses owned by Latinos or other ethnic and racial groups because they often represent essential elements in community life and can be a source of critical expressive and instrumental support. Furthermore, Latino communities are part of the broader urban fabric and as such help shape public perceptions of cities in this country.

Unfortunately, a national focus on unauthorized, or undocumented, immigrants has hampered the development of a more comprehensive and dynamic picture of a population group that numbered approximately 36 million in 2004 and is projected to increase to 103 million by 2050, which would represent 24 percent of the nation's total population (Scommegna 2004). "Race baiting" has politicized an economic trend and reality that requires careful attention and deliberation rather than reactive behavior with national and international ramifications.

This book attempts to fill in the picture of Latino life in the United States and thus assist community social workers and the nation as a whole to develop comprehensive and systematic interventions. This will facilitate understanding of the important role Latinos and other racial and ethnic groups play in making a better life for themselves and their communities. I provide many case illustrations and vignettes to illustrate the potential of small businesses to enhance community capacity through planning and program development methods and techniques, and of the social work profession to help create and expand ethnic and racial small businesses—particularly those that are Latino and urban-based.

DEFINITIONS OF KEY TERMS

It is necessary to pause and provide some definitions of key terms that appear in this book. This section highlights four terms that play a central role throughout the discussion. Is would be easy to provide whole chapters on the etiology of each of these terms and how they have evolved over an extended period of time, but space limitations require a briefer discussion.

LATINO

It is fitting to start with the term "Latino," although one could argue that this is a pretty straightforward term that is universally understood. Who has the right to be called Latino? Are we "white," "black," or "other"? And who does the labeling and calling? Such questions make for an interesting and at times provocative discussion (Davila 2001, 2008; Delgado 2007; Waterson 2008; Passel and Taylor 2009).

The term "Hispanic" did not exist prior to 1960, and it may now be the preferred term among members of this group (Montemayor and Mendoza 2004). Latino, which is the term I prefer, is often associated with an activist stance. Davila's observations on this matter are very similar to mine: "First, this terminology ['Hispanic Marketing'] is undoubtedly due to the business preference for the officially census-sanctioned category of 'Hispanic,' over 'Latino,' a term of self-designation more connected to social struggles and activism" (2001:15). "Latinization," a construct that appears throughout this book, has been defined by Benitez (2007:2) as "a movement. It is a force—a series of Latino trends that affect how we view the world. Not attributed to any isolated event, Latinization is born of a combination of influences."

SMALL BUSINESS

Terms such as "small business ownership," "firm," "self-employment," "enterprises," "micro enterprises," "family business," and "entrepreneurship" are often used interchangeably in the literature, as they are in this book (Astrachan and Shanker 2007; Valdez 2008). The term "small business" is popular among the general population. The 2008 U.S. presidential election illustrated the power of small businesses, and the emergence of "Joe the Plumber" as a symbol helped to capture this sentiment. However, this term can encompass a wide variety of perspectives and definitions (Blackford 2003; Greene and Owen 2004), so it is important to define what constitutes a "small business."

In functional terms, small businesses can best be defined as commercial establishments with relatively simple management; usually the owner personally runs the business, its clientele is generally bounded by geographical factors, and the service or product sold caters to a particular client base. When the owner hires employees, they often are relatives, friends, or members of the owner's church. In the case of Latinos, as will be seen in chapter 4, these establishments tend to hire a limited number of employees.

Reinecke and White (2004) characterize micro or small enterprises as low-level organizations, with minimal or no division between labor and capital as factors of production. Blackford notes that "the question of just what constitutes a small firm must be approached with caution. It is important to recognize that neither large nor small firms constitute homogeneous groups and to realize that a 'gray' intermediate area exists between these two groups. There are many gradations of 'smallness'" (2003:2).

Although it may not materially matter to the reader, it is necessary to pause and briefly address micro enterprises as a concept. Small businesses are different from micro enterprises, which have fewer than ten employees and are very popular in developing nations. Sanders (2004) estimated that there were three hundred micro-enterprise assistance programs in the United States as of 2004. These programs invariably involve provision of small amounts of direct loans or assistance in obtaining loans, technical help, training, and structured peer support. Latino small businesses are generally enterprises that have sprung up without formal governmental assistance. Critics of micro enterprises argue that encouraging low-income people, particularly women, to pursue businesses (most likely home-based and consistent with gender roles) by obtaining credit will continue to render them economically marginal without addressing the macroeconomic forces that have led to such a state.

ETHNIC AND RACIAL SMALL BUSINESS

The terms "minority," "ethnic," and "racial" have emerged to help develop the linkage between small businesses and sociodemographic groups. However, as with small business development, this subject is complex.

I do not like the term "minority," although judging by its popularity in the scholarly literature I am in the minority (pun intended). I prefer the term "people of color" as a unifying construct for bringing together people from different ethnic and racial backgrounds who have experienced discrimination in this country due to their physical appearance. Nevertheless, I use the terms "ethnic" and "racial" interchangeably throughout this book. Simply stated, a small business that is owned by a person of color (African American/black, Asian, Latino, or Native American) is designated as a small business of color.

INFORMAL ECONOMY

A definition of the informal economy is in order because of the influential role it plays in capturing the quest of Latino and other urban-based communities of color to carve out an economic livelihood devoid of criminal activity, and in a society that severely limits their economic options (Losby, Else, and Kingslow 2002; Light 2007). Simply defined, the informal economy comprises those economic activities that are legal but unregulated by government. Generally, this form of economic activity relies on cash transactions. However, bartering may also be a form of payment—one that is often overlooked when estimating the economic impact of this type of exchange.

Edgecomb and Armington (2003) identify four key aspects of an informal economy: (1) it is legal but unregulated; (2) it includes both employed and self-employed workers; (3) cash is the principle medium of compensation; and (4) working conditions are inferior to those found in the formal economy. The fourth aspect has profound implications for human services within a community because the precarious situations often encountered in an informal or underground economy often leave limited options for participants to seek redress.

TENSIONS RELATED TO SMALL BUSINESS

It is important to highlight the many social and economic benefits associated with ethnic and racial businesses in urban communities in the United States, but it must be done without romanticizing these establishments (Menzies et al. 2007). As a reflection of the reality of urban communities, this book also presents examples of marginalization and exploitation of both formal and informal ethnic small businesses. Small businesses are not a panacea for all of the ills associated with socially, economically, and politically marginalized urban communities; such businesses, after all, represent only one sector of a community's life and do not make up for substandard housing, health disparities, unemployment and underemployment, demographic upheavals, and other shortcomings. In other words, the well-being of the country does not revolve solely on the economy, although economics in its various manifestations does wield considerable influence, as evidenced by the economic turmoil of the past few years.

This section provides a perspective on small businesses that is rarely addressed in the professional literature. Ethnic and racial small businesses are not exempt from exploitative business practices. One Asian restaurant in New York is a case in point: in 2007 workers engaged in a number of strikes to dispute their pay and working conditions (Greenhouse 2007a). Food takeout delivery workers, a critical component of many restaurants in cities, protested wages that in some cases averaged a mere $1.40 per hour. Nail salons have also been the target of labor unrest because of poor working conditions and wage disputes (Greenhouse 2007b).

Examples of racial and ethnic small businesses providing poor-quality products and services at high prices, particularly when compared with supermarkets, are not uncommon either. Racial or ethnic small businesses are not necessarily community assets; they can also be the opposite.

Chaganti and Greene (2002) argue for a different system to determine how an ethnic or racial small business should be classified. They propose defining these businesses by their degree of involvement in the community rather than by ethnic grouping. Community social workers must be sensitive to these differences and carefully assess businesses before deciding which ones to encourage and support.

AMBIVALENCE OF THE SOCIAL WORK PROFESSION

Community social work practice with small businesses must be examined against the backdrop of social work attitudes toward involvement in the "corporate" sector. Historically the labor movement was a home for social work because social workers embrace the values of social and economic justice. More recently, the profession has also expanded into the field of industrial and corporate social work. Still, it would be fair to state that the social work profession has played a minimal role in the business sector, and this may be the result of a long-standing ambivalence toward the negative role that capitalism and for-profit corporations have played in the lives of millions of people around the world, including the United States.

The early part of twenty-first century may prove to be a fertile period to bring about a shift in attitudes. Bryce (2006) argues that nonprofit organizations are community social capital assets that can play influential roles beyond what is typically ascribed to them. Likewise, Bares (2007) advances the notion that community institutions such as Latino small businesses provide residents with increased social interactions and affiliations. Neighborhood social capital is enhanced by having institutions that both facilitate and encourage interactions within the community.

As noted earlier, the use of a social capital construct provides a means to understand how small businesses can increase the well-being of marginalized urban communities by making social work interventions in this economic arena more feasible. Furthermore, the emergence of social enterprises (in various manifestations, as described below) has opened the door to greater involvement of the helping professions and other social service organizations in businesses, thus providing community social work practitioners with an opportunity to reconceptualize the domains usually associated with their practice (Tracey, Phillips, and Haugh 2005).

Social enterprises can be defined as businesses that seek to meet a community need by using for-profit strategies and techniques, but with an underlying social purpose (Delgado 2004). Social goals and values underpin most commercial business practices, but communities play a central role in the actualization of these goals and values. This means that a company's bottom line transcends profits, with important community implications. Warner and

Mandiberg (2006:1488) identify the appeal of social enterprises for the human services field: "The growth of the social firm movement is aided by legislation that supports the businesses, policies that favor employment of people with disabilities, and support entities that facilitate technology transfer. Social firms can empower individual employees, foster a sense of community in the workplace, and enhance worker commitment through the organization's social mission."

Social work and other helping professions admittedly may prefer to work with affirmative or social firms—businesses created to employ people with disabilities and to provide a range of products or services—because such firms may be more compatible with social workers' previous experiences or their professional training (Warner and Mandiberg 2006). However, references in the literature to involvement of social workers in various types of businesses are not unusual. As early as 1938, for example, Gates argued for social workers' involvement in the service of small businesses providing loans.

Finally, Defilippis, Fisher, and Shragge offer a critique of community practice that cannot be ignored as merely an academic debate because it raises important interactional (political) considerations pertaining to the form of community social work practice advanced in this book:

> In the world of community practices, heavily influenced by decades of neoliberal [neoconservative] policy and politics, most community-based efforts have adapted to a conservative and constrained context for social change. . . . Practice has virtually eliminated prior social action and conflict models with community development and community building efforts better adapted to the shift right. An emphasis on "the bottom line," building "partnerships" with local businesses and corporations, developing "relationships" and focusing on "community assets" has narrowed conceptions of community activism. . . . Moreover, most contemporary models of community building and development focus exclusively on the local internal community, not the economic, political and social decisions, which rest outside the community and create community needs and concerns. (2006:675)

This critique converges with concerns that social workers may have about developing closer relationships with businesses, small or otherwise, and makes for an interesting dialogue. The field of community practice is certainly expansive enough to accommodate a wide range of practice models. The form of practice advocated in this book does not preclude social workers' use of conflict-related tools, particularly when social justice values and principles guide their perspective on social change.

SOCIALLY RESPONSIBLE CORPORATIONS

There is a growing awareness that businesses must rethink their relationships with the urban communities they market to: "Urban communities in 21st century America are facing severe economic challenges, ones that suggest a mandate to contemplate serious changes in the way America does business. The middle class is diminishing in many parts of the country, with consequences for the economy as a whole. When faced with the loss of its economic base, any business community must make some difficult decisions about its proper role and responsibilities" (Cava and Mayer 2007:263).

Hammel and Denhart (2007) argue that it is feasible for small businesses to meet their bottom line and still benefit their local communities in the process. Johnstone and Lionais (2004), in addressing "depleted communities" that can limit possibilities of conventional economic development, see the potential of community entrepreneurship to meet both community social and economic needs. The social responsibility of small businesses is influenced by commitment to the community (helping to explain family business performance) and by community support (which affects financial performance) (Niehm, Swinney, and Miller 2008).

When a business, small or large, engages in positive corporate behavior toward communities, there are definite social and economic returns. Irwin and Sharkova (1998:17) make this point in describing why small business owners would want to play an active role in their communities: "Small, locally-owned establishments reinforce civic engagement because the owners are heavily invested in the community. Owners and managers of small production firms participate in local community institutions in order to maintain local business contacts and supporters. Community involvement means that these businesses may be less likely to pull out of the community in an economic downturn, and more likely to support and lead local nonprofit institutions."

In their study of the impact of a corporate oral health initiative aimed at children in Latino families, Du, Sen, and Bhattacharya (2008) find that parents of participating children were willing to engage in reciprocal behaviors such as purchasing and supporting the company's products. Socially responsible small businesses benefit not only communities but also themselves and their employees (Hammann, Habisch, and Pechianer 2009). When there is a strong cultural tradition of small business owners playing an active social role in the life of a community, there is an added dimension of value when these individuals open new businesses in communities facing social and economic challenges.

The emergence and popularity of the construct of social capital can easily be applied to small businesses in urban communities of color. Newcomers to the United States with a desire to establish businesses bring with them psychological capital (hope, self-sufficiency, confidence, and resiliency) that can extend beyond their businesses to the rest of the community (Luthens, Norman, and Jensen 2007). Businesses owned and operated by civic-minded and community-focused individuals are in an excellent position to serve as social brokers within their respective communities (Sequeira and Rasheed 2006). Brokering can include advocacy on behalf of customers or community residents in an effort to correct a social injustice. This broker or advocate role is the result of the perspectives these individuals incorporate into their businesses, as well as their views of community assets and needs.

Monti et al. (2007) advance a different version of civic capitalism by stressing business ventures that must make a profit if their social role is to be achieved. These authors postulate that small businesses historically have been much more than profit enterprises and are best understood as civic associations with interests in community well-being.

Bibb et al. (2004) developed a five-stage continuum that helps define the place occupied by Latino-owned businesses. At one end of the continuum are financially focused firms (traditional for-profit corporations); next are organizations that practice corporate responsible behavior, social businesses, and social enterprises (with or without earned income). At the opposite end of the spectrum are traditional nonprofits with a social impact focus. Latino small businesses are located between firms that practice socially responsible behavior and social businesses.

This book seeks to expand what is usually considered to be within the purview of social work (and, more specifically, community social practice). In the process it addresses a wide range of topics and activities associated with this expanded vision of the practice. This perspective will surely test the imagination of community social workers and scholars. Transformation of urban Latino communities through small business development will also necessitate urban spatial and physical transformation.

Plazas, tourism, festivals, sporting events, and parades are but a few examples of the public spaces and activities community social workers must consider in planning and implementing projects that seek to encourage development of Latino small businesses and thereby create social, political, and economic change in their communities. Although this book focuses on one particular community of color, its implications go far beyond Latinos and can apply to other such communities.

The subject of defining a role for community social work in helping urban communities develop and sustain small businesses is rarely addressed in the social work curriculum or in a social work scholarship. Nevertheless, social workers have an instrumental role in helping communities to foster economic and social development. Furthermore, as this book will show, Latino small businesses themselves fulfill a multitude of roles within their respective communities: enhancing social capital, providing economic well-being for business owners, addressing community social and health needs, contributing to overall community economic development, and assisting in the cultural transformation of urban neighborhoods.

In this introductory chapter I have laid out a roadmap that I hope clarifies a variety of viewpoints and explains why community social workers should consider involvement in the creation and support of Latino small businesses. Clearly the nature of this topic is not meant to include all social workers. Nevertheless, even if social workers do not envision their role as entering the business sphere in communities, there is certainly a need to become aware of this world and how it impinges on the social fabric of urban communities of color across the nation. This awareness brings with it responsibility to aid community social workers who are addressing this goal.

This book is an effort to help the profession contribute to the economic well-being of the Latino community in this new millennium and, in the process, to embrace a broader vision for the profession. The potential of Latino small businesses can best be appreciated in the context of national demographics, particularly in the country's major cities, and that is the subject of the next chapter.

2

LATINO DEMOGRAPHICS AND GEOGRAPHIC DISPERSAL

> With more than a million immigrants entering the United States annually, their presence has become increasingly visible throughout the country. But there are other factors besides mere numbers drawing immigrants and their families away from Los Angeles, New York, and other gateway cities and toward small towns in Iowa, Georgia, and North Carolina.
>
> —C. Hirschman, *Immigration and the American Century*

AS HIRSCHMAN (2005) highlights, demographic trends sometimes contain contradictions, and therein lies the challenge for the practitioner (Booth 2006). The interpretation of demographic statistics is influenced by one's position regarding communities of color, newcomers, and native-born citizens and one's values and principles related to social justice. Fortunately, the social work profession has experience in viewing demographics within an urban setting and using this context to shape practitioners' perspectives and interventions.

The subject of demographics is a vital part of any systematic examination of small business activity in the United States (Brookings Institution 2009; Reamer 2009). It not only provides a context for understanding the dynamics of small business creation in urban communities of color but also helps forecast the population factors that will affect future businesses. In this chapter I present demographic data on a wide variety of topics, some rather standard or mundane and others highly unusual and rarely discussed in the literature. These data are critical to providing a basis for understanding how demographics have shaped the country and will continue to do so: "The news that Hispanics have become the nation's largest minority was no demographic surprise. Its fruition had been predicted at least 30 years ago" (Durand, Telles, and Flashman 2006:66). Latino demographic growth has been predicted since the early 1970s when the "decade of Hispanics" raised the nation's awareness of Latinos (Montemayor and Mendoza 2004).

This attention caused a great deal of anguish in other ethnic and racial communities—particularly among African Americans—because of its social, economic, and political implications (Delgado 2007; Vaca 2004). Latinos were replacing blacks as the largest "minority" group in the country. The emergence of Latinos as a major constituency has also played an influential role in the development of the concept of "minority-majority," which captures the demographic situation in which groups of color outnumber white non-Latinos in a geographical setting such as a city or town (Roberts 2008a).

Since this book is essentially about creating and supporting small businesses, readers might ask why I do not just focus on economic trends and skip the population demographics. My answer is that to do so would be a disservice to a serious analysis of Latino small business development. For example, in his 2004 study of Latino commercial establishments in Phoenix, Arizona, Oberle points out that Phoenix's Latino community almost doubled its economic purchasing power from 2000 ($3.6 billion) to 2006 ($6.4 billion), reflecting the growth of the Latino population in that city (Censky 2007). The relationship between demographics and small business development is significant, particularly in urban areas because of their sizable concentration of ethnic and racial groups (Oberle and Li 2008). The Latino population in the nation's thirty-two largest cities doubled between 1990 and 2000, further reinforcing why there is an urban concentration in this book (Knowledge @Wharton 2003). Nonetheless, some parts of rural and small-town America are also experiencing rapid changes in population composition, with Latinos playing a key role in these changes (Kandel and Cromartie 2004; Donato, Stainback, and Bankston 2005; Grey and Woodrick 2005; Griffith 2005).

Rapid demographic changes bring with them significant economic and social implications—or upheavals, depending upon one's perspective—because in many areas contact with groups viewed as "different" has been limited (Dunn, Aragones, and Shivers 2005; Shutika 2005; Diaz Mcconnell and Miraftab 2008; Miraftab and Diaz Mcconnell 2008; Orfield and Frankenberg 2008; Varsany 2008). Lack of experience with other ethnic and racial groups makes residents of these geographical areas more likely to view people who are different from themselves as a shock to their way of life and system.

Urban areas provide a unique set of circumstances (diversity, density, history, assets) that affect how Latino and other communities of color evolve socially, politically, and economically (Bradford 2005; Skop, Gratton, and Guttman 2006; Delgado 2008). Furthermore, cities are often high-profile media markets that shape national and international public opinion, adding to their significance (Padin 2005). Since most social work is practiced in metropolitan areas, it makes sense to emphasize urban-centered demographics in this chapter and throughout the book.

Finally, although demographic statistics and economic data can be dry and complicated, I try to make them as reader-friendly as possible by including stories about how Latinos are increasing their presence throughout the country. This chapter may require more than one reading to digest the implications of the important trends that will continue to unfold as Latinos gain more prominence in the nation's economy and society. No geographical sector of the country will escape this explosion.

THE ROLE OF DEMOGRAPHICS

Demographics have played a critical role in shaping public policy in this country, especially in urban centers (Frey 2009b). Marketing firms love demographics because such statistics help inform them about the profile of residents. Those of us in helping professions also embrace the value of demographics because of how they shape our responses to human needs. Statistics, however, cannot provide the entire picture of small business ownership by people of color; conversely, no picture of this phenomenon is possible without considering demographics. Consequently, I believe that readers must have a statistical grounding to understand and appreciate the qualitative importance of small businesses in the nation's urban communities of color.

The quantitative perspective goes hand in hand with a qualitative viewpoint to provide a more rounded picture of Latino enterprises. The latter approach helps provide pieces that are missing in a broad statistical overview. Jones (2008), in analyzing Latino immigrant residential patterns in San Antonio, Texas, advocates the use of micro-level analysis to counteract the limitations of broader-scale analysis often associated with statistical data on urban America. This level of analysis complements a qualitative approach.

McTaggart's observations bear out the close relationship between demographics and small business development and why these two aspects cannot be separated:

> It's an ironic turn of events. During the past decade several supermarket chains had declared the urban Southern California market a dead end and pulled out, leaving behind a fallow field of empty boxes. But for a few eager

local entrepreneurs, those abandoned stores looked ripe for cultivation into vibrant, community-oriented food markets, and those business owners set about figuring out how to serve the largely Hispanic populations the big guys hadn't been able to. Now some of these chains are clamoring to get back inside Los Angeles' ethnically diverse urban neighborhoods. . . . It's a tale of more than one city. Other multicultural hotbeds, including New York, Chicago, and Houston, are home to thriving independent retailers that made a commitment to Hispanic merchandising long before it became fashionable. (2004:1)

Likewise, Myers's (1999) concept of "demographic dynamism" is an attempt to capture the interrelation between demographics and the impact on the environment.

Rumbaut's (2006:60) historical overview sets an excellent backdrop to the primary goals of this chapter and highlights how demographics can help provide inputs into questions that must be answered in order for Latino small businesses can thrive: "Four decades into a new era of mass immigration, it has become commonplace to observe that the United States is undergoing its most profound demographic transformation in a century." Thus, present-day demographics have roots in history and will influence future demographics (Hirschman 2005). These three time periods are intricately tied together yet also distinctive; likewise, for Latinos, the demographic transformation is not only historical but also continues today, as it will into the future (Portes 2007; Salcido 2007).

This trend can be labeled in many different ways. Latino immigration, for example, can be labeled as the longest and largest in the history of the United States (Benitez 2007). Or, more specifically, Mexicans can be said to represent both the longest and greatest uninterrupted migration in the history of the country (Zuniga and Hernandez-Leon 2005). Regardless of whether this migration is viewed broadly or specifically, it has had profound social, economic, and political impacts on both the receiving country and the sending countries. Too often we think only of the impact on the host community and rarely about the consequences for the families and communities left behind (Delgado, Jones, and Rohani 2004).

Six demographic perspectives will bring these dimensions to life:

- What does the Latino community look like?
- Where is it located?
- What are the significant trends?

- How do small businesses contribute to the economic well-being of Latino communities and the nation?
- What are the significant demographic trends for the future?
- What are the particular demographic profiles of three major U.S. cities?

Although these perspectives are not mutually exclusive, I will treat them as entities unto themselves in an effort to disentangle central points and allow them to serve as the needed backdrop to an in-depth examination of Latino small businesses.

Garcia (2003:22) notes that commonalities of the Latino community are multifaceted: "The dimension of commonality—community linkages, bonds, affinity, interactions, and individual affiliation—is important in our discussion of Latino community." However, there are marked differences between Latino groups that this book can only touch upon. Fortunately, numerous other books focus on the uniqueness of each of the major Latino groups.

It is fitting to end this section on the role and limitations of demographics by stressing how the future may change our definitions of Latinos. Demographic projections, particularly those forecasting the next thirty to forty years, depend on common definitions of people. But as the Pew Hispanic Center (2002:1) notes: "While Latinos are likely to retain a strong self-identity, it is unlikely that they will be easily classified in the future. Hispanics also intermarry in significant numbers, with nearly 20 percent marrying a non-Hispanic." Thus, definitions of Latinos may change with children and grandchildren of multiracial and multiethnic unions. One key question is whether these offspring will be considered Latino. It is important to note that fifty years ago the terms "Hispanic" and "Latino" simply did not exist. Thus, we must be prepared to entertain the emergence of new categories of people who may not be considered Latino by today's standard definition. This, of course, has profound implications for future demographic projections.

WHAT DOES THE LATINO COMMUNITY LOOK LIKE?

Defining the Latino community is quite complex and is getting more challenging every year. Historically Latinos were far from being a monolithic group that shared similar backgrounds, customs, and language, although the popular media tended to lump all Latinos together to facilitate the telling of a news story or conveying of a particular, invariably negative image (Rumbaut 2006; Tienda and Mitchell 2006a, 2006b; Grenier et al. 2007). One study finds

Latinos severely underrepresented in the mainstream media: "While Hispanics make up 14 percent of the population in the United States, less than one percent of major mainstream news media stories are about Hispanics. In addition to a lack of air time and coverage, an annual study on Hispanics and news media revealed that news stories about Latinos concentrated primarily on immigration and crime" (Democratic Policy Committee 2005:5). Unfortunately, these stories often reinforce popular stereotypes about Latinos (Mastro and Behm-Morawitz 2005; Entman 2006; Rivera 2008). Trujillo-Pagan's (2007) analysis of the racialization of Latinos in post-Katrina New Orleans is an example that raises serious concerns about how Latinos are being portrayed in the media, though their rapid influx into New Orleans has caused tensions with African Americans (Dreier 2006).

There are both commonalities and differences between Latino groups, with significant differences arising from a range of human capital factors, such as level of formal education, English language proficiency, skin pigmentation, legal status, and level of acculturation. The days when one sentence could describe the Latino population are long gone, even for those who wish to treat this community as a monolithic entity. Creating a profile of the Latino community in the United States has never been more challenging than it is in the twenty-first century because of the immigration patterns of Latinos from the Caribbean and Central and South America and the emergence of acculturation as a key factor differentiating between those who arrived in the country as youths and those who were born and raised in the United States. Nevertheless, I will attempt below to provide a modern-day portrait of Latinos.

The Latino community in the United States comprises all major Latino subgroups, and it is certainly rare to find a geographic area that consists solely of one Latino group, as detailed later in this chapter. However, Mexicans are the largest group and account for 29.2 million residents (or 64.3% of the Latino community), followed by Puerto Ricans, with 4.1 million (9.1%); Cubans, with 1.6 million; Salvadorans, with 1.5 million; and Dominicans, with 1.2 million (Pew Hispanic Center 2009b–f).

Other groups are less commonly addressed but nonetheless represent significant portions of the Latino community in the United States (Falconi and Mazzotti 2007). For example, five additional Latino groups not represented in figure 2.1 account for 3.278 million residents (7.1% percent of the Latino population): Guatemalans, 860,000 (1.9%); Colombians, 797,000 (1.8%); Hondurans, 527,000 (1.2%); Ecuadoreans, 523,000 (1.2%); and Peruvians, 471,000 (1.0%) (Pew Hispanic Center 2009g–k).

Forty percent of Mexicans residing in the United States are foreign born, with most having arrived in the United States in or before 1990. Almost

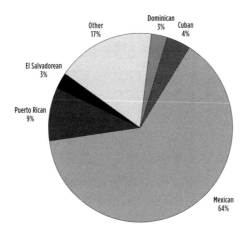

2.1 ORIGINS OF HISPANICS BY COUNTRY, 2007

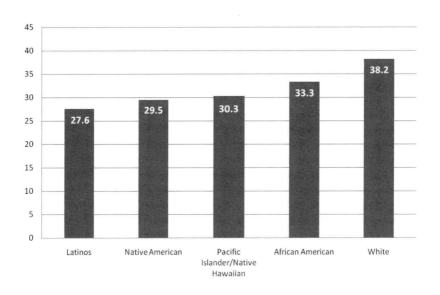

2.2 MEDIAN AGE BY RACE/ETHNICITY

Source: U.S. Census Bureau, 2008a

22 percent are U.S. citizens. Foreign-born residents make up more than 60 percent of the respective U.S. communities of Salvadorans (66.1%), Cubans (60.7%), and Dominicans (60.1%) (Pew Hispanic Center 2009c–f, 2010).

The Latino community is very young, relatively speaking, when compared with white non-Latinos and African Americans, as noted in figure 2.2 (Pew Hispanic Center, 2009a, 2009b). In 2007 the median age of a Latino was

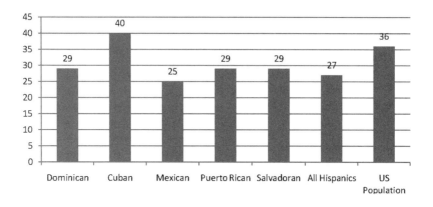

2.3 LATINO MEDIAN AGE BY COUNTRY OF ORIGIN

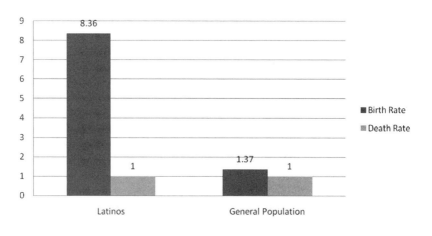

2.4 COMPARISON OF BIRTH TO DEATH RATES

27.6 years compared with 36.6 years for the U.S. population as a whole (U.S. Census Bureau 2008a).

Figure 2.3 shows that there are differences in median ages between Latino groups as well. Cubans, for example, are the oldest Latino group in the United States, with a median age of 40, followed by Dominicans, Salvadorans, and Puerto Ricans (29). Mexicans, in turn, are the youngest, with a median age of 25 (Pew Hispanic Center 2009c).

The majority of the Latino increases in population have been the result of births (60%) rather than net gains from immigration (Benitez 2007). In 2007, as shown in figure 2.4, the Latino birth-to-death ratio was quite dramatic, with 8.36 Latino births for every death, compared with 1.37 births for every death in the general population (Johnson and Lichter 2008a). The outpacing of deaths by births reflects the youthfulness of the Latino community and raises implications for further demographic increases as young Latinos enter childbearing age.

Latino population growth in 2008, as in 2007, was largely the result of births rather than immigration, with births accounting for 66 percent of the 1.47 million increase in Latinos. Births outnumbered deaths by a 10 to 1 ratio (Moore and Overberg 2009; Roberts 2009). This slight change from 2007 signals a population group that will continue to be composed in large proportion of children and youth, further decreasing death rates and increasing birthrates as these youths mature into adulthood and childbearing age.

Latino children represent 22 percent of all children under the age of 18 in the United States (Fry 2009). In 2008 Latino babies represented 24 percent of all newborns in the United States (Belanger 2009). The percentage of Latinos under the age of 18 in major cities is considerable: Houston, 36 percent; Los Angeles, 53 percent; Miami, 39 percent; San Diego, 39 percent (Grow 2004). Latino first graders are the majority in five of the nation's top ten cities, population-wise, and approaching the majority in four others: San Antonio (89.4%); Los Angeles (73.8 %); Dallas (68.6%); Houston (63.1%); San Jose (53.4%); San Diego (46.4%); Chicago (45.1%); Phoenix, (43.9%); and New York (40.6%). Philadelphia is the only exception in the top ten, with 17.8 percent of first graders there being Latino (Tomas Rivera Policy Institute 2009).

From a representation perspective, children and youth are heavily concentrated. California (Los Angeles, San Diego, and San Jose) and Texas (Dallas, Houston, and San Antonio) dominate the list of cities with sizable Latino first grades. In 1999 more than half of all Latino adolescents lived in two states, California (34%) and Texas (22%) (Institute for Health Policy Studies 2002). Concomitantly, Latino enrollment in suburban school districts increased by 296 percent from 1993–94 to 2006–07 (Gillium 2009). In 2009 Latinos (38.1%) surpassed African Americans (37.9%) as the largest group of color in Boston's public school system (Vaznis 2009). By 2050 Latino children in public schools will outnumber white non-Latinos in the nation's urban areas (Fry and Gonzalez 2008).

The youthfulness of the Latino community must be viewed from a national assets perspective rather than the conventional deficit perspective, which emphasizes that this group is an economic "sinkhole." As Tienda and Mitchell (2006b:61) put it: "This influx of young people into the United States is a potentially positive development, showing the nation's overall population aging while particularly offsetting the rising burden of dependency of an aging majority—what might be viewed as a demographic divide."

Latinos under the age of 35 constitute 70 percent of the overall Latino market, accounting for $300 billion in purchasing power, or half of all Latino spending in the country. If U.S. society embraces an assets view and thinks of young Latinos as a national resource in which to invest, the future looks very bright for this community and the nation as a whole.

Finally, Ramos and Gates (2008) present a demographic profile of a population group largely overlooked in most reports: California's Latino lesbian, gay, and bisexual community. Approximately one in four individuals in same-sex couples are Latino, whereas 12 percent of the individuals in heterosexual couples are Latino. Mexicans represent 81 percent of Latino same-sex couples.

WHERE ARE LATINOS LOCATED?

As noted earlier, Latino dispersal means that Latinos can now be found throughout all geographical sectors of the United States. Fischer and Tienda's (2006:103) comment on this dispersal shows why this trend is so significant: "The New Hispanic Destinations are of particular interest because of the number of places involved, their nationwide spread, their diverse growth rates, and the variable size of their black population." It remains to be seen, however, how the national recession of 2008 will impact the growth of the Latino community in states that have previously experienced enormous growth in this population, particularly those states in the Sun Belt (Cave 2009).

Prior to 1990, 75 percent of Latinos were concentrated in 65 of the country's 3,141 counties. Starting in 1990, however, dispersal across the country started to accelerate, most notably to the South and Midwest (Davis 2008). Since 2000 dispersal has shifted toward the West and the Northeast. However, the Latino population has increased in almost 3,000 counties (Fry 2008). New Mexico has the highest percentage of Latinos (44%), followed by California and Texas (36% each), Arizona (30%), and Nevada (25%) (U.S. Census Bureau 2008a). California, however, leads all states in the actual number of Latinos (13.2 million), followed by Texas (8.6 million). These two states account for 50.2 percent of the total Latino population in the United States.

California has often been looked upon as the bellwether of future trends in other parts of the country (Camarillo 2007). Thus, the statistics on Latino births signal future implications for the state and the country. Purdum

(2000) argues that California will become the first big state to epitomize what it will be like to live in a country in which no single ethnic or racial group predominates from a demographic perspective. The year 2003 marked a major milestone toward this vision, with two-thirds of births in Los Angeles and Southern California being to Latino parents (Murphy 2003). Percentage of workforce offers another perspective on how Latinos are transforming California. In 2006 Koehler and Koehler-Jones estimated that Latinos would constitute 45 percent of that state's workforce by 2010.

Although they may not be the fastest growing areas, ten states were considered to have the largest Latino markets in 2002: California, Texas, Florida, New York, Illinois, New Jersey, Arizona, Colorado, Georgia, and New Mexico. In addition, California, Florida, Illinois, New York, and Texas represent two-thirds of the Latino community in the United States (Goldman Sachs 2007). With the exception of Florida, none of these states has what is considered to be the fastest-growing Latino population; that distinction belongs, in addition to Florida, to Nevada, Washington, Oregon, Massachusetts, Virginia, and North Carolina (Furuseth 2005; U.S. Hispanic Chamber of Commerce 2007). The Latino portion of Nevada's population, for example, increased from 10.4 percent in 1990 to 25.1 percent in 2007 (Immigration Policy Center 2009). With the exception of Oregon, all the states listed above have a Latino population of over 500,000 (U.S. Census Bureau 2008b).

Not surprisingly, California ($202.7 billion), Texas ($127.4 billion), Florida ($75.1 billion), New York ($62.7 billion), and Illinois ($28.4 billion) also represent the top five states in Latino purchasing power (Cohn 2007). Incidentally, if we remove Illinois from this list, the remaining four states accounted for 73 percent of all Latino businesses (National and City Small Business Resources 2007). Other states, such as Wisconsin and Iowa, have also seen an increase in Latino economic power. In 2007 Wisconsin, for example, had 3,000 Latino-owned business, which generated $800 million in total sales, and the 850 such businesses in Milwaukee generated $225 million (Sava and Vill 2007; Monreal-Cameron 2008). Iowa, in turn, had 1,500 Latino-owned businesses, which generated a total of $285 million in revenue (Burns 2009).

Appalachia and the northern states, such as Minnesota, have benefited from this trend (Contu 2004; Fennelly 2005; Kandel and Parrado 2004, 2005; Kochhar, Suro, and Tafoya 2005; Powers 2005; Barcus 2007; Kleiner and Green 2008; Singer, Hardwick, and Brettell 2008; Wang and Li 2007). South Carolina, Alabama, and Georgia (like their northern neighbors Virginia and North Carolina), have also experienced dramatic increases in Latinos (Aponte 2001; Winders 2005, 2008; Young 2005; Grainer 2006; Ansley and Shefner 2009; McDaniel and Drever 2009; Schleef and Cavalcanti 2009).

Woodward (2006), in commenting on the influence of Mexican immigrants in South Carolina, notes that although this community represents a highly visible portion of the state's residents, most people, officials included, are uninformed about this trend. It is estimated that there were 131,000 Latinos—predominantly Mexicans—in the state in 2004, although when taking into account undocumented individuals the figures rises closer to 400,000.

Davis et al.'s (2009) book about Latino immigration in Dalton, Georgia, vividly illustrates how the ethnic landscape in nonurban Georgia has changed as the influx of Latino immigrants, primarily Mexicans from Mexico and the Southwest, has transformed Dalton from a social, economic, and political perspective. Dalton, in Whitfield County, is located eighty miles north of Atlanta and is often referred to as the "Carpet Capital of the World." However, the influx of Latinos has earned the city the designation of a "U.S. border town," even though it is located 1,200 miles from the Mexico border (Russakoff 2006). Latinos now constitute 50 percent (45,000) of the city's total population. Essentially, this city has been Latinized in the past decade.

Furuseth and Smith's comments on the Latinization of the "New South" apply to other regions of the country as well: "It is also important to point out that the Latinization of Southern places is only one of several major transformative forces reshaping the character and dynamics of the region in our era. The in immigration of both native and foreign born Hispanics and their role in the emerging Nuevo South cannot be understood fully without intersecting it with changes that are transforming the region's economy and culture through broader processes of restructuring and globalization" (2006:15). Cities such as Atlanta, for example, effectively serve as international corridors for directing newcomers, Latino and otherwise, in the South (Odem 2008; McDaniel and Drever 2009).

The emergence of a new service economy in southern states has been identified as one possible explanation for the attraction of Latinos to this region (Smith and Winders 2007; Vidal de Haymes and Kilty 2007). The influx of Latino immigrants to the South and its industries, such as poultry, has also fueled labor union drives (Greenhouse 2005). In essence, the ethnic and racial composition of the South is experiencing changes as a result of the influx of Latinos into the region (Sabia 2007).

New England has also experienced unprecedented population changes, primarily as the result of Latino migration and increased birth rates (Glasser 2006; Hernandez 2006; Torres 2006; Uriarte 2006; Montero-Sieburth 2007; Carey and Atkinson 2009). Latinos, primarily Puerto Ricans, are well represented (2005) in Connecticut (382,145) and in the state's major cities:

Hartford (40.5%); Bridgeport (31.9%); Willimantic (30.9%); New Britain (26.8%); Waterbury (21.8%); New Haven (21.4%); Meriden (21.4%); and Stamford (16.8%) (Credit Union League of Connecticut 2008). Willimantic has also seen Mexican migration (Nunez 2007) into what has historically been a community with Puerto Rican origins. Latino population growth in Connecticut has occurred in traditional immigrant centers, towns, and rural areas without histories of attracting Latinos. The Latino population in New England numbered approximately 900,000 in 2000.

The Latino population in New Hampshire totaled approximately 21,000 in 2000, representing just 1.7 percent of the state's population. However, it is noteworthy because twenty years earlier Latinos were almost nonexistent in the state (Camayd-Freixas and Karush 2006; Camayd-Freixas, Karush, and Lejter 2006). In 2007 there were 16,000 Latinos living in Maine. From 2000 to 2007, Maine's Latino population (primarily Mexican and Puerto Rican) increased by 67 percent, compared with a 3.3 percent increase for the total population (Maine Center for Economic Policy 2009). In 2002 Maine had 731 Latino-owned businesses, which generated a total of $113 million in revenue. This represents an increase of 117 percent from 1997.

As noted earlier, small changes in population size can have significant implications: "although a gain of 3 percentage points in terms of their proportion of the total New England population from 1990 to 2000 may seem small, it is useful to remember that New England has a population of some fourteen million and that Latinos constituted more than half of all population growth during the 1990s" (Marcelli and Granberry 2006:31). Latinos are no longer relegated to certain select cities within the region and have dispersed to small towns and cities (League of United American Citizens 2003).

Ironically, a community does not have to have an increased presence of Latinos to react in a racist manner. Martin's (2009) article titled "'No Dogs or Mexicans Allowed': Discourses of Racism and Ideology in Pahrump, Nevada," illustrates how the town's "English as the official language" policy was spurred by the national anti-immigrant climate and is another example of anti-Latino immigrant sentiments in the Southwest. In contrast, though, Nelson and Hiemstra (2008) illustrate how an increase in Latino residents in two small towns to the point that they became the majority population has altered Latino place identity and social belonging in the towns and brought about greater acceptance.

Borges-Mendez comments on the changing patterns of migration and dispersal of Latinos in the past decade regarding urban destinations other than large cities:

At the neighborhood level and in cities of all sizes, Latino neighborhoods will become, if they are not already, "fluid" urban ecologies, with a multiplicity of patterns of human circulation coexisting within, and pushing upon, the spatial boundaries (and identity) of barrios. . . . Central to this research is the path Latinos are undertaking, who seem to be climbing down the urban ladder to form barrios in small towns and mid-size cities. (2006:5)

Garden City, Kansas, typifies this trend whereby Latinos over a period of twenty years or so went from being a minority to a majority, population-wise (Stull and Broadway 2008).

In the case of Latinos in the United States, development of a community profile faces numerous challenges, although the rewards can be substantial. Even dramatic demographic changes in the Latino community generally take considerable time to be officially recorded by governmental agencies. I often argue that by the time these changes are reflected on paper, they are dated. However, the case of Mexicans immigrating to new sections of the country seems to be an exception: "In a few short years Mexican immigration has been transformed from a narrowly focused process affecting just three states into a nationwide movement" (Durand, Massey and Capoferro 2005:18). This remarkable shift will generate considerable scholarly interest and will surely have national social, economic, and political implications.

WHAT ARE THE SIGNIFICANT TRENDS?

This section highlights four significant trends that have direct implications for Latino community economic and social development and the use of small businesses to achieve these goals: population increases; dispersal across the country with an emphasis on Mexicans; presence of and changes among undocumented Latinos; and projected increases in the next forty years.

These four trends are by no means the only significant demographic trends that can be analyzed, nor should they be considered separately from one other. However, the centrality of these trends makes them stand out, and their implications for community social work practice are obvious.

Population Increases

The academic arena is notorious for creating debates about virtually any subject, but I believe I am on firm ground when I say that the increase in the number of Latinos in the United States in the past decade is universally accepted in all academic and political circles. Thus I will not devote significant space to debates about this fact. However, there certainly are legitimate debates about what the increases mean at the local, state, regional, and national levels (Delgado 2007; Lee 2008), as well as whether demographic trends today can be expected to continue into the next thirty to forty years (Shrestha 2006).

Population size is determined by the interplay of births, deaths, and migration. Each of these forces responds to a series of social forces on its own, yet the actions of one force can affect the other two and the totality. The key question is, is the population growing or shrinking and why? As noted above, the last several years have witnessed a rapid change in the demographic profile of the Latino population in the United States, with the number of Latinos increasing from 10.2 million in April 2000 to 45.5 million in July 2007, when they accounted for 15.1 percent of the total U.S. population (Fry 2008).

This increase resulted in certain cities becoming more Latinized, but without the cachet associated with Miami, such as the music, colors, palm trees, and food. Latinos account for almost 50 percent of the nation's population growth since 2000 (Pew Hispanic Center 2008). They are responsible for population increases in 221 counties that otherwise would have decreased in population from 2000 to 2005, and they also moderated overall losses in 1,100 counties (Johnson and Lichter 2008a). Latinos are the fastest-growing demographic group in rural and small-town America, with their numbers in these locations doubling since 1980 (Democratic Policy Committee 2005).

Suro examines demographic trends in the nation's hundred largest metropolitan areas based on the 2000 U.S. Census and concludes that there are four distinct patterns pertaining to Latinos:

> The Hispanic population is growing in most metropolitan areas, but the rate and location of increases varies widely. Four distinct patterns of growth can be discerned. *Established Latino metros* such as New York, Los Angeles, Miami, and Chicago posted the largest absolute increases between 1980 and 2000. However, *new Latino destinations* like Atlanta and Orlando charted the fastest rates, despite their historically smaller Hispanic bases. Metros with relatively larger Latino bases such as Houston, Phoenix and San Diego, meanwhile, became *fast-growing Latino hubs* during the past 20 years, with population growth averaging 235 percent. *Small Latino places*, such as Baton Rouge, posted much lower absolute and relative growth than the other locales. (2002:1)

Kasinitz, Mollenkopf, and Waters's (2004) study of New York's second-generation immigrants raises many themes and issues that also face Latino second-generation residents in other cities, including Los Angeles and Miami. As Suro and Passel (2003:9) note, "The rise of the second generation is the result of births and immigration that has already taken place, and it is now inexorable, undeniable demographic fact." The Latino population in the United States is relatively young, with 33 percent under the age of 18, similar to African Americans and Asian Americans. This relatively youthful population has the potential to translate into high fertility rates, increasingly the likelihood of this group remaining young compared with other ethnic and racial groups in the country (Johnson and Lichter 2008b). Another perspective on the size of the Latino community in the United States can be gained by comparing it with that of Spanish-speaking nations. Only Mexico has a larger Latino population, with 45.5 million; Spain has a population of 40.4 million (U.S. Census Bureau 2008).

The factors influencing the increase in size of the Latino community will shape its purchasing power and economic impact. There is arguably no more important segment of the future American consumer market than Latinos, particularly in major urban areas (Korzenny and Korzenny 2005). By 2025, for example, Latino purchasing power is estimated to surpass $3 trillion, making the Latino market the fourth largest economic force in the world, trailing only the United States as a whole, Japan, and China (Montemayor and Mendoza 2004).

Dispersal and Concentration Across the Country

Readers might rightly question a trend that involves both concentration and dispersal of Latinos at the same time, as Tienda and Mitchell (2006:65) note: "The spatial dispersal of Hispanics presents an interesting paradox. Even as Hispanics are experiencing less regional segregation, they are finding themselves re-segregated in both traditional settlement cities and their new destinations." Are Latinos dispersing across the country or staying in historical centers of immigration? Are they staying within major urban areas or moving to the suburbs? The answers to these questions are rather simple: it is both, and these trends will have profound implications for communities across the country (Brettell 2008; Donato et al. 2008; Parrado and Kandel 2008).

In 2006 white non-Latinos were a minority in thirty-five of the top fifty cities in the country, with Latinos playing a critical role in this demographic trend (Asthana 2006). Phoenix, Tucson, and Denver are examples of this shift in demographic composition, as are Arlington and Austin in Texas, Charlotte in North Carolina, and Las Vegas (Skop and Buentello 2008; Smith and Furuseth 2008). Latinos, nevertheless, like their Asian American and African

American counterparts, are also moving to the suburbs. In 2000, 51 percent of Asians, 43 percent of Latinos, and 32 percent of African Americans lived in the suburbs (Kotkin 2010; Singer, Hardwick, and Brettell 2008).

The Pew Hispanic Center studied Latino residential patterns based on the 2000 U.S. Census Bureau data and concluded the following:

> Rather than clustering in ethnic enclaves . . . most Latinos live scattered through neighborhoods where they are a small share of the population. Some 20 million Hispanics—57 percent of the total—live in neighborhoods in which Hispanics made up less than half of the population. . . . Of course, this leaves a sizeable share of the Hispanic population—43 percent—in neighborhoods where Latinos are a majority. These communities are large, and the Hispanic population that lives in such neighborhoods is growing faster than the Hispanic population that lives dispersed among non-Hispanics. (Soro and Tafoya 2004:1)

Thus, two countervailing trends have emerged—dispersal and concentration.

The dispersal of Latino groups from areas of the country where they have enjoyed a long history, such as Mexicans in the Southwest and California and Puerto Ricans in the Northeast, has started to make Latino communities in new regions even more diverse (Foner 2001; Dalla and Christensen 2005). Latinos are no longer concentrated in the primary ports of entry, over the past several decades—and, in the cases of some groups, the past decade—shifting the Latino composition of U.S. cities and regions (Fennelly 2005). Readers may be surprised to learn that Arkansas's Latino population, for example, experienced the fastest growth of any state (337 percent) from 1990 to 2000 (Bradley and Stuckey 2005).

Mexicans are a particular case in point. Zuniga and Hernandez-Leon (2005) present a dramatic picture of the new geography of Mexican migration in the early part of the twenty-first century, highlighting the changes that are occurring across the country. Leach and Bean (2008:51) also comment on these changes: "The Mexican-born were no longer concentrating nearly as much as before in the traditional states, the four border states of the Southwest—Arizona, California, New Mexico, Texas, and Illinois, mostly Chicago—but rather were dispersing elsewhere, which illustrated that such migration had become a national rather than a regional phenomenon. The magnitude of the shift was dramatic." McConnell (2008), in studying Mexican immigrant destinations within the United States, argues that the logic underpinning human capital theory can be applicable to these choices and offers a four-category typology of destinations: (1) large traditional urban areas; (2) small traditional urban areas; (3) nontraditional urban areas; and (4) rural areas.

Mexicans are the largest Latino group in the United States by far, as noted earlier in this chapter. They are both the oldest resident group as well as the newest group entering the country (Saenz, Morales, and Filoteo 2004; Diaz 2005; Rumbaut 2006). Mexicans in certain sections of the country predated European migration. Iber and DeLeon (2005) chronicle how Mexicans historically resided in the American West but have now expanded to states such as Hawaii, Oregon, and Utah.

Mexican newcomers are in fact changing the ethnic landscape of every region of the country, including cities that historically were not a destination for this group (Card and Lewis 2005; Borjas 2007; Massey 2008). For example, although Mexicans are heavily concentrated in California and Texas, they have started to disperse across the United States, as R. C. Smith (2005:4) observes in his important work. Fennelly and Orfield (2008) study the Mexican community in Minnesota's Twin Cities, Minneapolis and St. Paul, and find that suburbs there are increasingly attracting Latinos, predominantly Mexicans. Mexican small businesses in the suburbs found a receptive economic climate because of a lack of competition from other Latino enterprises.

The tremendous growth in Mexican migration to the state of New York over the past fifteen years reflects a larger trend. While most Mexican migrants still settle in the Southwest, during the 1990s migration to the East Coast increased and today more than 500,000 people of Mexican origin live in New York State, many of them in New York City. Mexicans also represent the second largest Latino group in Philadelphia, numbering approximately 12,000, with the majority having settled in that city during the 1990s (Balch Institute for Ethnic Studies 2004). The largest Latino group, Puerto Ricans, numbered 91,527 in 2000.

Florida (185,000) and Georgia (184,000) rank fifth and sixth among states with 100,000 or more Mexicans (Gutierrez, Wallace, and Castaneda 2004). New York (60,000) ranks ninth, although this figure is widely disputed as too low. This is considerably lower than Smith's (2005) estimate and highlights the difficulty in obtaining an accurate count of a group that is in high flux. Connecticut has the largest Mexican representation in New England (23,484), with Massachusetts a close second (22,288) (Montero-Sieburth 2007).

Presence and Changes Among the Undocumented

The upsurge in Latino undocumented immigrants into the United States has been labeled the new "civil rights movement" of the twenty-first century

(Robinson 2006). In 2006 hundreds of thousands of demonstrators, many of whom were newcomers to the United States, marched for recognition of their social and economic contributions to the country, with dramatic impact across the nation:

> Stores and restaurants in Los Angeles, Chicago and New York closed because workers did not show up or as a display of solidarity with demonstrators. In Los Angeles, the police estimated that more than half a million people attended two demonstrations in and near downtown. School districts in several cities reported a decline in attendance; at Benito Juarez High School in Pilsen, a predominantly Latino neighborhood in Chicago, only 17 percent of the students showed up, even though administrators and some protest organizers had urged students to stay in school. Lettuce, tomatoes and grapes went unpicked in fields in California and Arizona, which contribute more than half the nation's produce, as scores of growers let workers take the day off. Truckers who move 70 percent of the goods in ports in Los Angeles and Long Beach, Calif., did not work. Meatpacking companies, including Tyson Foods and Cargill, closed plants in the Midwest and the West employing more than 20,000 people, while the flower and produce markets in downtown Los Angeles stood largely and eerily empty. (Archibold 2006:1)

Unfortunately, the value of Latino and other undocumented groups in this country has essentially been reduced to their economic value as a low-cost labor force or a consuming group (Davila 2004a). Bolin's (2006) research on the economic and fiscal impact of immigration on the United States, interestingly, finds that these newcomers have a net fiscal and economic impact, contrary to frequent arguments put forth by anti-immigrant forces. Undocumented Latinos represent a significant economic force in the United States, and not just because they occupy low-paying jobs that are essential to the country's well-being. Their economic presence is greatest in areas of the country where they are concentrated or represent sizable proportions of the Latino community (Johnson 2004).

Chavez (2008) argues that Latinos, and more specifically Mexicans, are often portrayed in the media as an "invading force" that threatens traditional American values and way of life. DePalma's (2005a) reporting on undocumented Mexican immigrants in New York, for example, details the struggles they endure while seeking to make a living and support a family back in Mexico. New York's restaurant industry would be paralyzed without the supply of these low-wage workers. But the contributions of the undocumented go far beyond this limited view.

Suro's comments about Latino immigrants in general take on greater significance when discussing undocumented Latinos and highlight the negative views that many in society hold toward this group: "We should note that one of the curious things accompanying this business cycle is an extraordinary change in the way the poor are demonized. . . . The demonization of immigrants in this business cycle . . . is of poor people with too great a work ethic—people who work too hard. We now have this image of the workaholic Mexican as the demonized vision of the poor in this country" (2004:5).

The topic of undocumented residents is closely associated with any serious discussion of the Latino population in the United States (Passel 2006; Delgado 2007; Hagan and Phillips 2008). Two-thirds of the undocumented in this country are Latino (Preston 2009b). Further, any demographic picture of the Latino community is incomplete without consideration of this issue.

The economic crises encountered in 2008 resulted in severe consequences for undocumented Latinos: many increased the hours they worked, earned less for their labor, and curtailed remittances to their families. The recession has also resulted in a slowing of the movement of undocumented Latinos across the U.S. border (Preston 2009c). However, the lure of safety in the United States still motivates individuals to cross the border despite the more limited economic opportunities: "an expected wave of reverse migration, in which unemployed Mexicans would stream back home to their cities and villages, has been more like a trickle. . . . On top of the traditional economic reasons, a growing number of Mexicans feel unsafe in their own country" (Llana 2009:6). Although tough economic times in this country have often resulted in undocumented Latinos returning to their country of origin, there has been a reluctance to do so for other reasons than just safety: "Despite the mounting pressures, many of the illegal immigrants are resisting leaving the country. After years of working here, they say, they have homes and education for their children, while many no longer have a stake to return to their home countries" (Preston 2009a:1).

The subject of Latino children born in the United States to parents who are undocumented has important implications for national immigration policies. It is estimated that four million American children have at least one parent who is undocumented. In 2003, the parents of 2.7 million children were undocumented. Seventy-three percent of all children of undocumented residents are citizens of the United States. However, for the remaining 27 percent the consequences can be quite devastating because of the limitations on jobs and careers these youth can pursue in the United States (Gonzalez 2009).

Undocumented residents are not equally distributed across the United States. California, for example, has a high concentration, and cities such as

Los Angeles, as result, have an unequal distribution within the state. In 2004 California had 36.6 million residents, with 9.5 million being newcomers (81 percent were from Mexico and Central American). Some 2.4 million of these were unauthorized immigrants, or approximately one-quarter of the nation's total (Center for Continuing Study of the California Economy 2005).

Latino small businesses serving undocumented residents face considerable challenges not commonly found in small businesses serving citizens and those who have a documented status. It is tough enough making a small business profitable without also dealing with a host of political factors and considerations.

The case of Amalia Cerrillo from Weld County, Colorado, highlights the struggles that undocumented Latinos face in this country. Amalia's Translation and Tax Services, a Latina small business, was raided by the Weld County Sheriff's Office, which seized thousands of confidential tax returns in search of patrons with fraudulent Social Security numbers. The sheriff identified 1,300 undocumented Latinos who had filed tax returns using fake or stolen Social Security numbers (Frosch 2009). (Undocumented workers across the country paid the Internal Revenue Service $50 billion in taxes between 1996 and 2003.) A somewhat similar situation was reported in Dallas when U.S. Immigration and Customs Enforcement officers raided twenty-six Latino establishments (night clubs, pool halls, and other types of small businesses), arresting forty-nine undocumented Latinos who worked as security guards and charging them with a variety of felonies, including being in the country illegally (Kraft 2008).

These examples highlight the challenges Latino small businesses face as they seek to meet the needs of all Latino community residents, but those who are undocumented in particular. Latino undocumented residents have tremendous social needs that can only be addressed within the Latino community because of safety concerns. Thus, the intrusion of authorities into the life and social fabric of the community takes on even greater significance when it involves a small business.

Projected Increases in the Next Forty Years

Smith, Tayman, and Swanson (2008:1) provide a humorous, but not inaccurate, commentary about the appeal of predicting the future:

> People are fascinated by the future. Palm readers, astrologers, and crystal-ball gazers down through the ages have found eager customers for their predictions and views of the future. Modern-day analysts and forecasters—

using computers and mathematical models instead of tea leaves and chicken entrails—continue to find willing audiences. The desire to see into the future is seemingly insatiable and apparently has not been diminished by the relatively low success rates achieved by visionaries and forecasters.

A word of caution is called for concerning the projections that follow. A 2009 estimate of Latino and Asian American population growth shows a slowing in the growth rate in the future because of lower immigration (influenced by economic swings) and birthrates. For example, Latino growth slowed from 4.0 percent in 2001 to 3.2 period in 2008 (Associated Press 2009b).

Projecting far into the future requires a certain degree of trust, and projecting the size of the Latino population to the year 2050 is such an example. Nevertheless, the past is prologue to the future, and this is very much the case in demographics (Montemayor and Mendoza 2004). Barone (2007:1) notes the importance of this field and why it is necessary to pay close attention to how the composition of this country is changing: "demography is destiny." Pinal stresses the current and future contributions of demographic changes to the nation, highlighting an assets rather than a deficit perspective: "The rapid growth of the Hispanic population in the last three or four decades has in effect rejuvenated the aging U.S. population by adding children and working-age adults, at the same time making it more ethnically diverse" (2008:57).

This country is turning two shades of color—graying (the population is increasingly growing older) and browning (groups of color continue to increase numerically) (Lopez 2005). Much of the emphasis in the professional literature has focused on the youthfulness of the Latino community, and this is understandable. However, from a demographic perspective, Latino baby boomers have largely been invisible, although they too, like their younger counterparts, will prove to be a group to be dealt with in the near future (Torres-Gil 2009).

The U.S. Census Bureau has made startling predictions involving Latinos in the United States, with profound implications for the nation, particularly when examined within a hemispheric or global context. It is important to pause, however, and note that critics of immigration, which plays a significant role in Latino population increases, tend to focus on short-term problems rather than long-term gains (Kuznets 1971). A short-term prediction has the U.S. population increasing by six million people between 2006 and 2010, with Latinos accounting for three million, or 50 percent of the growth (Goldman Sachs 2007). Latinos will continue to increase in representation and account for 20 percent of the U.S. population by the year 2030. The cohort of Latino children in schools in 2015 will be in the workforce by 2030 (Tienda and Mitchell 2006).

A long-term view of the Latino population also shows a continued increase. The Latino community is predicted to triple in size between 2000 and 2050. Numerically, Latinos will go from 35.6 million (12.6% of the total population) to 102.6 million (24.4%). This represents an increase of 188 percent in the fifty-year period. The nation's other groups of color will also increase, particularly Asian Americans, so that the nation will comprise approximately 50 percent people of color in 2050 (Cohn 2007). States such as Florida have drawn particular attention because of the current and projected changes in population within the Latino community and their implications for emerging markets (Will, Cobb, and Cheney 2008).

By 2050, according to the U.S. Census Bureau (2008b), children of color will constitute 62 percent of the nation's children, up from 44 percent in 2008. Latino children, in turn, are expected to constitute 39 percent of the youth population in this country, up from 22 percent in 2008 (Institute for Health Policy Studies, 2002).

The two states with the largest current Latino population (Texas and California) will continue to experience dramatic increases in their respective population profiles. In 2000 Texas became the fourth state (along with California, Hawaii, and New Mexico) to have a minority-majority population, with Latinos playing a critical role in this development (Caldwell 2005). By 2020 the number of Latinos will surpass white non-Latinos in Texas, and by 2040 they will reach 18.8 million (State of Texas 2008). There will be two Latinos (59.1 percent) for every white non-Latino (24.2 percent) in Texas in that year (Mudock and White 2002; Harris 2007). Close to half (49%) of Arizona's population (5 million) will be Latino by 2030 (Underwood and Ducker 2007). Latinos will triple in size in Arizona cities, from 5.9 million to 17.2 million, and almost double in rural areas, from 777,000 to 1.6 million.

California will also witness dramatic changes. In 2020 it will have 44.135 million residents, of which Latinos will count for 18.261 million, or 41.3 percent. In 2040 the population will increase to 49.240 million, and the Latino community will number 26.551 million (53.9%). Finally, in 2050 California's population will top 50.507 million, and the Latino community will number 31.028 million, or 52.1 percent of the total population (California Department of Finance 2007). These projected estimates are predicated on a number of assumptions pertaining to births, deaths, and migration. For example, estimates for California for the year 2025 have ranged from a low of 41.5 million to 52.5 million (Thomas and Deakin 2001). Nevertheless, regardless of which estimate one accepts, all sectors of the state—from the economy to the school system to health and social services—will experience the racial and ethnic transformation.

DEMOGRAPHIC PROFILES OF THREE CITIES

I have selected three cities to profile in this section, based on their geographical location, demographic trends, the strategic position they hold in the Latino community nationally and internationally, and the media publicity they generate: Miami, Los Angeles, and New York. Clearly there are numerous other cities across the country with histories of attracting Latinos—Chicago being one (Badillo 2004; Klein 2008). Ready and Brown-Gort (2005) find dramatic increases in the Latino population of Chicago's metropolitan area, with this group accounting for more than 26 percent of the city's total population. The influx of Latinos was primarily responsible for Chicago not experiencing a decrease in population between 1990 and 2000. Mexican Americans accounted for 15 percent of the city's population in 2000, followed by Puerto Ricans with 2.5 percent (Tienda and Raijman 2004). Almost half of Latinos living in Chicago's metropolitan area reside outside the city itself. Nevertheless, I have elected to focus on Los Angeles, Miami, and New York because these three cities have historically held and/or currently hold important roles in shaping how Latinos are viewed nationwide and internationally.

The cities are unique but share much in common beyond being ports of entry into the United States for different Latino groups (Saenz, Morales, and Ayala 2004; Fischer and Tienda 2006). For example, Latinos account for $28.9 billion in purchasing power in Los Angeles, $17.6 billion in New York, $9 billion in Miami (compared with $6 billion in San Francisco and Chicago, respectively) (El Nassar 2005). The demographic trends that are occurring in these cities may well surprise readers but reflect the dynamic nature of immigration and dispersal in the United States as a whole (El Nassar 2008; Fischer and Tienda 2006).

Below I discuss each city from four perspectives: a brief historical demographic overview; their current demographic profile; their current small business profile; and projected trends. These categories are not mutually exclusive, each seeks to capture a particular portrait or glimpse of the urban Latino community in the early part of this century.

LOS ANGELES

Brief Historical Demographic Overview

The history of the Latino community in Los Angeles is as long as the history of settlement in California (Macias 2005). This history, not surprisingly, is closely tied to Mexico. However, the Latino community has recently started to diversify to include other groups. Nevertheless, Los Angeles is still heavily represented by Mexican Americans. In 2006 Latinos surpassed African Americans as the largest group of color in Los Angeles (Wood 2008).

The Latino community in Los Angeles elicits a wide variety of images at the national level. East Los Angeles is to the city's Latino community what Little Havana, Miami, is to Cubans and El Barrio (Spanish Harlem), New York, is to Puerto Ricans (Davila 2004a). These Latino centers represent ethnic symbols, social and intellectual centers, and cultural capital (Wood 2008).

The impact of Latinos in Los Angeles and its surroundings also goes beyond the Latino community itself, as Hayes-Bautista (2004b: 202) notes: "Southern California is becoming a region with a Latino population majority. The way that Latinos define the activities of daily life—family, work, diet, religion, dreams, fears, the common good—soon may become characteristics of the entire region, not just of Latinos."

Current Demographic Profile

As in other major cities, Latinos are no longer concentrated in Los Angeles's historically Latino centers (Ochoa and Ochoa 2005). Nevertheless, in 2007 Los Angeles County had 4.7 million Latinos, making it the largest "Latino" county in the country (U.S. Census Bureau 2008). Los Angeles itself had 3.75 million Latinos, constituting 50 percent of the city's total population (Cohn 2007).

The upsurge in Latinos has manifested itself in both traditional Latino neighborhoods such as East Los Angeles and neighborhoods that were historically African American. For example, in the 1980s South Central Los Angeles was predominantly African American, but by 1990 it was equally divided between African Americans and Latinos (47% each). By 2006 Latinos constituted 62 percent of the population, with African Americans reduced to 31 percent (Marquez 2008; Ong 2008).

Current Small Business Profile and Data

The Latino small business community in Los Angeles has been the subject of numerous scholarly and government reports (Richardson and Gordon 2005). In 2002 more than 50 percent of all businesses owned by people of color in the Los Angeles region were owned by Latinos (Latino Business Review 2009). Latino-owned businesses in the region are estimated to have generated $35 billion in sales from 2002 to 2008 (*Latino Business Review* 2009a).

A 2005 study of 205 Latino business owners finds that 68 percent originated in Mexico (Minority Business Atlas 2005). Eighty percent of this sample have been in existence for at least nine years; 36 percent, for at least sixteen years. Seventy percent are owned by men, and 11 percent by women (19% of respondents did not answer this question). Latino owners are well educated: 64 percent are college graduates. Nearly 60 percent of the owners are between 30 and 50 years old; 33 percent are over 50. Services (55%) and retail (21%) represent almost three-fourths of all businesses. Finally, 38 percent access bank loans and 6 percent use government financing. Credit cards (42%), personal loans (29%), and home equity loans (17%) provided the bulk of their startup financing.

The informal economy of the Latino community in Los Angeles, not surprisingly, has received considerable scholarly attention, particularly in relation to informal enterprises. Lopez-Garza (2001) highlights the toll that an informal economy extracts on Latino immigrants. Similarly, Rosales (2001) focuses on the personal histories and work experience of Latina domestic workers documenting the hardships encountered that led to their employment as domestic workers.

Chinchilla and Hamilton (2001) study both formal and informal Central American enterprises and show how this newly arrived group has grown and contributed to the well-being of Los Angeles. Weber (2001) illustrates how political will translated into the development of a street vendors' association as a means of dealing with established business owners who resent both the street business and the increase in the Latino population. Bernhardt et al. (2008), however, express concerns about the "gloves-off" informal economy and how individuals in these types of industries are increasingly being subjected to harsh work conditions and a higher likelihood of abuse.

Projected Trends

The economy of Los Angeles has undergone dramatic changes in the past decade, as Corraiejo 2009) explains:

> We can no longer depend on Hollywood, the defense industry or home builders to expand our economy and create hundreds of thousands of job opportunities. . . . The future of America, and particularly for Los Angeles, can no longer depend on global corporate giants or "too-big-to-fail" financial institutions, most of which have laid off tens of thousands of workers and outsourced jobs to Asia. Instead, we should focus on the resources that

are available to Greater Los Angeles. The most unique is the hundreds of thousands of small minority-owned businesses, and, in particular, the approximately 200,000 Latino-owned businesses in Los Angeles County.

It is estimated that Los Angeles will continue to become more Latinized in the near future. For a complete picture, demographic projections for the city also need to be viewed in the context of changes predicted for the state of California (Myers, Pitkin, and Park 2005).

MIAMI

Brief Historical Demographic Overview

There is little question that the nation has developed a particular image of Latinos in Miami, and that this picture has largely been shaped by the Cuban community and its arrival in large numbers after the revolution that overthrew Fulgencio Batista and installed Fidel Castro in his place. This is not to say that Latinos had not been part of Miami's landscape before 1959 (Bauzon 2007; George 2007; Nijman 2007). However, 1959 marks what was arguably the beginning of the Latinization of Miami, a trend that has continued largely unabated for fifty years (Stepick et al. 2003). Miami has been forever transformed by this influx of Cubans and other Latino groups (Orum 2005; Portes and Shafer 2007).

It is important to note that the "Miami experience" of Cubans does not represent that of Cubans in other parts of the country. Skop (2008) argues that the Miami model has dominated the public and scholarly discourse on Cubans in the United States, virtually negating their experiences in other parts of the country and limiting a comprehensive understanding of this Latino group. To counteract this phenomenon, Prieto (2009) focuses on Cubans' experiences in Union City, New Jersey, and provides an ecological perspective on the Cuban experience in the United States.

The success of television shows like *Miami Vice* has probably had a greater influence in shaping national images of Miami and Cubans than have all the scholarly papers and books on the subject. These observations take on added salience as dispersal patterns create new geographical realities and models for better understanding the presence and economic influence of Latinos in this country. Nevertheless, Miami and Cubans are synonymous in Latino folklore.

Current Demographic Profile

Today Miami is a highly diverse city in terms race and ethnicity. According to the U.S. Census Bureau (2008), Latinos account for almost two-thirds (65.8%) of Miami's population of 363,470. Metropolitan Miami, however, has an estimated 2.2 million people, of which 1.3 million, or 57 percent, are Latino. Miami's Cuban community represents about half of all the Cubans in the United States, although they can be found in sizable pockets in the Northeast as well as other parts of the country. Cubans are the largest Latino group in Florida, representing 41 percent (900,000) of the Latino community in the state (Montemayor and Mendoza 2004), followed by Puerto Ricans and other Caribbean and Latin American groups (Aranda 2009).

Current Small Business Profile and Data

The Miami business landscape is dominated by Latinos, which is to be expected based on the numerical representation that this demographic group enjoys in the city. Tourism, for example, has played a strategic role in helping to elevate Miami to international prominence. Moreno, like other scholars, attributes Cubans' business success to their geographical concentration (forming an ethnic enclave) within select Miami neighborhoods:

> The economic enclave is the second factor that has contributed to the rapid political empowerment of Cuban-Americans. Cuban-Americans are not only concentrated in South Florida but they are also concentrated within South Florida in well-defined neighborhoods. Cuban immigrants first settled in Southwest Miami along Flagler and SW 8th Street. This neighborhood quickly developed into Miami's vibrant Little Havana district as businesses catering to Latin tastes sprang up along this corridor. The arrival of more and more Cuban refugees between the 1960 and 1980 caused the Latin population to expand west along Flagler and SW 8th Street (which became known as "Calle Ocho"), encompassing new neighborhoods such as West Miami, North Coral Gables, Westchester, West Dade, and the working city of Hialeah. The establishment of a large Hispanic population in Miami-Dade served as an incubator for Latin-owned businesses. Cuban-American entrepreneurs quickly established a network of businesses (grocery stores, pharmacies, restaurants, construction, banks, newspaper, furniture stores, etc.) to serve Miami's growing Hispanic population. Professional services quickly followed as Spanish-speaking lawyers, doctors, real estate and insurance agents, and dentists established offices along the Flagler and 8th

Street corridors and in the city of Hialeah. The size and institutional completeness of these businesses and services have allowed the residents of these areas to conduct all their personal affairs in Spanish. Miami's Cuban population in those central neighborhoods became a self-contained ethnic enclave. (2005:3–4)

This is not to say, however, that discrimination against Latinos is no longer a factor. Carvagal (2004), in a study of Hispanic-owned architecture and engineering firms in South Florida, finds discrimination against these firms, including those owned by women, based on their earnings compared with those of white non-Latino firms with similar characteristics.

Projected Trends

The Miami of the twenty-first century will share much in common with the Miami of the late twentieth century, with the trends that began in the last century simply continuing into the next. Nevertheless, there will be changes, and that should be expected in a port city such as Miami. Although Little Havana still has a strongly Cuban identity, it is no longer predominantly Cuban in composition. This community has gradually been transformed from a Cuban to a Latin American community with numerous other Latino groups calling it home. This transformation occurred in full force in the 1980s when Central Americans started to settle there in large numbers, and it continues today (Alberts 2006).

Latino small businesses in Miami and southern Florida are destined to continue wielding tremendous influence on the economic and social life of the city, with regional, national, and international (Caribbean and Latin American) ramifications. The strategic position of the city will help ensure that the image of Miami as a multicultural and multilingual city will continue to endure. This does not mean, however, that ethnic and racial tensions will disappear. The economic dislocation that has occurred in Miami is well-known, and efforts must be made to help reduce the possibility of future conflicts and tension.

NEW YORK

Brief Historical Demographic Overview

New York has a long and distinguished history as a haven for newcomers to the United States, and the Statue of Liberty stands as testimony to the role this port of entry has played for millions of people in the past two centuries. New York's history is integrally associated with immigration to this country. Roberts (2008b) captures this sentiment in describing the situation since 2000: "In almost every category, the results demonstrated the city's diversity and dynamism . . . the proportion of foreign born who are American citizens passed a tipping point, to 50.8 percent in 2007 from 45 percent in 2000. The city's prominent position as a media center has propelled the presence of newcomers, documented and undocumented."

Current Demographic Profile

Foner's (2001:1) assessment of New York sets a good foundation for this section and highlights the role of immigrants in shaping the city's past, current, and—in all likelihood—future composition: "At the dawn of a new millennium, New York is again an immigrant city. In the last four decades, more than two and a half million immigrants have settled in New York City." After a brief period of slow immigration, New York again occupies its rightful place as "America's immigrant city."

Based on the 2000 U.S. Census, more than one-third of the city's residents are foreign born, and an estimated 2.2 million are Latinos, or 27 percent of the total population (Foner 2001; Montemayor and Mendoza 2004). The Latino community has changed dramatically in the past fifty years (Lobo, Flores, and Salvo 2002; Miyares 2004). Historically Puerto Ricans and Dominicans have dominance as the two largest Latino groups, although there are noticeable shift toward new Latino groups entering the area.

The history of Latinos in New York is intrinsically tied to the history of Puerto Ricans. Puerto Ricans are still the largest Latino group in the city, though their concentration has decreased over the past fifty years. In 1950, 80 percent of all Puerto Ricans in the United States lived in New York; in 1970 that number declined to 62 percent, falling further to slightly under 40 percent in 1990 and 25 percent in 2000, with approximately 850,000 Puerto Ricans living in the city in 2000 (Fischer and Tienda 2006).

Dominicans are the second largest Latino group in New York, and approximately 50 percent of Dominicans living in the United States are located in that city (Pantoja 2005; U.S. Census Bureau 2008). Other large groups of Dominicans reside elsewhere on the East Coast, with Florida, other parts of New York, New Jersey, and Massachusetts being the most popular states. Marwell (2004:230) reinforces the importance of New York to Dominicans in the United States: "New York City is the focal point of the Dominican community in the United States. It contains the largest Dominican population outside of the Dominican Republic, and remittances from New Yorkers supply 25 percent of the country's GNP."

It is estimated the 2000 U.S. Census seriously undercounted Dominicans in New York, with the actual number being closer to one million rather than the approximate 800,000 reported (Scott 2001; Chun 2007). Other Latino groups were also undercounted: Salvadorans by 42.6 percent, other Central Americans by 47 percent, and South Americans by 41.3 percent. It should be noted that significant undercounting of Latinos also translates into significant underreporting of income and sales in the informal economy (Delgado 2007).

Mexicans, both immigrant and native-born, numbered an estimated 250,000–275,000 in 2000 and form the third largest Latino group in the city (Smith 2001; DePalma 2005a, b). The Mexican influx has spread throughout the city: "Mexicans are the fasting growing Latino group and they are actively reshaping the city's landscape. In the past decade, Mexicans have formed vibrant communities in Corona, Sunset Park, and Jackson Heights, but because of its location in Manhattan, El Barrio's Mexican community has surfaced as one of the most visible and well known" (Davila 2004a:153). The Archdiocese of New York, in response to this demographic change, instituted a program to bring nuns from Mexico to give spiritual support to the 25,000 Mexicans in the South Bronx (Filkins 2001). Nonetheless, Mexicans, like other Latino groups in the city, are far from being homogeneous in composition (Davila 2004a).

Current Small Business Profile and Data

Ethnic and racial small businesses are certainly an integral part of many New York neighborhoods (Morawska 2004). In 2002 there were 129,461 Latino businesses in the city, ahead of such cities as Los Angeles, Miami, Houston, and San Antonio (Associated Press 2006). In 2009 New York had an estimated 185,000 small businesses, with 42–45 percent of them owned by Latinos. Eighty-five percent of the 16,500 bodegas (grocery stores) had Latino owners (Graglia 2009). Latino-owned enterprises have been estimated to generate a total of $8.7 billion in receipts, with payrolls of approximately $250 million (Samaad 2009).

Latino business ownership increased by 57 percent from 1997 to 2002, five times the national average (Gerson 2006). More specifically, the Bronx, one of New York's five boroughs, saw Latino-owned firms increase by 159 percent during that period. In 2002 the Bronx was home for six thousand more Latino-owned small businesses than Manhattan, and three thousand more than Queens. However, profits in Manhattan and Queens firms were higher profits than in the Bronx (Gerson 2006).

Puerto Ricans owned 20 percent of all Latino businesses in the city. However, Dominicans were a close second, and Mexican ownership rose to 7 percent in just five years. The president of the New York State Coalition of Hispanic Chambers of Commerce commented on this trend: " 'The Mexican community is growing very fast. They bought the bodegas from the Dominicans,' he said, noting that the bodega, once dominated by Puerto Ricans, has now become a tradition to be used as a launching pad to other entrepreneurial ventures" (quoted in Gerson 2006).

Projected Trends

New York will no doubt continue to be home to countless numbers of new groups, and to their children in unprecedented numbers. In the early twenty-first century, almost 66 percent of the city's population under the age of 18 consists of children of immigrants (Kasinitz, Mollenkopf, and Waters 2004). In addition, immigrants have played an influential role in New York's post-9/11 economy (Hum 2005), and there is no reason to believe that this will cease to be the case in the future.

This chapter placed heavy emphasis on providing the latest data on Latino demographics. Further, I made a conscious effort not only to focus on the most pertinent demographic data but to highlight often overlooked data as well. This perspective on communities serves as a backdrop for examining the interplay and interrelationship of numerous social and economic factors. In addition, the demographics in this chapter set the stage for subsequent chapters to examine the key social and economic roles that Latino businesses are playing in the largest and fastest-growing Latino areas in the country.

Some readers may take exception to the urban concentration of this chapter, and particularly my selection of Los Angeles, Miami, and New York for more focused discussion. I did this as a means of showing how demographic trends are shifting in major cities across the nation. Suffice it to say that Latino representation is not static, and its dynamic nature, as evidenced in this chapter, is alive and well.

Development of effective social programs cannot transpire without a proper grounding in demographics, regardless of the population group being targeted, and this is particularly the case when examining the role of small businesses in the Latino community (Toussaint-Comeau, Smith, and Comeau 2005). This type of information is invaluable in creating a profile of who is being targeted for services, and in determining how we can become more strategic as a profession and as a nation.

The United States is clearly at a crossroads. People can take stock of how the country is changing and view these changes within a global context, making the nation economically competitive on a world stage. The presence of multilingual and multicultural population groups with insights into their countries of origin provides invaluable information from an economic perspective (Jones 2005; Johnson and Sengupta 2009). A negative or alarming viewpoint on demographics, however, which unfortunately seems to be the prevailing perspective, will not make the United States competitive on a world scale but will result in valuable resources being expended to incarcerate, deport, and suppress millions of people, with international repercussions.

The demographic trends discussed in this chapter have a tremendous impact on the nature, well-being, and ultimate success of racial and ethnic small businesses. The next chapter presents theoretical and empirical information to assist in developing a foundation from which to better understand and appreciate these enterprises.

3

RACIAL AND ETHNIC SMALL BUSINESSES IN THE UNITED STATES

▪▪▪▪▪▪▪▪▪▪▪▪▪▪▪▪▪▪▪▪▪▪▪▪▪▪▪▪▪▪▪▪▪▪▪▪▪▪

> As the fastest growing business segment in the country, Hispanic
> business owners are a large indicator to the economic stability of
> the U.S. Quite bluntly, if the Hispanic small business community
> falters, the small business community is weakened. If the overall
> small business community fails, the U.S. economy fails.
>
> —M. L. Barrera, "Back to Business: Giving Small Businesses a Voice"

THE DEMOGRAPHIC PICTURE of the Latino community in the United States
presented in the previous chapter has established a foundation from which to
understand the relationship between small businesses and population size,
profile, and demographic trends. This chapter details the historic role such
enterprises have played in urban communities of color in the United States
and a variety of conceptual ways of viewing these establishments (Pages 2005).

As the quote above attests to, there really is very little that is small about
"small businesses" in this country, regardless of their geographical setting
and the ethnic and racial background of the owners (Korsching and Allen
2004; Reynolds 2007). Nevertheless, ethnic and racial businesses are generally labor intensive and low profit, with social and economic implications for
communities of color. Yet they increasingly provide an alternative path to
economic wealth and mobility in the United States (Halter 1995).

More than twenty years ago, Bates reported on findings from a study of
"minority" small businesses in urban inner cities, arriving at conclusions that
unfortunately are still prevalent today:

> Within the minority communities of large SMSAs, neither the black-owned
> nor the small nonminority enterprises are flourishing. Facing limited access

to financial capital as well as constrained markets, the ghetto firms that do persist are typically quite small in terms of sales and employment. Among black establishments, the ghetto firms that do persist are typically quite small in terms of sales and employment. Among black establishments, the least educated entrepreneurs are the ones who are most likely to remain in business. Unless greater financial capital is forthcoming and better educated owners are induced to remain in business, the business community that is located in minority neighborhoods of large urban areas may be destined to stagnate. (1989:625)

Small businesses account for 60–80 percent of new jobs in the country and represent a powerful economic engine. However, they are also the sector that is hardest hit by economic downturns since approximately 94 percent of them employ 20 or fewer workers. These businesses are firmly grounded in the communities they cater to.

According to the U.S. Department of Labor, small businesses and immigrants played a huge role in helping the nation's major cities achieve economic recovery during the recession of the 1980s: "The commercial recovery of New York City in the 1980s and the continued vitality of Los Angeles and Miami have been fueled by voluminous increases in small business activity. Immigrants are directly responsible for a substantial share of this activity" (Lofstrom 2010:94). It remains to be seen whether the same will hold true when the results of the recession of 2008–2009 are assessed, but we do know that women and newcomers have played important roles in the growth of self-employment in California during this period.

Fairle (2005:2–3) notes that there has been an upsurge in interest concerning small business development in general, and particularly in urban communities of color: "The intent in entrepreneurship and business development has been spurred by arguments from academicians and policymakers that entrepreneurship provides a route out of poverty and an alternative to unemployment or discrimination in the labor market." This same argument can also be made for social work and other helping professions.

Small businesses are credited with job creation, innovation, and economic growth (Acs and Kallas 2007). As Bernard and Slaughter note, the ultimate success or failure of enterprises owned by people of color will largely be responsible for the success or failure of the U.S. economy in the twenty-first century:

The United States today faces unprecedented demographic changes, the net result of which will be dramatic changes in the size and racial and ethnic composition of the U.S. labor force. In future decades the U.S. labor force will grow much more slowly than in the past, and any growth that is realized will be accounted for entirely by minorities—whose growth, in turn, will be accounted for largely by immigrants. The success or failure of minority-owned businesses will increasingly drive the success or failure of the overall U.S. economy. (2004:1)

This assessment of the current and future contribution of racial and ethnic small businesses highlights the long-term implications for the country, and for cities in particular.

From a purchasing and economic power perspective, there are four major economic groups in the United States: Latinos, African Americans, Asian Americans, and European Americans (Misonzhnik 2008). For example, Sriram, Mersha, and Herron (2007) and Cooke (2005) advance the notion that African American small businesses will play an influential role in any solution addressing economic distress in the nation's inner cities.

African American purchasing power is estimated to be $913 billion as of 2008 and is expected to rise to $1.2 trillion by 2013 (Miley 2009). In 2008 the Latino and African American markets amounted to about $1.7 trillion (Misonzhnik 2008). If Asian Americans are added ($453 billion), the amount goes up to $2.26 trillion. Humphreys (2006) notes that the African American and Latino consumer markets are larger than those of all but nine countries in the world and therefore need to be viewed from this perspective to more fully appreciate their significance for the U.S. economy. However, when businesses owned by white non-Latinos are compared with those owned by people of color, a tremendous disparity in the amount of money these businesses generate becomes apparent (Lowrey 2007).

Hutchinson (2005) cautions against viewing African American small businesses as a panacea for all the social ills confronting this community, advocating that solutions need to involve large-scale federal intervention. Similar cautions must be made about Latino- and Asian-owned small businesses. Small businesses can wield tremendous influence on positive community outcomes. However, they must be considered as part of the economic solution, not the entire solution.

Barth, Yago, and Zeidman summarize important economic data on racial and ethnic small businesses that place these institutions in context and highlight why they cannot be expected to be the social and economic engines for social reform:

Entrepreneurship drives economic innovation and job formation. Business-ownership participation rates vary dramatically among those ethnic groups accounting for the largest demographic growth rates. For example, Hispanics constitute 13.5 percent of the U.S. population, but just 7 percent of business ownership; they employ just 13 percent of the work force and represent less than 1 percent of the revenues. Similarly, African-Americans account for 12.4 percent of the population, but only 5 percent of the firms and less than 1 percent of both employees and revenues. (2006:3)

SCHOLARLY ATTENTION TO ETHNIC BUSINESSES

The subject of ethnic or minority businesses in the United States received considerable attention in the scholarly literature during the 1990s (see, for example, works such as Halter 1995; Waldinger et al. 1990; Light and Rosenstein 1995; Bates 1997; Yoon 1997; Park 1997; and Waldinger 2000). This work highlighted the excitement and importance of a nation looking at small businesses through a different lens—one that helps portray communities of color in a positive light.

However, since that period the literature has at best been spotty, although newspaper accounts of small businesses in urban communities of color have increased, and scholarly articles and official reports of various kinds have surfaced on a regular basis (Greenhouse 2007a, b). For example, there has been no book targeting the Latino community from this perspective. Latino-owned businesses as a dimension of community assets holds much appeal for community social work practice because of how this field of practice and scholarship embraces indigenous community assets. Nowak (2007:3) notes: "Significant development always builds from existing assets and points of strengths." These Latino establishments clearly are community assets and represent a bridge, or link, between the "old country" and the "new country."

There is general agreement that the broader business establishment has historically viewed urban communities of color as undesirable or abandoned, with the possible exception of the alcohol and cigarette industries, sometimes referred to as "merchants of death" in the 1980s (Hacker, Collins, and Jacobson 1987; Maxwell and Jacobson 1989). Hudson (1996) developed the concept of "merchants of misery" to illustrate how corporate America profited from marketing to low-income communities. There is evidence, however, that this neglect has started to shift because of an increase in population and purchasing power (Delgado 2007; Garcia 2004). Tobacco and alcohol availability and point of sale, for example, continue to be highly concentrated in poor urban communities (Grier and Kumanyika 2008; Hyland et al. 2003; Kyeyoung 2004; Laws et al. 2002).

Existing books, with notable exceptions, have emphasized the economic role of ethnic and racial small businesses and largely ignored their social and cultural impact, including the potential role these establishments can play in providing health and human services. For example, Song (1999) examines the social consequences of reliance of Chinese small businesses on child labor. There are no books where such firms are explored as potential vehicles for helping severely marginalized subgroups, such as those with histories of persistent mental illness or those with criminal histories (Delgado, forthcoming).

In his book titled *SIDEWALK*, Duneier (1999) presents a dimension of contemporary urban life that I would like to build on in this chapter—that is, individuals can make their livelihoods from selling wares on street corners in urban places like New York. These informal businesses often represent an avenue for marginalized groups to be part of the American entrepreneurial spirit, yet this phenomenon generally goes unnoticed by society. These ventures must be considered part of the subject "small businesses" if we are to obtain a more comprehensive perspective on economic enterprises within urban Latino communities.

Finally, the subject of ethnic small businesses is quite complex and becoming increasingly more so as new scholarly attention is paid to it. There certainly are different motivations on the part of entrepreneurs for engaging in social enterprises (Zahra et al. 2009). For example, Danes et al. (2008:229) seek to broaden the context in which to examine ethnic small business development in order to more fully grasp its richness and its importance to their respective communities and to the broader society:

> Entrepreneurs have been traditionally epitomized as rugged individuals garnering creative forces of innovation and technology. Applying this traditional, limited, and narrow view of entrepreneurship to ethnic firm creation and growth is to ignore or discount core cultural values of the ethnic contexts in which these firms operate. It is no longer possible to depend solely on human capital theory and household characteristic descriptions to understand the complex and interdependent relationships between the ethnic-owning family, its firm, and the community context in which the firm operates.

Erick and colleagues (2009), in a study of Latino entrepreneurs in New England, find that social capital, conceptualized and measured as family support, plays an influential role in venture preparedness and the startup decision. This finding reinforces Harris's (2009:293) conclusions related to the important intersection of family and race/ethnicity in small business creation in communities of color and the need to go beyond a narrow view of capital to better understand this phenomenon: "Both family and ethnicity are viewed as 'upstream factors' that may help a business gain a favorable identity with potential stakeholders. Family businesses that have an ethnic background in common with customers, employees, and suppliers may receive preferential treatment. Communities may patronize a business simply because of an associated group identity. Thus, ethnic collectivism may alter some assumptions about family businesses and how they compete."

Rodriguez, Tuggle, and Hackett (2009) draw on family social capital theory to examine the relationship between family capital characteristics and new venture startup rates in the United States. The results of this study show how families and other factors such as health and wealth influence decisions to start a business, lending credence to the complexity of the decision-making process and the importance of factors beyond human capital.

THE INFORMAL ECONOMY

This is a good time to revisit the informal economy and why it plays such an influential role in the life of Latino communities. An informal economy goes under many different terms, such as "underground," "shadow," "invisible," "space of hope," "black," and "alternative economic space," most of which convey the generally negative public perceptions of this sector of the economy (Harvey 2000; Leyshon, Lee, and Williams 2003; Vogel 2006). The informal economy is characterized as small-scale and generating little revenue, but it wields a tremendous amount of social and economic clout. Economists, for instance, estimate that the informal economy in the United States is anywhere from 4.4 to 27 percent of the nation's gross national product (GNP), with 10 percent being the most widely accepted figure (Thelford and Edgcomb 2004). This translated to $1.067 billion in 2003.

As initially addressed in chapter 1, the informal economy may not be formal or official, but it does have a prodigious amount of influence in urban communities of color. This economy wields a duel-edged sword: it provides a much needed avenue for entrepreneurship in places where a formal economy does not exist, but it carries a potential for poor working conditions and exploitation as real threats to the health and well-being of business owners and their employees. The largely invisible nature of this form of business brings with it a host of potential negative consequences. Rinehart (2004), who notes that efforts to improve working conditions in the informal economy have drawn increased attention, identifies eleven compromising conditions: occupational safety and health, maternity protection, work–family issues, working time, home-based work, wages and income, work organization, sexual harassment, violence at work, workload, workers' welfare facilities.

The conditions listed are not mutually exclusive and take on added significance in the case of people who are undocumented and thus afraid to seek assistance from formal organizations. Poor working conditions (long hours, low pay, difficult or dangerous conditions), low status, and poor relationships between workers and supervisors have a negative spillover effect onto family life (Delgado and Canabal 2006). The familial consequences of workers who are emotionally drained, frequently in a bad mood, or often tired can be profound.

Drawing a line between informal and formal businesses may do a disservice to the development of a critical understanding of small enterprises within Latino and other ethnic and racial communities. The concepts of "layering" and "patching" are often used to describe the informal economy and the use of multiple streams of income, including formal employment. Thus, it probably is best to view the informal and formal economies on a continuum. Lofstrom and Wang (2007) argue that viewing small businesses as a binary (self-employed or not self-employed) outcome hides important factors and considerations and oversimplifies a complex community socioeconomic system. Latinos, for example, invariably turn to the informal economy for one or combination of the following reasons: lack of documentation; desire for hidden income; competitive advantage in pricing; avoidance of costs of compliance with regulations; or limited business size and lack of intent to grow a business (Thelford and Edgcomb 2004).

Lopez-Garza (2001) provides an interesting observation that facilitates the understanding of the informal economy. Any occupation that can be carried out in a formal economy can also be performed in an informal economy, at a less expensive price. Furthermore, it is not out of the ordinary to find a Latino worker performing the same job in both the formal and informal economies. One study finds five types of informal economy prevalent in the Latino community: specialty foods/catering (24%); child care (18%); cleaning (10%); construction and home improvement (10%); and retail (8%) (Thelford and Edgcomb 2004). Thus, there is a thin line between these two forms of economy, with frequent crossing over from one to the other.

Williams, Round, and Rodgers (2007) note that the historical view that a robust informal economy deters the formation of a formal economy does not hold true. In fact, a robust informal economy can be considered a vehicle for nurturing enterprise creation by serving as a laboratory or incubator for emerging entrepreneurs in the nation's central cities. Edgcomb and Armington (2003:20) also address the blended nature of the informal economy: "The patching these entrepreneurs do may involve a steady combination of income sources, with the primary wage job generating a regular return. For some, however, both the job and the enterprise are somewhat fluid with each rising and falling, depending on the availability of work or customers."

Diaz brings a historical perspective pertaining to Latino home-based enterprises that still holds merit today in the twenty-first century but has its roots over a century ago:

> Businesses in barrios have, historically, utilized homes for commercial activities, often conducting retail and service transactions in front rooms. The planning profession has staunchly opposed this nontraditional use of space, yet it remains a staple in barrio business life. In fact, the commercial use of "private" space dates back to the early twentieth century, a time when Euro-American property owners refused to rent commercial space to Chicano(as). [Consequently] numerous retail and crafts small businesses that developed prior to the 1950s began in home-based locations. (2005:122)

Zlolniski (2008:73) echoes a similar theme based on his research on janitors and street vendors in Silicon Valley: "Santech is one of the favorite sites of street vendors, who daily come to sell a large variety of products, including fresh fruits and vegetables, tortillas, beauty products, kitchen cookware, jewelry, pirated CDs, and others. Many residents of the barrio are themselves also directly involved in the informal economy." Consequently, home-based businesses have a historic place in Latino communities but are largely invisible to nonresidents, and their origins have been shaped by discriminatory local social circumstances.

The theories on ethnic and racial small business development that follow can best be appreciated and understood against a backdrop of informal enterprises and the conceptual, economic, social, and political implications this business has for Latino and other groups of color in the nation's urban communities.

THEORIES ON ETHNIC AND RACIAL SMALL BUSINESSES

The scholarly literature on ethnic small businesses has generated a number of theories to help explain the phenomenon of self-employment within communities of color. Some of these theories have caught the attention and imagination of many scholars, while others have minimal support and following. Nevertheless, there is no absence of theories to help explain the presence and proliferation of ethnic small businesses among communities of color.

It is important to pause and note once again that it is ill-advised to lump together all ethnic and racial groups when developing approaches to encourage and sustain small business development: "Not only has the scholarship retained a culturalist lens, but, for the most part, it has also suffered from a myopic tendency to treat ethnicity as a monolithic construct, overlooking within group variation. In fact, members of the same ethnic group often harbor dissimilar values and face distinct opportunities due to class, gender, religious, racial, and/or other stratifying cleavages" (Verdaguer 2009:1).

The increased attention given to ethnic businesses has resulted in a greater awareness and understanding of the role these institutions play in the tradition of small businesses in the United States. As a result, there is a call to embed ethnic small businesses within this context (Jones and Ram 2007). An integrative (universal) model of small business development and growth considers social, economic, political, and psychological factors (Wiklund, Patzelt, and Shepherd 2009). However, there is no denying the particularistic aspects attributable to cultural influences.

Bates, Jackson, and Johnson (2007) postulate that small business creation depends on the presence of and interplay between three critical factors: the skills of the owner, access to necessary financial capital, and access to a market. I would add to this list access to competitively priced products and technical assistance. Each of these factors, in turn, is greatly influenced by racial and ethnic forces that either facilitate or hinder small enterprise development and expansion within the broader society.

Zhou (2007) breaks ethnic small business ownership into two schools of thought: "middlemen minorities" versus "enclave entrepreneurs." Middlemen seek to trade or broker between society's elites or dominant group and the masses (community). These owners have few if any intrinsic ties to the social structures and social relationships of the community their business serves. Ethnic enclave entrepreneurs, however, are firmly grounded in the community because of coethnic group membership and are embedded in community life. Immigrants, who are predominantly either Latino or Asian, for example, are 10–20 percent more likely than native-born residents to start a small business. However, there has been no systematic measurement of immigrants' entrepreneurial impact on the nation's economy (Bolin 2006).

In a review of the literature, Le (2007) identifies four theories to help explain the characteristics of individuals who choose self-employment, their reasons for doing so, the types of businesses they own, and the success and failure of such enterprises: labor market discrimination; cultural traits and ethnic resources; class resources; and structural opportunities. Le summarizes these theories from the perspective of the Asian community, but they have implications for other newcomer groups as well, which I discuss below.

LABOR MARKET DISCRIMINATION

For newcomers, opportunities to work at regular jobs are very limited because of language, cultural traits, and discrimination (Oh 2008). Lack of alternatives, as a result, necessitates that newcomers develop their own employment opportunities. Edgecomb and Armington's (2003) research on informal Latino enterprises finds that 42 percent of those engaged in this form of enterprise did so because of necessity rather than choice.

Hum's (2001) study of immigrant economies in Los Angeles concludes that newcomers remain largely excluded in the general labor market, necessitating creation of their own small businesses. However, those who are not able to do so and are relegated to working in these enterprises can suffer from exploitation and further increase isolation and segregation.

CULTURAL TRAITS AND ETHNIC RESOURCES

Inherent cultural traits, such as an ability to delay gratification, willingness to work hard and to tap informal savings and loans, and willingness to sacrifice for the next generation, facilitate a pull of newcomers toward small business development and are a central thesis of theories related to cultural traits and resources. Jones and Ram (2007), for example, stress the need for embedding ethnic ventures within the cultural context in which they operate in order to better understand the forces that lead to small business creation. Baycon-Levent, Masurel, and Nijkamp (2006) study gender differences in ethnic entrepreneurship and note important cultural and familial forces fostering development of businesses owned by females. Puryear and colleagues (2008), in turn, place ethnic enterprise development within the understudied context of family to develop a better understanding of the forces and resources operating in small business development. Model (2008) illustrates how a series of cultural and ethnic factors have converged and combined with opportunities to encourage and support West Indian immigrants owning their own small enterprises. Finally, Pastor (2001) finds that the presence of a strong work ethic has the potential to be tapped for economic development.

Religious associations are another dimension that is worthy of greater research. Marte's (2004) study of Brazilian small businesses in Massachusetts describes how Pentecostal Brazilian small business owners were able to effectively reach out to fellow parishioners and encourage them to become loyal customers. Siqueira's (2007) research on Brazilian newcomers' human capital and family social capital finds that the presence of a cohabiting spouse greatly increases the probability of starting a business in this community, adding an important dimension to discussion of human and social capital.

CLASS RESOURCES

Human capital, such as advanced educational degrees and managerial experience, is closely related to class resources when it comes to small business development. Possession of a solid formal education, language skills, legal status, and "Americanized" attitudes, norms, and values makes it easier to develop a small business catering to newcomer communities (Oliveira 2006; Zhou et al. 2008). Robb and Fairlie (2009) study the role of class resources (financial and human capital) of Asian-owned small businesses and find such businesses to be more successful than white, non-Latino small businesses because Asian-owned businesses have higher levels of human capital and substantial startup capital.

Possession of high levels of human capital results in significant advantages for entrepreneurs (Kim, Aldrich, and Keister 2006). An increase in the number of Latinos and other groups of color being educated in business programs and schools has opened up options of engaging in enterprise development outside of enclaves (Diaz 2005; Kirton 2009). Bates (2006) notes that highly educated African Americans have a greater likelihood of owning larger firms and hiring larger numbers of African American employees than do their less well educated counterparts.

Bogan and Danity (2008) argue against the position that low ownership rates among African Americans are the result of cultural factors, instead attributing them to socioeconomic forces that undermine small business creation. These authors cite implications of a theory that essentially blames the victim for lack of progress in the United States. Kollinger and Minniti (2006) conclude, based on their research, that blacks are more likely than whites to start a business. However, their underrepresentation in business ownership is the result of stronger barriers to entry and higher failure rates rather than lack of optimism or initiative.

Opportunities to enter into a small business can be the result of one of three structural situations that effectively direct involvement in being one's own boss: the "middleman minority" model, ethnic enclaves, and the "economic openings" model. These structural situations present options that otherwise would not be available.

The middleman minority model is premised on the belief that because of fear of crime, loss of status, or lack of profits, the dominant culture is not interested in serving the needs of newcomer communities. Therefore, the market in these communities is wide open for small businesses. Another underlying assumption of the middleman theory is that newcomers participate in the economy through the traditional means of the labor market (Grey, Rodriguez, and Conrad 2004).

Halkias (2007:5) brings a different dimension to this theory:

> The middleman minority theory makes an assumption that many immigrants start out as temporary residents in a host country and that they plan on returning to their home country. The immigrant's main goal in the country is to make money quickly to either send back home to his or her family or to take back with him or her upon returning home. Therefore, immigrants who are sojourners are inclined to seek self-employment in industries where start-up costs are relatively low, where competition is minimal, where capital can be raised quickly, and where assets can be easily liquidated and turned into cash.

Oh (2008) concludes that the closing down of manufacturing jobs in central cities leads to self-employment because of the large number of individuals with limited options to enter other businesses, particularly those requiring a high level of formal education. Diaz-Briquets' (2004) research on the evolution and characteristics of Cuban-owned firms in the United States finds that these small businesses prosper because of the middleman role owners play within their communities.

The availability of ethnic enclaves serves to protect newcomer owners from hostility and discrimination from the mainstream labor market (Montero-Sieburth and Melendez 2007b; Orum 2005). Ethnic enclaves stress the importance of bilingualism and biculturalism as a means of connecting with a loyal patronage base (Diaz 2005). In their study of Mexican self-employment rates along the U.S.–Mexico border, Mora and Alberto (2006) note that

Mexicans have higher self-employment rates but lower earnings than their counterparts in the rest of the United States primarily because of access to a steady customer base.

Ethnic ventures are able to survive by having both ready access to a continued supply of low-wage labor—often provided through kinship networks—and flexibility to respond quickly to emerging market needs (Edwards and Ram 2006). However, less reliance on strong social networks has been found to facilitate Latino newcomers' movement outside of these networks and greater employment opportunities outside the community (Pfeffer and Parra 2009).

Lee and Park (2008) argue that transnationalism has effectively altered the conventional views of ethnic enclaves. These communities have been the targets of global flows of both capital and labor. The authors cite Los Angeles's Koreatown, often referred to as the "overseas Korean capital," as an example of these changes, which are not unique to this ethnic group.

An economic openings model stresses the availability of a market in newcomer communities as white residents move out of the neighborhood and sell to newcomers. However, Salaff et al. (2002) note that the primary reason for starting a small business may be in reaction to an emergency rather than because ownership is preference or a dream. Oh's (2008) study of the quest for self-employment in urban areas finds that the decline in manufacturing jobs and an increase in immigrant population lead to an increase in self-employment.

Drever's (2008) research on the influx of Latinos to post-Katrina New Orleans also fits well with an economic openings perspective on Latino small businesses. The arrival of Latinos has brought with it a corresponding growth of Latino-owned small businesses:

> For the first time since it was a Spanish colony some 200 years ago, New Orleans is getting revitalized by Spanish speakers. One of the more dramatic and immediate impacts of Hurricane Katrina has been the influx of thousands of new Latinos who have moved to the city to detoxify, renovate and rebuild storm damaged roads, flood walls, businesses and homes. Following a mini-boom in Latinos has been a growing number of Latino-owned businesses, especially in retail and service sectors. (Liberto 2009)

In fact, the first establishment to open its doors in the ravished Lower Ninth Ward of New Orleans was a Latino grocery store named La Tienda Latina (Harris 2007). This is particularly significant because small businesses usually are slow to recover from natural disasters (Tierney 2006).

Baraya, Budden, and Escobar (2008) speak to the importance of Latino small businesses in creating post-Katrina New Orleans, noting that Latino small businesses recovered quite well. Two years after the hurricane, 60 percent of Latino-owned enterprises reported earning either the same or more revenue, with 28 percent reporting revenues 100–200 percent higher than before the hurricane, and 3 percent more than doubling their revenue (Turner, Varghese, and Walker 2007). The upsurge in the Latino workforce helping with the reconstruction of New Orleans was instrumental in these increases. Concerted and highly focused support efforts on the part of the nonprofit sector also played an important role in helping small businesses recover (Lacho, Bradley, and Cusack 2006).

Baraya, Budden, and Escobar (2008) address employment opportunities in a variety of sectors for Latinos. Zentgraf's (2001) identification of the forces behind economic restructuring in Los Angeles highlights how market availability, in this case involving Latinas, creates opportunities for small business creation and fits well with the economic opening theoretical orientation.

Readers may rightfully be confused about all these theories focused on essentially the same topic. The theories, however, are not necessarily mutually exclusive, and this both complicates and makes it easier to assess community situations and opens up a wide range of opportunities for social interventions. Cervantes-Rodriguez's (2006) study of Nicaraguans in Miami-Dade County, for example, finds that this group's small business development activities require a combination of several different elements or theories because no one theory offers a sufficiently comprehensive understanding of this community.

The theories summarized by Le (2007) above, as well as the other theories I have touched on, help policymakers and practitioners develop a better understanding of the social dynamics at play in fostering the creation of ethnic and racial small businesses. Social interventions, be they led by community social workers or other helping professions, must seek to incorporate theories related to ethnic small business development in order to conceptually ground interventions in a manner that stresses both social and economic community gains and makes evaluation of these efforts meaningful.

COMMUNITY ECONOMIC DEVELOPMENT: BUSINESS PROFILES

Gruidl and Markley's (2009:220) comments on the "discovery" of entrepreneurship by community economic developers highlight why this arena has so much potential for community social work practice: "A profound change in community economic development strategy over the past decade has been the emergence of entrepreneurship. Now, as never before, community developers recognize that entrepreneurship is critical to the vitality of the local economy." The authors speculate that globalization has effectively made manufacturing jobs in the United States economically unprofitable, which has opened the door for entrepreneurs to create new jobs that are more locally based.

Community economic development represents a vast arena that encompasses many different perspectives, and it has the potential to touch every facet of community life (Villa 2000). The role of small business development is one dimension that is receiving increased attention because of the opportunities it presents for newcomers to the United States and the central role these establishments play in the social and economic well-being of urban communities (Penaloza 2007).

Small businesses open up possibilities for economic advancement that also serve to strengthen community well-being in the process, particularly when these institutions are viewed from a multifaceted perspective that includes both social and economic considerations. The entrepreneurial process is capable of being modified to include pursuit of community well-being goals, thereby creating new and exciting contexts for community economic and social development (Harvey and Lionais 2004).

Fairlie (2004), in researching recent trends in ethnic and racial business ownership in the United States, concludes that rapid growth rates have continued and have largely been fueled by rapid growth in population and the labor force. In 2002 people of color (both newcomers and native-born) owned approximately 1.8 percent of the nation's twenty-three million businesses (Lowrey 2007). Latinos were the largest group of color owning their own businesses (6.6%), followed by African Americans (5.0%) and Asians and Pacific Islanders (4.7%). Relatively few small businesses (1.6%) are inherited, suggesting a set of dynamics in small business development that are not intergenerationally influenced (Fairlie and Robb 2004).

The term "small business," as noted in chapter 1, can be misleading from an economic and sociocultural perspective. Fairlie (2008), in a recent study estimating the contribution of immigrant businesses ownership to the U.S. economy, finds that newcomers contribute $67 billion of the $577 billion in U.S. business income. Their impact, however, is more considerable in California (25% of all business income), Florida, New York, and New Jersey (20% in each). Not surprisingly, immigrant business ownership is geographically concentrated in California (30%), New York (25%), Florida, Hawaii, and New Jersey (20% each).

Fried identifies the importance of sociocultural outcomes of economic transactions that are often overlooked in discussions about fostering ethnic and racial small business development:

> Public markets, unlike more conventional economic development projects, must not only succeed as businesses but also meet community goals. Indeed, a market is much more likely to thrive economically if it has deep roots in the surrounding community. Whereas a big box retail development relies on cheap prices (and low-wage labor) to draw customers, a market must offer a public space experience and mix of products tailored to the people it serves in order to be economically competitive. Just as crucial, the economic opportunities it creates are more lasting and meaningful. (2009:1)

Thus, to view ethnic small businesses, as in the case of Latinos, for example, as simply economic enterprises would do a disservice to this field. I explore this notion in the next chapter.

Ethnic and racial small businesses also provide a window on a community for outsiders who have difficulty envisioning how best to reach and serve its residents. Menzies et al. (2003), for example, acknowledge in their study of Canadian entrepreneurs' ethnic involvement using personal and business characteristics that there is greater diversity among small business owners than in the general population. They propose an index of ethnic involvement, which they call the Ethnic Inventory (EI) Index, that uses R. D. Putnam's concept of social capital. Their index targets a set of key factors, such as gender, education, years of employment, experience prior to immigration, immigrant status, and prior ownership of a business, to determine the level of ethnic involvement in a business.

Latinos, as will be noted in the following chapter, have not been the only community of color that has embraced small businesses as a means of achieving the "American Dream." In 2002 there were 1.1 million U.S. businesses owned by Asian Americans, generating over $326 billion in revenues and employing 2.2 million people. Among foreign-born Asians 25 years of age or older, Koreans have the highest percentage of self-employment (27.8%), followed by Taiwanese (16.6%), Japanese (14.0%), Asian Indians (11.5%), and Chinese and Vietnamese (11.2% each). Foreign-born blacks had the lowest rate of self-employment (6.6%), as did U.S.-born African Americans (4.8%). Latinos born in the United States had the highest rate (7.02%) among the various groups (Le 2007).

It is important to examine the income generated by ethnic and racial enterprises compared with their white, non-Latino counterparts. On average,

Pacific Islanders made fifty-nine cents for every dollar whites made. Latinos, Native Americans, and Asian Americans made fifty-six cents on the dollar. Finally, African American businesses made the least amount, with forty-three cents (Lowrey 2007). The disparity in income generated by small businesses raises important social implications about their role in the economy of the United States.

As noted in chapter 1, a number of scholars have expressed concerns about small business development. Johnson, Burthey, and Ghorm (2008) warn that economic globalization will have a dramatic impact on the African American community, further limiting the possibilities for this group to make significant progress in economic terms. Blackburn and Ram (2006), too, caution about too much optimism in relying on small business creation as a solution to inner-city economic distress. Such ventures must be a part of any economic initiative targeting inner cities, but they are just one part, and attention must be paid to a host of other economic and social factors.

FACTORS FACILITATING AND HINDERING BUSINESS CREATION

Ethnic and racial small businesses do not succeed or fail for no particular reason, and these outcomes must be viewed within the lifespan of the enterprises in order to better understand the forces that foster success. Community social workers, as a result, must have a keen understanding of the forces that are operative in facilitating and hindering business creation, particularly in the case of those businesses reaching out to various subgroups.

FACILITATING FACTORS

The upsurge and existence of ethnic and racially owned small businesses is the result of interplay of at least four key factors.

Limited Employment Opportunities Outside the Community

As noted earlier, limited viable options for people of color outside their neighborhoods are often cited as a major motivation for opening up a business. There are numerous interpretations as to why opportunities outside of the neighborhood are limited. Nevertheless, the need to earn a living can converge with the excitement of being one's own boss, particularly in the case of newcomers who may have to support an immediate family in this country but still must send remittances back to their country of origin to support family members there. Furthermore, earning a living can also converge with a desire to make sociocultural contributions to the community.

Availability of Role Models and Technical Support Within the Community

An assets perspective on communities of color would uncover a wealth of experiences in businesses within these communities, particularly in the case of newcomers who either owned or worked in such enterprises in their country of origin, and their willingness to venture into the informal economy. Mind you, the individuals with these experiences may not have MBA degrees, but this does not detract from this asset.

The resourcefulness of people who have endured countless hardships is inspiring, if those external to these communities are willing to entertain such a perspective. Indigenous role models are readily available within communities of color. However, they may not fit the stereotypical views held by the dominant society. The emergence of business associations, as I will discuss later, often provides small business owners with an opportunity to mentor and support other new owners. Much research needs to be undertaken, however, to develop a clearer picture of how small business owners of color gain instrumental and expressive support from each other.

Knowledge of Market Niche

Belonging to the same ethnic/racial (co-ethnic) group brings with it a tremendous understanding of and insight into markets that businesses hope to reach (Galbraith, Rodriguez, and Stiles 2007). This insider knowledge translates into knowledge about what products and services are going to meet community needs, how best to advertise and sponsor community events that will have the greatest impact, and where the businesses will have the greater visibility within the community, to mention but three advantages.

Bates and Robb (2008) conclude, based on their study of recently started urban neighborhood businesses, that it is critical for their survival to expand their customer base beyond neighborhood co-ethnics. This expansion, however, represents a challenge. On one level, the nature of the products and services being offered, combined with a highly personalized and community-invested set of values and actions, requires that any expansion of the customer base to include other ethnic and racial groups entails a shifting in marketing. Expansion beyond the immediate neighborhood necessitates a shift in thinking about profits and how labor-intensive personalized services will become if it is possible to make this leap; thus there is tradeoff in selling goods and services that have appeal beyond a business's current customer base.

Such a decision brings with it a set of realities concerning the profitability of the business, and this broadening of the customer base may not be desirable for small business owners. However, the motivation for opening a business will serve as a guiding frame of reference in the decision-making process. If the motivation is social and civic in nature, namely, a desire to be an integral part of the community, to be held in high esteem by residents, or to give back to the community, to name but three, then profits take on secondary importance.

The proliferation of books on how to market to the Latino community stands as a testament to the importance of non-Latino corporations' better understanding this market and positioning themselves with products and services that cater to its needs. Nevertheless, regardless of the marketing firm these corporations enlist in their quest to turn a profit, the local knowledge that small business owners possess is of immense importance.

Low Startup Costs

The potential opportunities that small businesses provide often outweigh the tremendous odds against their eventual success (Lofstrom and Wang 2007). The ability and willingness to venture into small business creation with minimal startup funding can be viewed as both a facilitating and a hindering factor. Businesses with low startup costs take on particular attraction in communities where there is a built-in need for a product or service that can be delivered with minimal outlay of cash. Often the initial cash infusion can be obtained from close family and friends and does not require the elaborate paperwork and eligibility criteria associated with banks.

The emergence of meal businesses whereby Latinas cook native meals and go from home to home of Latino laborers to sell the meals is an example of an innovative venture with low startup costs. These entrepreneurs develop a market for their meals and establish an extensive customer referral base that not only generates other customers but also ensures that cultural and language barriers will not interfere with the business. In addition, the reputation of the individual preparing and selling food takes on added significance in cases where the customer is undocumented, necessitating implicit and explicit trust.

HINDERING FACTORS

Operation of small businesses within urban communities of color also involves a number of challenges. These characteristics generally fall into three areas, which are not mutually exclusive. Each of these hindering factors, detailed below, is quite formidable, and the first is particularly challenging, but they also offer social workers an opportunity to make important contributions to community social and economic development.

Interethnic or Interracial Tensions and Safety Concerns

One of the most challenging factors hindering the potential of small businesses has to be the impact of interethnic and interracial tensions on ethnic businesses reaching out beyond their own ethnic group (Klotkin and Friedman 1993; Bean 2000; Pedraza 2000; Aja 2006; Wahl 2007). A rapid expansion of Latinos into historically black areas is one example of this form of tension (McClain et al. 2007; Barreto and Sanchez 2009).

Le (2007:4) reminds us of the images often shown of ethnic and racial tensions and strife between small business owners, often Asian, and their consumers, generally African American or Latino, as manifested in urban riots in which businesses are looted and burned:

> [T]he most graphic example of these tensions has to be the Los Angeles riots of 1992. For years and decades, much of the Black community in Los Angeles had built up resentment and anger against institutional racism they faced. At the same time, many Korean store owners tried to improve their lives by opening up stores in low-income areas. But cultural and language differences between Korean owners and Black customers eventually produced even more hostility. The acquittal of the four police officers who beat Rodney King was the spark that ignited all those tensions. It was not a coincidence that 40% of all stores that were burned down, damaged, or looted belonged to Koreans.

Some 850 Korean-owned small businesses closed after the riots, at an economic cost of $300 million (Grey, Rodriguez, and Conrad 2004). Park (2004) documents a different grassroots campaign in Los Angeles in which African Americans and Latinos targeted Korean-owned liquor stores. Amoruso (2005) examines interracial and interethnic tensions from yet another perspective by looking at the demographic changes experienced in Los Angeles and California as a whole. Shifting demographic trends have witnessed the numeric decline of African Americans and the ascension of Latinos around the same time.

This shift in demographic composition in cities such as Los Angeles has translated into shifting of economic and political power, causing tension between African Americans and Latinos, as observed by Gay (2006:982):

Rapid growth in the size of the Latino population has increased the ethnic diversity of urban neighborhoods, transforming the residential experiences of many black Americans. . . . In environments where Latinos are economically advantaged relative to their black neighbors, blacks are more likely to harbor negative stereotypes about Latinos, to be reluctant to extend to Latinos the same policy benefits they themselves enjoy, and to view black and Latino economic and political interests as "incompatible."

It is important to note, however, as Ryoo (2005) does, that there has been a disproportionate focus on negative and conflictual relationships between Koreans and African Americans at the expense of positive interactions. Thus, these tensions must be viewed from a historical perspective in order to better appreciate the current situation in communities where these two groups interface in the economic sphere.

The economic viability of small businesses is significantly increased when ethnic/racial businesses can extend beyond one group to encompass a cross-section of a community (Kim 2004). The tension between Asian business owners and the community they serve is not restricted to Los Angeles but can be found in virtually any urban community across the United States (Park 2001; Lee 2002; Meyerson 2007; Min 2007). Tensions in Miami between blacks and Cubans in the mid-1980s, for example, were instrumental in leading to race riots in that city (Portes and Stepick 1993), and tensions that arose after Hurricane Andrew have continued, although to a much lesser extent (Kessner 2007).

McClain and colleagues' (2007:2) research on the influx of Latino immigrants into a southern city found concern on the part of African Americans pertaining to the shifting demographic profile of the city: "Results suggest that blacks and non-blacks perceive a potential economic threat from continued Latino immigration, but that blacks are more concerned about the effects of Latino immigration than are whites." Intergroup tensions between African newcomers and African Americans can also exist and spill over into the commercial sector, as in Dolnick's description of incidents in a Bronx neighborhood in New York: "The owner of Café de C.E.D.E.A.O. . . . , named for the coalition of West African nations . . . could count the number of American patrons on one hand. Meanwhile, he [the owner] and his customers have been tainted . . . and his restaurant's windows urinated on. Someone tried to break into a diner's car. Then there is the bullet hole in the front window, a mark from a gunshot through the window late one night last summer" (2009:A23).

Finally, using a different dimension of crime that generally gets overlooked, money laundering has an affect on commercial rental space in urban communities and the tensions that result from this activity. The consequences of laundering drug money can take a toll on a neighborhood by preventing new businesses from entering the neighborhood. Drug-fronted businesses are able to pay exorbitant rents and thereby push commercial rents up to several times the going rate. The added expense for new businesses can be considerable.

Limited Access to Capital and Technical Advice

Finances, not surprisingly, play a critical role in the startup and ongoing operations of ethnic and racial small businesses in the United States (Beck and Demiguc-Kunt 2006; Bates and Bradford 2007; Blanchflower 2009). Blanchard, Zhao, and Yinger (2007) find that lenders do discriminate against people of color and women. Other scholars note substantial differences in denial rates between firms owned by African Americans and those owned by white males (Cavalluzzo, Cavalluzzo, and Wolken 2002; Cavalluzzo and Wolken 2005; Coleman 2005; Sweet 2006; Weller 2009). Latinos have not escaped this barrier (Congressional Report 2005; Green and McNaughton 2008; Holguin, Gamboa, and Hoy 2008).

Consequently, racism plays an insidious role in preventing communities of color from having access to the same credit resources found in white, non-Latino communities. The emergence of ethnic banks has helped to fill this void by providing alternatives to mainstream banks (Li et al. 2006). However, this does not absolve dominant-culture commercial banks from reaching out to these communities.

Pathways to small business ownership share much in common regardless of the ethnic and racial background of the owners. Huck et al. (1999:46) note a number of reasons for lack of small business success:

> Small business access to capital is an important policy issue because business owners may face funding limits, known to economists as liquidity constraints. . . . [S]tudies have shown that liquidity constraints affect entrepreneurs both upon start-up and after the business is underway. These constraints deter entry into self-employment and force would-be owners to save for longer periods before launching a business. The effects of start-up constraints extend to on-going businesses, because starting with more capital increases an owner's prospects of developing a viable, growing business.

Startup capital and the role of institutional informal resources (loans and support from family and friends) have been identified as particularly important because of limited access to commercial financing (Puryear et al. 2008; Tienda 2001). Rueda (2008) identifies lack of Latino access to capital, struggles with overcoming bad credit, finding contacts, and balancing their business's finances as principle reasons for small business failure.

Senator John Kerry, in testimony before the U.S. Senate Small Business and Entrepreneurship Committee on May 22, 2007, notes: "While the numbers of minority-owned businesses are a source of optimism and hold promise for the future, much more needs to be done to encourage and strengthen the minority business community. The potential for small business growth and entrepreneurship has not been fully tapped and there are barriers to entry that continue to exist." Senator Kerry goes on to note: "One of the keys to small business growth is access to capital, an area where minority firms also still lag behind. . . . Small business cannot grow unless they have access to working capital and loans. As our nation is changing, we must preserve our commitment to equal opportunity. We can only do that when we appreciate the value that all of our citizens bring to the table, and when we invest in every segment of our society" (*U.S Fed. News* 2007).

The Latino Foundation (San Francisco) has launched the Isabela Project, an initiative to raise between $75 million and $100 million to close the Latino parity gap in the San Francisco Bay Area (Aviles et al. 2004). The Latino Foundation notes: "Too often, entrenched market players use their political or financial muscle to undermine or eliminate emerging markets because they fear the competition created by open access to capital. In other words, the problem with capitalism is that, too often, the capitalists don't share it." The growing Latino community does not have access to the necessary capital. The Latino Foundation seeks to accomplish three goals through the Isabela Project: (1) to provide an innovative source of financing for Latino business owners; (2) to increase capacity to successfully execute real-time procurement opportunities; and (3) to increase job growth and career opportunities for Latinos.

Access to technical advice is another critical concern for Latinos and other groups of color wishing to start a formal business. For example, Chinchilla and Hamilton (2001:207), in their study of Central American businesses in Los Angeles, identify the challenge of Latinos negotiating what they perceive to be a legal maze in formally establishing a business:

> Perhaps the greatest need expressed by small-business owners was for assistance with the complicated legal and financial procedures involved in setting up and maintaining a business. . . . "The number one problem is a lack of information in every aspect including where to buy cheap products, loans, laws of this country." Some business owners stated that "back home"

all that was necessary was to put out a sign, and "you're in business." Many were confounded by the extensive legal and tax requirements for small businesses in the United States. "Here one needs a license for everything, and pays taxes for everything, which isn't the situation in El Salvador."

Tension Within Racial and Ethnic Groups

Readers may be surprised by this category if they embrace the assumption that ethnic and racial small businesses face competition only from outside of their respective communities. However, competition between small business enterprises can take a variety of forms. For example, newcomers can face tension from established members of their communities. In Salinas, California, for example, there is tension between Latino owners of licensed mobile catering vehicles ("taco trucks") and Latino owners of restaurants (Marshall 2007). The latter have expressed concerns about losing business to taco trucks and have proposed passing ordinances limiting their ability to park near restaurants. Similar tensions have been reported in New Orleans, where, however, the tension is between Mexicans and established restaurant owners who are non-Latino (Bustillo 2007). New Orleans residents also complain about these trucks being considered a blight on the neighborhood, as some do in East Los Angeles (Renaud 2008a, b; Steinhauer 2008). The upsurge in Latinos in New Orleans since Katrina, where they now constitute 20 percent of the city's population, has largely fueled the need for the Latino food sold by taco trucks.

Taco trucks are not restricted to the Southwest or the West Coast. Providence, Rhode Island, for example, also has an East Coast version, called "chimi trucks." Marcelo's (2009:2) vivid description illustrates the symbolic and economic role these mobile establishments play in Latino communities:

> Where Broad Street straddles Elmwood and Lower South Providence is a bustling center of commerce of the small mom-and-pop variety. Latino grocery stores, hairdressers and restaurants serve a community that is more than 75 percent black and Hispanic. Broad Street is also where many of the city's "chimi" trucks—the converted trailer homes and ice-cream trucks serving cheap fried eats. . . . Around dinnertime, anywhere from 10 to 15 of them are lined up along Broad Street, in the few blocks around the nightclubs and bars. . . . The chimi trucks also reflect the cultural shift of Providence, from a largely working-class Italian and Irish to a city of working-class Latinos.

In New York there has been tension between Latino restaurant owners and Latinos setting up food stands close to restaurants: "This summer . . . tensions worsened when several Mexican restaurants complained to the police about a group of Mexican women selling tacos and empanadas on the sidewalks in front of their doors. The women, they said, were stealing customers. The women, in turn, have said that selling street food is the only way they can survive" (Feuer 2003). Puerto Rican owners have expressed concerns about losing business to Mexican stands because their costs are considerably higher and they simply do not have the mobility to move when business suffers.

The subject of crimes against Latino small business owners is another potential manifestation of interethnic and intraethnic group tensions (Taylor 2004). Victimization rates against Latino small businesses have generally escaped attention within the criminal justice arena. Both intra- and intergroup crime are key factors in the success or failure of a small business. As hate crimes against Latinos increase, the safety of small business owners will only become more significant (Mock 2007; Sandoval 2007; National Council of La Raza 2008; Olivo 2008; Juffer 2009).

Crimes of profit, too, are prevalent and are often tied to overall crime rates within communities (Rhodes and Conly 2008). In New York bodegas (small grocery stores) are often the targets of crime because they are cash business and are very hard to see into from the outside (small windows are often covered with advertisements). The president of the Washington Heights Bodega Association of the United States highlights this problem: "The No.1 problem for bodega owners is still safety" (Ramirez 2007). In 1993 there were five hundred violent crimes committed against *bodegueros* (owners of bodegas). In 2006 there were twenty-five recorded crimes. The association instituted a training program with the New York City Police Department to train bodegueros on how to deal with crime through the use of surveillance cameras and other techniques. Ramirez notes that crime against bodegas was the reason the association was formed in the first place. Home invasions of Latino small business owners represent but the latest type of crime targeting Latinos. Business owners invariably have large sums of cash in their homes, making them attractive targets (Chayes 2009).

TYPOLOGY OF SMALL BUSINESSES

Sanchez-Jankowski's (2008) conceptualization of small businesses is particularly useful for understanding theories of ethnic and racial small business development. That study of social change and resilience in poor urban neighborhoods focuses a great deal of attention on the role, function, and importance of small businesses, or what the author refers to as "mom-and-pop stores." Based on his findings, Sanchez-Jankowski developed a four-pronged typology that has implications for Latino small businesses.

The first type, the "imperialist," captures the spirit of the "American Dream" and fits into the ethnic niche or enclave school of thought. In this type, the store owner does not share the racial or ethnic background of the customers, does not live in the community, and is interested primarily or only in profits. The following quote captures the sentiments of patrons of this type of store in a New York neighborhood: "Every time I go to that store I get mad. The Indian, or whatever he is, just charges so much for things. He and his brother are so unfriendly when you ask for something and especially when you check to see if the price is right. . . . You know them guys make so much money off us, and then they just take it to the Island [Long Island] and spend it. They just take so much advantage of us. They're so disgusting" (Sanchez-Jankowski 2006:115).

The "holdout" store represents the second type of small business. The owners of these stores stayed behind after their ethnic or racial group left the neighborhood. Concerns about relocating their business, including the cost of doing so, have necessitated that they remain. The store represents a source of livelihood but, just as important, has strong sentimental value from an era that no longer exists. Sanchez-Jankowski (2008:118) presents the case of Hector, a Mexican grocery store owner: "To sell this store to someone right now would just kill me. I love this store. I have been working here for thirty-two years. . . . I was so proud of the fact that I could own a business. . . . When I got this store and started to run it, it was the best time of my life. As a matter of fact, I married the daughter of one of the women who used to come into the store all the time. When I am in this store I have good thoughts." It is clear that a small business is much more than a source of revenue for these types of owners.

"Trailblazer" represents an economic opportunity that presents itself when the community changes demographically. These types of establishments represent demographic markers of a community in transition. A Puerto Rican community, for example, may be experiencing an influx of Mexicans. As Mexicans buy and open up their own businesses, Puerto Ricans soon find that their needs are not being met by the new establishments. They may continue to shop in these new establishments, but it is just a question of time before the neighborhood no longer has a significant Puerto Rican population. These demographic shifts can cause resentments, as captured by Sanchez-Jankowski in the following quote from a Brooklyn resident: "No, I ain't going to Sippley's anymore since it now is for them foreign blacks. They got food and stuff for them, and I don't cook with that stuff. . . . Yeah, just like that there store, there is going to be lots of them [Jamaicans] coming here to live, and that's a shame" (2008:119).

The fourth type of store is referred to as "indigenous," with the owner sharing many similarities with the residents of the neighborhood, in addition to living there: "Owners of this type of store were socially integrated into the community, and although they might make very modest living, they found satisfaction in their interaction with members of their community. Some of the establishments might well have been trailblazers in the past, but as the population of their group increased and their tenure in business lengthened, they became indigenous" (Sanchez-Jankowski 2008:120).

Sanchez-Jankowski's conceptualization of small businesses brings to life the theories outlined earlier in this chapter and emphasizes the importance of viewing urban small businesses within an ecological model, with special attention being paid to the motivation for starting a business and staying with it. The demographic composition of urban communities has historically been dynamic, and small businesses have served as effective markers of these shifts in profiles.

This book falls into Sanchez-Jankowski's "indigenous mom-and-pop store" category, as the reader has probably realized. From a community empowerment and assets perspective, indigenous small businesses bring to the fore endless possibilities to strengthen Latino community from a social, economic, and political standpoint. The next chapter will elaborate on the cultural dimensions of Latino small businesses, particularly those that can be classified as Sanchez-Jankowski's indigenous type of business.

A LIFE-CYCLE PERSPECTIVE

Pittman and Roberts (2009:210) issue a word of caution about community economic development overemphasizing new business creation and ignoring existing businesses and how to prevent them from closing and/or expanding their economic reach: "While the recruitment of a new business into a community usually garners front-page headlines, the retention or expansion of an existing business rarely does. Communities tend to take their existing businesses for granted, which can be a big mistake." Viewing small businesses in urban communities of color from a multifaceted perspective, with attention being paid to all phases of business development, opens up opportunities for community social workers and others interested in community economic development to make important contributions to a marginalized community economic base.

Efforts to better understand the life of a racial or ethnic small business have recently received attention from scholars interested in a life-cycle developmental perspective (Churchill and Lewis 2004). This perspective resonates with social workers and other helping professions because they are familiar with looking at individuals and families from a developmental viewpoint. This viewpoint borrows from the well-known life-cycle perspective used in human development and applies it to small business development. Like its human development counterpart, a business life cycle generally consists of four key developmental stages: birth, adolescence, maturity, and death. Churchill and Lewis (2004) offer a different, five-life-cycle framework specific to small businesses: existence, survival, success (profitable status quo), take-off (obtaining resources for growth, return, and resource maturity).

Each of these stage models brings with it a host of rewards and challenges for the business owner and has implications for community social workers and other helping professions practicing in this arena. Churchill and Lewis (2004) are critical of most small business life-cycle models because of an assumption that all business must go through all stages of development or perish. Most models seem to place equal value on the importance of all stages and as a result do not emphasize the importance of the initial stage, the business's origins. Finally, there is a bias or focus on using sales to determine success and minimal or no attention paid to factors such as value added, rates of change, and other nonmonetary sources of rewards.

Applying a life-cycle model gives researchers a multifaceted view of small businesses, with each stage providing a range of key factors to be considered. As Bernard and Slaughter note:

> To develop such a general framework, we conceptualize a firm having a life cycle analogous to that of an individual: starting with birth and ending with death. To understand how minority firms prosper or fail, we must understand how they behave at each point during the life cycle. More importantly, our methodology requires that we follow the path of individual firms over the course of their existence. Answering the most important questions facing minority-owned firms is not possible with snapshots of the minority business community taken every five years. (2004:13)

The life cycle of Latino small business must be examined against the backdrop of small business survival in general, and that of small businesses of color in particular. It is estimated that more than half (56%) of all small businesses fail within the first four years, and 85 percent fail within the first five years of inception (McQueen, Weiser, and Burns 2007; Mendoza 2008).

Consequently, the failure rate of Latino small businesses can only be appreciated within this context. Interventions, as a result, must target the knowledge needs of businesses based on their stage in the developmental cycle in order to maximize their potential to succeed (Phelps, Adams, and Bessant 2007). For example, relatively little is known about the final stage of the business cycle, failure (Shephard, Wiklund, and Haynie 2007). This stage would benefit from strategic intervention to help owners navigate its social, psychological, and financial aspects.

This chapter has provided an insight into racial and ethnic small businesses that will be built on in the next chapter. The subject of small businesses is an emerging area of scholarship as well as of popular interest. This interest is based on the economic, social, and political importance these establishments have in the life of urban communities of color. The role these businesses play, however, must also be viewed from an ecological perspective in order to appreciate more fully their significance and the need for community social work involvement in fostering their development.

In this chapter I did not attempt to provide community social workers with a highly detailed primer on small business theories and economics. My goal instead was to provide an overview. There are very few social work programs in the country where students get an introduction to the world of business and economics. Thus, much work needs to be done in this area for small enterprise development to be viewed as an option for social work practice.

Social work, however, does have an interest in people of color and their geographical settings. Thus it is not a tremendous leap to also be interested in small businesses and the role they play in shaping the social and economic fabric of such communities. The theories and other content presented in this chapter provide social workers with a wide variety of ways of looking at ethnic and racial small enterprises and can accommodate a range of social work theories related to oppression, capacity-enhancement practice, participatory democracy, life-cycle development, and community development. This is important because community social work practice is not monolithic, and no one theory or school of thought dominates discourse in the field.

There is little that is small about small businesses, and there certainly is nothing simple about them either. The next chapter presents various ways of thinking about Latino small businesses that encompass social, human, economic, physical, and cultural capital. The richness and importance of these establishments will quickly become apparent.

4

LATINO SMALL BUSINESSES AND COMMUNITY ECONOMIC DEVELOPMENT

> We, as Hispanics, as Mexican Americans, Puerto Ricans, and Cuban Americans, must look to economic stability in our communities. We must look to solutions that bring money into our neighborhoods. We should seek to end redlining by banks, remove bureaucracies that prevent small business development, and look for any creative way to encourage enterprises and economic development for our people.
>
> —G. Rodriguez, *The New Civil Rights Movement: Economic Empowerment*

LATINO SMALL BUSINESSES can best be appreciated when viewed within the broader context of the history of racial and ethnic small businesses in the United States and the role these institutions play within their respective communities. Rodriguez's (1990) provocative statement made over thirty years ago to the conservative think tank the Heritage Foundation raises the importance of economic empowerment of Latino and the active and meaningful role they can play in the social and economic destiny of the United States.

Latino economic and social advancement in this country depends on this community's ability to enter the business world in sufficient numbers and positions to significantly alter its earning capacity. The option to enter the business world must be available to Latinos who are not interested in other careers.

Latino small businesses cannot be understood without a grounding in demographics and racial and ethnic small businesses, as noted in chapters 2 and 3, and without viewing these establishments against the backdrop of Latino economic well-being. Furthermore, there needs to be an appreciation for the role that sociocultural factors play in influencing whether small business development is viable, as well as the interplay of such factors as acculturation, economic status, documented status, formal educational level, and geographical location. There is no doubt that the association between Latino inclinations toward small business ownership and the actual undertakings is far from being linear, and any serious effort to understand the Latino small business phenomenon must take this into consideration.

LATINO SMALL BUSINESSES

The themes identified in the previous chapters on Latino demographic profiles, dispersal, and projected future numerical increases have direct implications for enterprise development and community economic survival in all sectors of the United States. The Latino community has been the subject of considerable national attention in the past five years, particularly with regard to immigration and the presence of those who are undocumented. However, the role of the business sector in emerging Latino communities has been neglected historically, though its importance is well documented in a wide variety of academic forums (Delgado 2007).

Grossman's observations of Latino small businesses and the challenges they face set the tone for this chapter:

> The Latino community is full of entrepreneurs. Latinos own manufacturing companies, construction firms, restaurants, and real estate. Their businesses are small but successful: their many businesses are each individual family's main source of income and the foundation on which the family will build future generations. Yet the founders do not look like the typical American entrepreneur. They don't think like the typical American entrepreneur. And they don't see themselves as the typical American entrepreneur. In many instances, Latino entrepreneurs' early goal when starting their business wasn't necessarily to make a profit, but to put food on the table. And when they pass the business on to the next generation, their children often see the legacy of the family business from a more Americanized point of view— without emotional attachment and with an eye toward either selling it or bringing in outside investors to facilitate a large-scale expansion. (2007:8)

The potential of Latino small business owners to serve as role models, mentors, and leaders in the community has generally escaped attention in the literature, though it is starting to be recognized in the field of practice. "Small business owners are like homeowners. They're committed to the neighborhood; they're a committed citizenry. The hope is that entrepreneurship brings more civic engagement by immigrants. That they'll have their voices heard more. That they'll be anchors, developing roots in the community, and serve as role models" (Hispanic Advocacy and Community Empowerment Through Research 2004:5).

Coetzer and Perry (2008) stress the process and role of employee learning from small business owners and categorize this learning into four areas: external business environment; factors in the work environment; learning potential of the job itself; and learning orientation of employees. This orientation toward employee learning has important implications for employees wishing to move on and become owners themselves.

Latino small businesses can also be a source of community leaders and elected officials, as experienced in Lodi, California (Adams and Armstrong 2005). These individuals invariably have high-profile positions within the community and have intimate knowledge of residents' needs, concerns, and assets. Consequently, since community social work practice is always concerned about enhancing indigenous community leadership and empowerment, Latino small business owners are a fertile source for exploration on both counts. Sweeney (2008), for example, reports on a Miami University of Ohio project whereby students are paired up with Latino small businesses as a means of learning real-world business practices, but also giving back to their mentors by helping them automate some of their business practices.

The development of an accurate census of Latino small businesses is complicated. Raijman (2001), for example, concludes, based on a study of Mexican self-employment in Chicago, that national rates of Latino small business ownership severely underestimate the prevalence and role of such enterprises in Latino communities. This undercounting may be the result of a general lack of understanding of the informal economy, combined with difficulties in actually measuring economic activity in this realm. There has, however, been a systematic bias against counting informal businesses, which have a long tradition in many developing countries, including those in the Caribbean, Central America, and South America (Tipple 2006). Transplanting these enterprises to the United States can be viewed as a natural response to limited employment opportunities for Latinos.

The future for Latino small businesses is considered quite promising. They are expected to grow 55 percent from 2006 to 2011 and number 3.2 million, with a 70 percent increase in revenues, totaling $465 billion (Esmalloffice.com 2007). One recent estimate has Latinos as the largest group of color owning their own businesses, with 6.6 percent of the approximately 23 million firms in the United States (Ibarra 2007). These businesses employ 1,536,795 workers (Democratic Policy Committee 2008).

It is estimated that 10 percent of small businesses are Latino-owned, and 40 percent of business owners who are women of color are Latinas (United States Hispanic Chamber of Commerce 2007). Latina-owned businesses generated $44.4 billion in sales in 2004 and increased by 64 percent between 1997 and 2004 (Torres 2007). Thus, Latino small businesses are not the exclusive domain of males.

The economic impact of Latino small businesses can be considerable, as evidenced in Richfield, Minnesota. A qualitative study of six Latino-owned businesses in that town finds that they annually generate $693,900 in employee wages; $393,000 in supplies and equipment; $165,600 in rent and utilities; $89,000 in publicity; $17,500 in property taxes; and $11,700 in sales taxes. (Data were not gathered on payroll taxes.) These expenses totaled $1.37 million, or $228,600 per business. If one uses a conservative multiplier effect of 1.55, it results in an annual economic impact of 3.46 million (Hispanic Advocacy and Community Empowerment Through Research 2004).

Ricourt and Danta, in a detailed inventory of Latino small businesses in a neighborhood in the Jackson Heights, Queens, section of New York, identify twenty-four types of businesses owned by nine different Latino groups and show the diversity of small businesses that can exist in a Latino neighborhood:

> These included businesses one might expect in a heavily Latin American immigrant area: ethnic restaurants (Argentinean, Colombian, Cuban, Dominican, Ecuadorian, Peruvian, Latin American Chinese), bakeries (Argentinean, Cuban), a botanica selling religious articles (Puerto Rican), and an English-language school (Colombian). They also included firms one might find in any New York City neighborhood: accountants (Chilean, Dominican), realtors (Argentinean, Colombian, Cuban, Dominican, Venezuelan); beauty salons (Colombian, Cuban, Dominican, Peruvian, Puerto Rican); women's, men's, and children's clothing stores (Colombian, Dominican, Ecuadorian); jewelry shops (Colombian, Cuban); an optician (Colombian-Italian); a discount goods store (Dominican); dry cleaners (Colombian, Uruguayan); coin laundries (Colombian, Peruvian); camera shops (Cuban, Dominican, Puerto Rican); refrigerator repair businesses (Dominican, Ecuadorian); furniture stores (Dominican, Ecuadorian); a copy center (Dominican); car services (Colombian, Peruvian, Cuban-Ecuadorian); driving schools (Ecuadorian, Latino nationality undetermined); a bicycle shop (Colombian); a florist (Dominican); video rentals (Colombian, Ecuadorian); bars (Uruguayan, Latino nationality undetermined); and a billiards parlor (Dominican). (2003:43)

Santiago and Jennings (2004) undertook a detailed profile of the Latino business sector in a very different community, Lawrence, Massachusetts. They identify a similar range of types of businesses, but the vast majority are owned and operated by Puerto Ricans and Dominicans.

The small businesses listed for both New York and Lawrence cover only formal types and neglect the informal economy, which some would argue is far greater than the formal economy. In a historical study of the Latinization of Lawrence, Borges-Mendez (2007) concludes that the steady increase in the Latino population is largely responsible for the increase in services and businesses to meet the needs of the primarily Puerto Rican and Dominican community.

Formal businesses, too, can look rather unconventional. TATs Cru, a mural/graffiti company based in the New York's South Bronx, illustrates this point quite well. It is arguably the first and one of the few Latino-owned businesses using this art form as a business venture. It was officially incorporated in the mid-1990s by a group of Puerto Rican artists who had their start painting graffiti on subway trains and eventually expanded to painting murals, accepting contracts from hip-hop artists like Fat Joe to design compact disk covers. Corporations such as Coca-Cola, McDonalds, and Sparkle have contracted with the group for design work targeting urban-based communities of color. TATs Cru employs Latino staff with urban backgrounds and conducts a variety of community-centered projects, teaching youth how to paint murals and giving formal talks at community-sponsored events, both as a means of giving back to the community and to help ensure that the company stays connected to it (Delgado 2003).

The development of informal health care businesses is another sector that has generally gone unnoticed in the literature. Zlolniski (2008) analyzes the emergence of an informal dental care operation in California's Silicon Valley involving a Latino dental assistant who decided to open up a business in a garage. Botanical shops (cultural variations of pharmacies) are another example of small health care businesses that may appear unconventional but are ubiquitous in urban Latino communities (Delgado and Santiago 1998; Viladrich 2006). These establishments cater to a range of social and health needs within the Latino community. Their unconventionality does not mean that they are not major businesses, however. One botanica in the Bronx, Original Products Company (not owned by Latinos but employing them), annually generates $3 million in business (Semple 2010).

Finally, Siu's (2007) vivid description of Cuban–Chinese restaurants brings into the discussion historical as well as current themes in Latino culture—in this case, how Cubans and Chinese crossed during the nineteenth century in Cuba and were transplanted to New York. Just walking into a Cuban–Chinese restaurant brings to light the richness of nineteenth-century Latino history and culture. Davis (2006) offers a different perspective, coining the term "Asian Latino" as a concept that is emerging in the marketing literature, not to capture of results of intermarriage but to encapsulate the demographic prowess of these two groups.

On a different note, Furuseth (2010) examines Latino businesses from a place-making perspective and draws conclusions similar to those I have made. Latino small businesses select where they will be located based on a host of factors, such as space availability, rental costs, personal relationships with building landlords, and advice from other owners. Small, food-related stores, or tiendas, invariably are the first businesses to open up in an emerging Latino community. Tiendas fulfill multifaceted commercial functions, such as selling of food, newspapers from back home, and money transfers. These businesses are often followed by restaurants, which eventually lead to spin-offs of other forms of businesses to meet the growing demands of an expanding Latino community.

As the reader can surmise, the enterprise types, developmental histories, and backgrounds of small business owners are indicative of a vibrant community with endless possibilities for small business ventures and potential involvement of marginalized groups within the community. The dynamic and influential nature of Latino small enterprises takes on added significance when informal businesses are counted alongside formal businesses. Accounting for both types makes the process of assessment more difficult but presents a more accurate picture of small enterprises in this community. This form of assessment brings a different dimension to nontraditional settings by focusing on the economic role of these institutions (Delgado 1999).

Latino small businesses have a role to play in helping the community reaffirm its Latino identity. As will be addressed later in this chapter, these institutions' presence and active support of community celebratory events help establish and reaffirm Latinos' positive sense of self. Their role in creating a sense of community is similar to that played by Latino businesses elsewhere in the world. Reyes-Ruiz (2005a, b, c) finds small businesses playing such a role in Japan. Latino nightclubs, for example, bring Latino music and community together in one Japanese setting. Block's (2008) study of Latinos in London, England, reports on a similar situation there.

Marcias (2005) arrives at a similar conclusion. His study of Latino music and dance settings in postwar Los Angeles shows how these small businesses serve to reinforce Latinidad, merging Mexican pride with "urban elegance" to create culturally affirming places and spaces. Latino investment (social, political, psychological, and economic) in localities is manifested in a variety of forms. There is a symbolic relationship among music, place, and community, reinforcing Latino identity: "People invest a broad range of values in places and localities. Belonging, identity, and meaning are aspects of the human experience that depend in large measure on place" (Singer and Martinez 2004:180).

LATINO BANKS AND BANKING

Access to bank loans and lines of credit by small businesses of color has been identified as particularly crucial for successful startup and growth, as noted in the previous chapter. Dymski and Weems (2005) argue that the creation of the black-owned banks represents one of the most critical responses of blacks to their exclusion from access to credit and capital markets. Further, they postulate that black-owned banks will play an important role in economic development in their communities in the twenty-first century.

Dymski et al. study ethnic banks in Los Angeles and conclude that they are significant in communities of color:

> Banks owned by racial-ethnic minorities usually flaunt banking industry trends in one or more ways—by retaining both "relationship banking" and branches as offices for delivery of services, by focusing on culturally specific growth rather than "plain-vanilla" growth, by making loans for purposes and to customers that have been written off by non-ethnic banks and so on. They often target different categories of ethnic customers differently, in ways that differ from the conventions of mainstream banking. (2010:163)

Similar conclusions can be drawn about Latino-owned banks. Latinos are expected to be responsible for $200 billion in banking business by 2015, or half of all the retail growth in this sector during this period of time (Ordonez 2006). For example, in 2008 Latinos wired $20 billion to Latin America and the Caribbean (Kelderhouse 2009). Although the amount will fluctuate with the economy, it represents a significant level of business for banks. One estimate has California's Latino small businesses numbering 340,000, including 25,000 that generated more than $1 million in annual revenue (Flanigan 2006). These businesses, as a result, should benefit from banking (Iwata 2008). Since almost half of the nation's Latino community does not yet have financial services, this group is attractive for the banking sector (Credit Union League of Connecticut 2008).

Access to banks is a challenge for both Latino customers and banks wishing to reach this community: "Unfortunately, neither the Latino community nor the financial industry fully understands how to access one another or take advantage of economic opportunities. This is due in part to L.A.'s changing demographics" (Alliance for a Better Community 2008:2). Obviously, this challenge is not restricted to Los Angeles.

Latinos as a group have a high percentage of members who do not use conventional banks. Fifty-one percent of Latinos do not own a credit card (*Hispanic Market Weekly* 2008), and one-third do not bank at all. More specifically, the majority of Mexicans (53%) do not use banks. Lack of legal identification (55%), language barriers (50%), distrust of banks (25%), financial illiteracy (21%), and use of money service businesses (20.5%) are the five primary reasons for Latinos' reluctance to use banks (Giese and Snyder 2009).

This distrust, however, must also be looked at from a historical perspective to fully appreciate its depth. Experiences with banks in Latinos' countries of origin often lead to distrust of such institutions because of corruption, mismanagement, and association of banks with the wealthy and privileged (Klim and Gresham-Jones 2001). This historical distrust is further compounded in this country, making conventional banking an unattractive option for many Latinos (Sichelman 2007).

Lack of access to banks may also be the result of economic disincentives:

> Low wages and remittances also can reduce income to the point where bank fees and minimum balances make checking or savings accounts financially out of reach, leaving many immigrants "unbanked," without bank accounts or credit cards. They live in a cash-only economy. They are paid in cash, use money orders to pay bills, and cash checks at local supermarkets or fee-based check-cashing agencies. Not only does this leave a large proportion of the Latino community out of the financial mainstream, it also has created a group of consumers who think their only option is to deal with alternative institutions such as payday lenders, businesses offering tax refund anticipation loans, and fee-based check cashers. (Grossman 2007:12)

It is estimated that 22 percent of Latino borrowers of mortgage and auto loans have no credit score, compared with 4 percent for white non-Latinos and 3 percent for African Americans (Stegman et al. 2001). Living a cash-only existence essentially translates into having no credit history on which to draw when needed to establish a small business (Fonseca et al. 2009).

This inability to use banks and distrust of these institutions can carryover into small business development, making it arduous to seek financial backing (Caskey, Duran, and Solo 2006). For example, one study of Massachusetts' Latino small businesses finds that more than 66 percent used their own savings to start up businesses. In Lawrence, Massachusetts, only 18.8 percent actually used conventional bank loans (Barrios 2005). In East Boston, all the Latino-owned small businesses were either self-or family-financed (Hohn 2005). A Lodi, California, study of Latino small businesses finds similar results concerning financing of startups, with only 16 percent of Latino-owned small businesses turning to a bank or the Small Business Administration for financial assistance (Spence 2006). Two Latino owners in Los Angeles state why they eschewed financial institutions for loans: "'There's too many requirements and red tape.' Another said, 'I'd rather ask a person because you pay it off faster. If you get the money from a bank, you pay monthly, but all you are paying is the interest'" (Minority Business Atlas 2005:35).

Latino-focused banks have emerged to service the specialized and growing needs of this community: "For banks, focusing on a niche is a way to set themselves apart from the competition" (Galst 2008). These banks have the potential to reach Latino small businesses because of their language capabilities, hiring of Latino staff, and understanding of Latino cultural values and history. However, although in 2004 there were some nine thousand banks in the United States (Hoffman 2004), three institutions accounted for 77 percent of all Latino-owned banks in the nation (Dymski and Weems 2005).

According to Matasar and Pavelka (2004) there were a reported total of 125 "minority-owned" banks in the country, with Asian Americans and Pacific Islanders owning 53 (42.4%), followed by African Americans with 33 (26.4%), Latinos with 22 (17.6%), Native Americans and Alaska Natives with 16 (12.80%), and 1 being multiethnic. In 2006 California had 40 Asian-owned banks, and that year marked the opening of the first new Latino bank (Promerica) in thirty-five years (*Banderas News* 2006). In 2008 Vibra Bank opened in San Diego, seeking to reach the six thousand Latino-owned businesses in the county (Soto 2008). Florida, in turn, had 14 Latino-owned banks (Reckard 2006).

The paucity of banks owned by people of color necessitates that mainstream banks be prepared to undertake special outreach to the Latino community if they hope to attract customers and make loans to small businesses: "After lagging behind other industries in their efforts to reach Latino consumers, banks, investment companies, brokerage and mortgage firms, and credit card companies recognize that this group can no longer be considered a niche market. Many have retooled their marketing strategy with a focus on multicultural efforts as part of a plan designed to increase market share among Hispanics" (*Hispanic Market Weekly* 2008:1–2).

Reaching the Latino market has necessitated new ways of delivering banking-related services that make them more accessible (Stein, 2005; Flanigan 2006; Garcia 2006; Credit Union League of Connecticut 2008). Innovative efforts such as those undertaken by Banco Popular, which sends trucks outfitted with teller booths to construction sites to help Latino laborers deposit their checks into bank accounts, are illustrative of what banks can do to reach out to this growing market (*Business Week* 2005). Nuestro Banco in Raleigh, North Carolina, hosts a monthly luncheon for local Latino pastors, with attendance ranging from twenty-five to thirty (*Hispanic Market Weekly* 2008).

Non-Latino banks have started to pursue an aggressive campaign to reach this community, which probably typifies the thrust of future efforts in the financial sector:

> Events and community outreach allow the brand to integrate itself into the Hispanic community and build awareness from within. . . . The investment firm sponsors Celebrity Domino Nights in Miami and works with Amigos for Kids, a group of young professionals who focus their efforts on disadvantaged children and teenagers. Nationwide, ING started a project—Corre Por Algo Mejor [Run for Something Better]—to promote running programs in schools to help combat obesity among children. (*Hispanic Market Weekly* 2008:5)

Corporations such as Wal-Mart and Target have moved in to fill the gap in the financial sector by providing many of the services usually offered by traditional banks, and they have done so in a manner that is more Latino-friendly from a cultural viewpoint.

CHARACTERISTICS OF LATINO SMALL BUSINESSES BY SECTOR

A better understanding of the types of small businesses provides community social workers and helping professions with the necessary background to encourage community residents to consider undertaking such ventures. Although much of what we know about the characteristics of Latino business owners comes from formal businesses, these data still provide important clues as to how best to develop interventions that encourage small business development in Latino communities. One study of Latino small businesses came up with a profile: "Hispanic-owned businesses follow this general profile. They are small with annual revenues of less than $250,000. They typically have fewer than four employees and do business within their home state and particularly in their own neighborhood" (Grossman 2007:20).

It is important to note that although profile statistics do provide important information, they also serve to mask differences within and between categories. In essence, numbers replace stories and individual voices. Verdaguer (2009), for example, issues a scathing critique of existing Latino small business scholarship and research for its narrow focus on select Latino groups (Mexicans and Dominicans) with high-profile status at the expense of Latinos who are less visible, such as Salvadorans and Peruvians.

Length of residence in the United States also influences the decision-making process. The longer an immigrant resides in the United States, the more he or she is able to take advantage of information provided through ethnic enclave networks (social capital). Citizenship and documented status also affect self-employment. Consequently, it is necessary to examine the characteristics of Latino small businesses from a variety of perspectives, such as definition, prevalence, and themes.

Also relevant is that the nature of Latino-owned small businesses is significantly influenced by geographical location. For example, Los Angeles and New York City are the two capitals of the garment industry in the United States, and these two cities are gateway cities and home to a large portion of the Latino community (Bonacich 2004; Light 2007; Sullivan and Lee 2008). A study of Latino-owned businesses in Nevada found that retail (32%) and entertainment, accommodations, and food services (23%) are the two largest concentrations of Latino businesses in the state (Grady 2007). Washington, D.C., when compared with other metropolitan areas, has a larger proportion of Latino small businesses in high technology, legal, accounting, engineering, and translation services (Williams and Kang 2006). In 2002 the Washington metropolitan area had 8,593 construction businesses, 4,947 administrative and cleaning firms, and 4,079 Latino professional service businesses. In 2007 Massachusetts had but one Latino accounting firm in the entire state. That business, incidentally, was owned by two Latinas (DeBaise 2006). Not surprisingly, Los Angeles County had the highest number of Latino-owned businesses in the country (188,422), followed by Miami-Dade County (163,187) and Harris County, Texas (61,934) (U.S. Census Bureau 2008). The New York, New Jersey, and Connecticut tristate region had 225,000 Latino-owned small businesses, or an estimated 10 percent of the national total (Gerson 2006).

A 2002 study of Latino-owned businesses identifies twenty different categories of businesses (U.S. Census Bureau, 2006). For the purposes of this discussion, these categories will be combined into six types. According to the

Small Business Administration (Lowrey 2007), Latino-owned businesses are concentrated in construction (13.5%); administrative and support (13.2%), which can also involve remediation services; and health care and social assistance (11.5%). The "other category" is the largest grouping (15.8%) and covers repair and maintenance and personal services. Almost 43 percent of Latino-owned businesses are in the construction arena, followed by administrative and support services, waste management and remediation services, and other services such as personal services, repair and maintenance (U.S. Census Bureau 2008). It is important to emphasize, however, that this distribution refers to formal businesses and does not include the informal sector, which is estimated to be considerable.

SERVICE SECTOR

The service sector has historically seen the most frequently started type of small business by people of color (Mendoza 2008). This sector usually consists of multiple categories, with personal, business, and health services being the most frequently identified in the Latino community. The service sector is a broad sector that is structurally complex and consists of numerous types of businesses. The cleaning sector, for example, can include big firms that are national in scope as well as small enterprises. Small enterprises, in turn, can be formal or informal. Small businesses that are independently operated can be owned and operated by one person. That person can book jobs and may also drive employees to and from sites (Hondagneu-Sotelo 2001). It is generally agreed that informal sector cleaning businesses are the most prone to having poor working conditions.

Small businesses in the service sector often do not necessitate large investments in equipment and or startup costs. Consequently, the popularity of this sector for Latinos should not come as a great surprise. For example, the mass influx of Latinos in California, particularly in Los Angeles and San Francisco, resulted in a rejuvenated labor movement as well as presenting opportunities for Latinos to enter various business sectors, such as janitorial services (Laskett 2006). The service sector is the largest sector of Latino-owned businesses and is expected to account for 50 percent of all Latino-owned businesses by 2010, up from 48 percent in 2005 (Cohn 2007).

Huerta (2007) concludes, based on a study of Mexican immigrant gardeners in Los Angeles, that these entrepreneurs have managed to carve out a niche market that has allowed them to succeed as small business owners within an informal economy. However, working conditions among these enterprises, as typically found in informal economies, are less than optimal.

Smith-Hunter's (2006) study of 140 Latina-owned businesses drawn from a Dun and Bradstreet listing of business owners found that these firms are concentrated in services (beauty and consulting, 11.6% each), followed by retail, clothing, and janitorial/cleaning services (9.3% each). Florida (23.4%), California (18.6%), and New York (14% percent) have the highest concentrations Latina-owned businesses of any states in the country. These states, incidentally, are also well represented among firms owned by Latino males.

CONSTRUCTION SECTOR

The construction industry has opened up opportunities for Latinos with low levels of formal education to break into the U.S. economy. This industry has provided an avenue for Latinos, particularly newcomers, with construction backgrounds in their country of origins. Latino-owned construction businesses, as noted earlier, are ubiquitous among Latino small businesses. The construction sector is expected to increase to 12 percent of Latino-owned businesses between 2005 and 2010 (Cohn 2007). In 2002 Latinas owned 7.5 percent of all women-owned construction firms in the United States (*Latino Business Review* 2009b). California, Colorado, and Texas had the heaviest concentration of these firms.

The recent downturn in the economy has had a devastating impact on the construction industry because fewer houses have been built. This, in turn, has translated into a particular economic setback for Latinos because of their large presence in the industry: "Because Latino immigrants are so heavily concentrated in construction work, they appear to have been hardest hit by the mortgage crisis and subsequent housing slump" (Alzenman 2008). Nevertheless, the construction industry offers Latinos a viable way of entering the business world because the skill set they bring from their country of origin generally does not require additional advanced training.

DOMESTIC SECTOR

Domestic small businesses, although a part of the service sector, have been separated out from that category and made into their own category because of their influence in the Latino community, particularly among females. Latino domestic small businesses have a long history in the United States and in many of the countries represented today in neighborhoods across the nation. Blum (2004), for example, traces historical developments leading to the role of domestic servants of various kinds in Mexico City during the 1900–1935 period. Most Latinas engaged in domestic service can be considered part of the informal economy, although there are operations that are formal in nature. This form of business necessitates minimal startup capital, allows for integration of workers with varying degrees of formal education, and does not require fluency in English to be able to operate economically.

Romero's (1992) research on domestic service and women of color in the United States stresses the importance of this form of self-employment and the inherent employer–employee strains found in this informal economy. Hondagneu-Soto (2001) studies Latina domestic workers who do cleaning and caring and concludes that this form of informal economy constitutes the bedrock of U.S. culture and economy but has remained largely invisible and disregarded. However, any comprehensive effort to understand small businesses, whether formal or informal, within the Latino community cannot be accomplished without including this form of employment.

Dresser (2008) raises serious concerns about how these self-employed women are paid as well as about abuses in working hours and conditions that make them a prime target group for exploitation. Domestic service businesses almost exclusively consist of Latinas; as a result, this form of business is critically important to women.

FOOD-RELATED SECTOR

The food industry has been an excellent social and economic indicator of the presence of Latinos in the United States. These establishments generally mark the first formal appearance of the Latino community in the small business world. The need for food from home countries often serves to help bridge the gap between the country of origin and the United States. Latino-owned restaurants and grocery stores are two of the most visible indicators of the transformation of a neighborhood from one dominated by another ethnic or racial group to a Latino neighborhood. These establishments, particularly grocery stores, or bodegas, often fulfill important nontraditional functions in the community (Delgado 1996).

It is worth noting that Latino food is the fastest-growing ethnic food category in the United States, and there is every reason to expect continued growth in the near future as the Latino population increases and the broader community discovers this type of food. Los Angeles is considered the world capital of Mexican food. Companies such as La Tapista (a tortilla maker based in Compton, California) and Case Herrera (a South Los Angeles food-processing-equipment maker) are examples of the popularity of Latino food-related businesses.

The success story of Luis Reyes highlights a variety of themes raised in this chapter and throughout this book.

When Luis Reyes opened Amigo's Deli and Groceries in 1991, shortly after arriving in the United States from the Dominican Republic, he offered two things that build business anywhere in the world: good service and good prices. Reyes especially reached out to the growing Brazilian population, he said. "I wanted to give the Brazilian community a place where they could find Brazilian products for less than everywhere else," Reyes said. For instance, he was able to sell Café Pilão at a less expensive price than in other stores in Danbury. "Because I was selling cheaper Brazilian products, more Brazilians came to my place, and I made more Brazilian friends," Reyes said. As the deli grew, the Reyes family started helping out in the store. And now they also help run the newest addition to Reyes' growing business, Minas Carne, which he bought in September. Richard, 23, graduated with a business degree and helps run that side of the operations. Juan, 25, is a trained chef and works with his mother Generosa to develop menus for the deli and Minas Carne. Javier, 16, also works in the kitchen. "We kept the food the same but also incorporated what we have used at Amigo's, which is household ingredients," Richard said. "At Amigo's, my mother, who was the chef there for a long time, used ingredients that she would use at home and we wanted to do the same here." And, he added, his father is "the face of the business and basically in charge of hospitality." In other words, he makes sure that customers are satisfied. Minas Carne clearly reflects the many contributions of Reyes' children. Richard, who graduated from New York University in Economics and Sociology, said that Minas, for him, "is like a home." "Like I said my dad is hospitality, but he also manages the store like I do; I'm a business administrator. My brother Juan graduated from Johnston Wells in Culinary Arts, so he and my mother made the menu in Amigo's. At Minas, we kept the Brazilian food the same as before and now my brother Javier is working in the kitchen." "It's good to know that I can call up any one of my brothers and ask them for help in either one of the stores," Richard said. "It's good to know that I can depend on them." In the future, Richard said, he hopes to develop partnerships with other local businesses and organizations that might need food service. "In the next six months we want to remodel, especially making the dining area more spacious for our customers so that they can sit and relax. And we hope to grow our clientele not only within the Hispanic and Brazilian community, but also within the [U.S.] American community." (Kostek 2009:2)

GARMENT SECTOR

The garment industry has enjoyed a long tradition of being a source of economic support for newcomer women in the United States, with this industry witnessing changes in the ethnic composition of those involved in the sector (Zhou 2007). It is estimated that there are 2,500 small contracting shops (sewing, cutting threads, ironing, and checking garments for delivery to retailers) in Los Angeles (Buddle 2006).

Latinos, probably more than certain Asian groups, are considered the backbone of this industry (Ambruster-Sandoval, Munoz, and Reese 2008). For example, Hamilton and Chinchilla (2001) note that in the 1980s Central Americans accounted for 75 percent of all apparel workers in California, largely due to the influx of emigrants from that area. Latinos, as a result, have made significant strides in establishing their own small businesses in this sector (Narrow 2005).

Latinas represent but the latest group to make its presence felt in this industry. The garment industry historically has played an influential economic role among Latinas in urban areas throughout the country (Waldinger 1984). The exploitation and abuse of Latinas and other women of color, however, is legendary (Su and Martorell 2001). Latinas owning their own businesses as part of the informal economy may also be employed in garment factories during certain periods of the day; at the end of their day, they go home and partake in their own garment business. Consequently, the formal and informal sectors are not mutually exclusive. It is important to note, however, that garment ventures face incredible challenges because their survival rates are far lower than those for other types of businesses (Pearce 2005).

AGRICULTURE SECTOR

Although this book is focused on urban practice, I include the agriculture sector for the simple reason that urban farming is a phenomenon that is increasing in prominence, as evidenced by the presence of community gardens and farmers' markets in virtually every city. Furthermore, the relationship between Latino farms and urban Latino consumers is yet to be fully explored and realized.

In this section I seek to start this dialogue and potential collaboration by providing what little data we have on Latinos and agriculture. Latino small farms are important community and national assets: "Like other small businesses, these farms are valuable community assets, generating both income and employment opportunities. Above and beyond their economic contributions, family owned and operated farms serve critical environmental, aesthetic, cultural, and social functions that benefit all members of society" (CSANR 2005:1).

Agriculture-based small businesses may elicit an image in readers' minds of Latino-owned and operated landscape companies that are ubiquitous in suburban communities across the United States. However, agricultural businesses are far more expansive than what is commonly assumed, particularly regarding Latinos (Lewis 2009). Valentine (2005), for example, studies Latino immigrants in the Wisconsin dairy industry and highlights the potential for Latino small business development in this sector if government loan programs targeted Latinos.

Latinos can make important contributions to the industry beyond just working on farms:

> Latinos in Van Buren County [Missouri] and elsewhere in the United States are keeping an American tradition alive—the family farm. In fact, they are entering farming at a time when land concentration is on the rise and the family farm of old is under the imminent threat of vanishing. More than individual initiative and hard work, farm ownership among Latinos is made possible through social capital available in social networks. Making USDA [United States Department of Agriculture] resources available to Latino farmers will allow more of them to become farmers and to continue growing food for the region and the nation. (Martinez and Garcia 2004: 5)

Small farms, generating less than $250,000 in annual gross receipts and with day-to-day management done by the farmer and family, comprise 92 percent of all farms in the United States (CSANR 2005). In 2007, according to the U.S. Department of Agriculture (2007), there were 82,462 Latino farmers and ranchers in the United States, a 12.3 percent increase from the 72,349 in 2002. The lure of land is very strong among many Latinos with agricultural and ranching backgrounds in their family history: "Once they have achieved economic success in Texas, many Latino entrepreneurs and professionals crave land, buying it and then relaxing or working it. Regardless of whether they hail from Mexico, Panama or other parts of Latin America, owning their own ranch is a part of their Hispanic heritage, they say. Their families worked on rural land or their relatives owned ranches or farms" (Moreno 2009).

This phenomenon of wanting to own land is not restricted to Texas. In southern Oregon, for example, Latinos make up a significant sector of forest contracts to go along with a growing Latino community (Sarathy 2006). Martinez and Garcia (2004) identify the increase in Latino-owned family farms in the Midwest and why this form of small business is attractive to Latinos: many are familiar with farming, and this activity lends itself to family members working together. A survey of 111 Mexican and Central American newcomers in Marshalltown and Denison in Iowa finds that 83 percent grew up on farms and 93 percent want to continue farming on their own farms. However, buying or leasing a farm has proven to be an obstacle for them (Kilen 2009).

In a rare study of Latino-owned farms, Garcia (2006) finds that there were 72,329 farmers in 2002, with the vast majority of falling into the small and midsize categories. One-third were beef cattle farms, followed by nontraditional crops (almost 16%) and fruit and tree nuts (15%). Not surprisingly, 90 percent were either individual or family farms.

Martinez and Garcia (2004), in a study of 31 out of 34 Latino farmers in Van Buren County, Missouri, find that Latinos own farms with acreage that is too small to yield sufficient income to support their families. These farms, as a result, take on greater meaning than a business firm. These ventures (hybrid) represent an additional source of income but also, probably more important, a return to a way of life that had great symbolic meaning to the owners.

In their study of Mexican immigrant gardeners, Ramirez and Hondagneu-Sotelo (2009) conclude that this form of business lends itself to the proliferation of hybrid forms of entrepreneurship and service work by blending the informal and formal economies. This business sector effectively taps Latino agricultural backgrounds in their native countries. The relatively low capital investment inherent in this form of enterprise facilitates the crossover from formal to informal businesses.

LATINO NEWCOMERS AND SMALL BUSINESSES

Economists have identified three critical elements of entrepreneurship: risk taking, resource creation, and innovation (Hispanic Advocacy and Community Empowerment Through Research 2004). Risk taking is a quality often found in both entrepreneurs and immigrants, particularly those who are undocumented. The motivation for a better life for themselves and their families is often mentioned as a reason for entering into small business development (informal economy).

Immigrant neighborhoods often thrive socially and economically in ways that native-born groups cannot fully appreciate, but the popular media has been dismissive in its coverage of this population group. There is a joy of life and a willingness to undergo hardships and sacrifices because conditions back home offer little of the hope for economic and social mobility that accompanies formal educational attainment, because of the feelings associated with sending money back home and knowing that loved ones are dependent on this act, or because of the sensation that accompanies opening up a small business and being a part of a community that both respects and is dependent on the business owner for services and products.

Immigrant residents often display a tendency to stay within the neighborhood and spend their time and money there because they are familiar with their surroundings and, especially in the case of those who are undocumented, are somewhat safe from the risk of being arrested and deported. Local Latino small businesses have been found to be important social anchors for these newcomers (Mcilwaine 2005; Waters and Jimenez 2005).

Pages (2005:4) issues a call to view newcomers from a contributing rather than a deficit perspective: "Nurturing new entrepreneurs can help revitalize distressed communities in both the inner-city and in rural regions. New immigrants will play a particularly important role in addressing the demographic pressures of rapidly graying populations in many developed Western societies." Latinos are certainly a case in point with regard to cultural, social, and economic assets.

Opportunities to engage in civil society do exist, including development of formal and informal businesses, and are often taken advantage of by newcomers, depending on their documented status and gender (Theodore, Valenzuela and Melendez 2006; Bogan and Darity 2008; Theodore and Martin 2007). Datel and Dingemans (2006) provide a vivid and colorful description of how sports teams (primarily soccer) and festivals bring newcomer Latinos and sponsoring businesses together in shared public spaces in Sacramento, California. Kilgannon's (2004) description of the Golden Age League in Queens, New York, which consists of Latino soccer players who are over 40, illustrates the transnational identity.

Latino transnational identity is reinforced in social gathering places (Cravey 2005). Latino small businesses can take advantage of these gatherings and be viewed as vehicles for increasing community social capital and reducing barriers to economic attainment, particularly for those who are the most marginalized within the community (Larson-Xu 2008).

BUSINESS SURVIVAL RATES

Although the professional literature invariably pays greater attention to establishing Latino small businesses, equal attention must be paid to helping these enterprises survive and prosper once established. To focus only on starting a business without understanding the forces it will encounter would be foolhardy. For example, from 1997 to 2001, survival rates for Latino small businesses were 68.6 percent compared with 72.6 percent for white, non-Latinos enterprises. Manufacturing and retail businesses had the highest survival rates, with 72 percent each. Wholesale businesses and finance, insurance, and real estate firms were close behind, with 71 percent each nationally. South Carolina had the highest survival rate for Latino businesses, with 88.6 percent, and North Carolina had the lowest rate, with 54.7 percent (Lowry 2004; Watson 2005).

Georgarakos and Tatsiramos (2009) study the entrance of Mexicans and other Latino immigrant groups into small businesses and find that, unlike what was found in previous studies, they have lower survival rates when compared with their predecessors. However, they also find that entrepreneurship is an alternative (intermediate stage) to unemployment and not a goal. This conclusion has profound implications for any form of Latino community economic development involving small businesses.

As noted in chapter 3 in the discussion of the life-cycle of ethnic and racial small businesses, much is still unknown about how cultural and ecological factors interact to facilitate or hinder the development of Latino business ventures. There is a general consensus, however, that a critical population mass must be present to foster such development. Nevertheless, a deeper understanding of the developmental stages, including the ultimate stage (failure), is still missing in the literature.

Furthermore, survival rates must be viewed within an ecological perspective. Curran and Hanson (2005), for example, study small businesses in the Williamsburg neighborhood of Brooklyn, New York, and find that local government can play a significant role in creating a business climate that effectively hastens the demise of ethnic-owned small businesses. Thus, ecology must play a role in enhancing our understanding of how the environment shapes small business survival.

PROFILE OF LATINO SMALL BUSINESS OWNERS

The sociodemographic characteristics of Latino small business owners provide important insights into who is creating businesses and, more specifically, what are the types of small businesses that attract Latino entrepreneurs. This profile, in turn, provides guidance for outreach to and support for potential owners. It can assist community social workers and community economic development centers, for example, in developing interventions that are specific to a community.

Alvarez nicely sums up the need to develop a better understanding of who owns Latino enterprises: "There are hundreds of thousands of Latino small business owners, Hispanic entrepreneurs with an appetite for growth. Their backgrounds are varied, their experiences distinct. They are part of America's economic success, each with a story to tell, a role to play. Yet there are very few serious studies of the Latino small business sector" (2009:71).

Much research needs to be undertaken to develop a better understanding of the factors that facilitate or hinder Latinos entering into enterprise development. Differences in generational status and personal and familial economic circumstances wield considerable influence on the business creation process, as Torres (1990) finds in a study of Latino small business owners in Tucson, Arizona, in which he develops a two-tiered view of the motivations behind establishment of an enterprise. One group falls into a mainstream category that emphasizes capitalism and the importance of profit; another group stresses a traditional cultural perspective of service to the community in addition to seeking profits.

ETHNICITY

Latinos owning their own businesses in the United States come from all twenty-one Latino countries. There is a prevailing attitude, largely based on the success of Cubans in Miami, that Cubans have the highest rate of small business ownership; nevertheless, approximately 45 percent (701,078) of all Latino-owned businesses in the United States are owned by Mexicans, Mexican Americans, and Chicanos (U.S. Census Bureau 2008). Cubans own 10.2 percent (161,688), followed by Puerto Ricans, with 7 percent (109,475). Other Latino groups combined account for 37.9 percent (596,125) (Lowrey 2007).

Not surprisingly, there are strong geographical factors influencing Latino groups in the establishment of small businesses. Mexicans, for example, are particularly well represented in California and Texas. Cubans, in turn, are well represented in Florida. Puerto Ricans in Orlando and central Florida bring a different dimension to geographical setting. By 2020, 33 percent of the population of "New Orlando" will be Latino—more specifically, Puerto Rican (Ramos 2006). In 2004 there were 370,000 Latinos in Orlando, of which 200,000 were Puerto Rican. According to one Latino expert, Angelo Falcon, the Orlando area is the fastest-growing Puerto Rican area of the country (Ramos 2006). And the 2000 U.S. Census Bureau cites 5.4 percent of Puerto Ricans over the age of 15 in the central Florida region as being self-employed, compared with 4.2 percent in New York and 7.7 percent in Puerto Rico (Duany and Matos-Rodriguez 2006).

LEGAL STATUS

The legal status of Latino small business owners must be viewed from two distinct perspectives: those owners who are legal residents in the United States, and those who are undocumented. Legal residents either are U.S. citizens or have a green card. As a result, they have the option of engaging in enterprises that are either formal or informal. Those who are unauthorized, however, can participate only in the informal economy. Salazar (2005) found that Latinas born in the United States have a distinct advantage over those who are immigrants. This is probably due to a host acculturation factors, such as English language proficiency, education, and knowledge of how to navigate U.S. society.

In a qualitative study of twenty undocumented Mexican women in South Carolina, Campbell (2008) finds that these women possess assets and are quite resilient. The following description highlights the motivation and abilities of these women to run small businesses that are very visible in many Latino communities across the United States:

> Some ran businesses out of their homes, recreating a small-scale version of their former lives in Mexico. Selena, for example, operated an informal day care center out of her home for children of family members and friends. . . . Ana and her husband built a bakery in a shed behind their trailer. Using one wood-burning and two electric ovens, Ana baked more than 300 different kinds of breads and pastries each week and sold them to local markets. Another woman, Ruth, sold tamales and tacos every weekend in her predominantly Hispanic/Latino neighborhood. Juana, a seamstress, made dresses for weddings, baptism, and girls' 15th birthday celebrations. Delia worked

the night shift at a meat-processing plant and during the day as a beautician for friends and relatives. The women were skilled at entrepreneurship even though many of them had never run a business in Mexico. (2008:236–37)

Undocumented Latinos, on the other hand, have many limitations pertaining to business ownership. The informal economy plays a particularly strong role in dictating the type of business activity they can engage in. In the informal economy they can operate a business with less fear of identification by immigration authorities and deportation back to their country of origin. Consequently, residency status takes on great significance in shaping options available to Latinos.

Fairlie and Woodruff's (2007) study of Mexican American entrepreneurship based on the 2000 U.S. Census, Outgoing Rotation Group Files of the Current Population Survey from 1994 to 2004, and the Legalized Population Survey finds that the legal status of Mexicans who are unauthorized in this country reduces business ownership rates by approximately 0.7 percent for both men and women. This is yet another indication that small business ownership for those who are undocumented is limited to the informal economy.

In an article for the Hoover Institute, Pamaffy (1998) tells the story of a Mexican named Bartolo Lopez. Bartolo entered the country unauthorized in the early 1970s and learned the business of landscaping through work with a Japanese gardener. Eventually he obtained legal residence and opened up his own business. "The qualities that promoted Lopez to launch his own enterprise are the same ones that brought him to America in the first place: a penchant for risk-taking and a willingness to sacrifice and work hard in pursuit of a better life. These attitudes are typically strong among immigrants, and they help to explain why a vibrant entrepreneurial culture is developing within the Hispanic community." Pamaffy's asset perspective toward newcomers is shared by many others in this country and interjects the importance of community advocates and scholars providing a different spin on the role and contributions of immigrants, particularly those who are undocumented.

Local efforts at addressing the issue of undocumented Latinos have had an impact on Latino-owned small businesses, as in the case of Mesa, Arizona, where recent legislation (see epilogue) has created a divide between those facing relaxed standards and those facing harsh standards: "The businesses catering to Latinos are suffering. At Mi Amigos, a bodega, the manager, Rigoberto Magana, glanced at the emptiness of the store at midday and said it was typical. 'Our business is way, way down, and so is everybody else's here. . . . Nobody comes out" (Archibold 2010c). Mr. Magana's experience can be multiplied countless times, with implications going far beyond undocumented

Latinos to those who are citizens or have the necessary resident papers but also rely on these small businesses.

EDUCATIONAL LEVEL

The role of small business ownership takes on even greater significance in the case of those with limited formal education because they have fewer employment options (Fairle and Woodruff 2007). It is estimated that in 2002 small business owners (12% of the U.S. population) accounted for almost 40 percent of the total U.S. wealth (Bucks, Kennickell and Moore 2006). At the same time, 44 percent of Latino small business owners were under the age of 45 (Lowrey 2007). Not surprisingly, native-born Latino owners have more formal education than immigrants, following a pattern similar to native-born Latinos in general when compared with their newcomer counterparts (Watson 2005).

Higher levels of formal education (human capital) capture a host of factors that can translate into greater success at owning and operating a small business. Toussaint-Comeau (2008), for example, finds that characteristics such as English language proficiency and formal education level increase the likelihood of a decision to pursue self-employment, reinforcing the class resources theoretical approach to ethnic/racial small business development addressed in chapter 3.

Lofstrom and Bates stress the importance of formal education in determining the financial viability of Latina small business owners:

> To allow for a meaningful comparison of earnings between self-employed and wage/salary women, we generate different earnings measures addressing the role of business equity. We compare earnings of Hispanic female entrepreneurs to both Latina wage/salary workers and to self-employed female non-Hispanic whites. Latina entrepreneurs are observed to have lower mean earnings than both white female entrepreneurs and Latina employees. However, our findings indicate that Latina entrepreneurs often do well, once differences in mean observable characteristics, such as education, are taken into account. Self-employed Latinas are estimated to earn more than observationally similar non-minority white female entrepreneurs and slightly less than observationally similar wage/salary-employed Latinas. (2009:427)

Human capital, as represented through formal educational attainment, increases the likelihood of success for Latina entrepreneurs as well as for their male counterparts.

There is little dispute that the majority of Latinos owning small businesses tend to be males, as Salazar (2005) notes:

> Why is it that Latinas are still underrepresented among business owners? The business field is predominantly a man's world. Even though the numbers of Latina-owned firms have grown in the past few years, they still make up a small number of Latino/businesses. Latinas have to work twice as hard to receive the same rewards. Because of the difficulties of gaining access to education, language, capital, and training and the unfamiliarity with U.S. business laws and regulations, Latinas often encounter discrimination in the business world.

Nevertheless, Latinas do wield considerable influence in the business world. It is estimated that women-owned enterprises totaled 10.4 million in the United States and employed more than 12.8 million, accounting for $1.9 billion in annual sales (*Banderas News* 2006). A study of businesses owned by women of color in Southern California shows that their ownership, as evidenced by the number of firms, sales and receipts, and job creation, increased between 1987 and 1997 (Community Development Technologies Center 2002a). Los Angeles is considered the top metropolitan area for such businesses.

Latina-owned small businesses also witnessed dramatic increases between 1997 and 2006, with the service sector (286.2%), real estate, rental, and leasing (186.4%), and wholesale trade (115%) showing remarkable growth. In 2006 Latina-owned businesses accounted for 37 percent of the 2.5 million Latino-owned businesses in the United States and were responsible for generating $45 billion in sales (Holvino 2008).

Gender characteristics of Latino small business owners have generally been overlooked or only minimally addressed in the literature (Salazar 2005; Smith-Hunter 2006). As a result, there has been a tendency to lump together both genders when representing Latino-owned small businesses. More than fifteen years ago, Sarason and Koberg (1994) advocated for more research on Latina small business owners. Unfortunately, the field did not heed this call to action, with some notable exceptions (Delgado 1997, 1998b; Shim and Eastlick 1998; Salazar 2005; Smith-Hunter, 2006).

Despite this gender bias in reporting and scholarship, there is a growing recognition of Latinas in the small business arena. In 2002 there were 553,618 Latina-owned small businesses in the United States, generating $44.4 billion in sales, and Latina-owned small businesses grew by 39.3 percent from 1997 to 2002, far outpacing the growth all women-owned businesses during that period. Not surprisingly, the five states with the most Latina businesses were California (17%), Texas (18%), Florida (16%), New York (14%), and Arizona (13%) (Hispanic Business and Entrepreneurship 2007).

Cruz's (2005) ethnographic study of Latina's business ownership in Denton, Texas, addresses the role of gender in influencing the nature of the enterprises Latinas seek to establish within a community. Salazar (2005) finds that Latinas who own their own businesses tend to be younger than their male counterparts, with 53 percent of Latinas being between the ages of 35 and 44 compared with 30 percent of their male counterparts.

Latinas, however, face challenges that their male counterparts do not, as noted in several sections earlier. In my earlier study of Latina-owned businesses such as botanical shops and beauty parlors (Delgado 1998a), I find that Latinas have limited venues for leadership and service to community as a result of cultural expectations—for example, women are not supposed to own their own businesses, and they are not expected to know finances as well as men. Furthermore, in cases where they have young children, they are expected to care for them, even when their businesses require long hours. Nevertheless, these and other limitations have not stopped Latinas from entering a world that has historically been dominated by men. The nature of the small businesses that lend themselves to Latina entrepreneurial spirit (garment businesses and domestic service) severely limits their earning potential and leads to exploitation in both the formal and informal sectors.

Latino males, as noted earlier, are well represented in the construction industry. This has had a corresponding impact on the community because of the economic slowdown in the building sector, which lost almost 250,000 jobs from 2007 to 2008. This loss in employment has had a disproportionate impact on Latino males (Kochhar 2008). Latinas, in turn, tend to be concentrated in the service (54.5%) and retail (31.8%) sectors (Davies-Netzley 1999).

NAMING OF SMALL BUSINESSES

The naming process involved with Latino small businesses provides a unique viewpoint on the community:

> These owners [Latinos] of grocery stores and restaurants, at the point that they began their business in a new setting, are drawing from the cultural foundation that grounds their identity. Grocery store and restaurant names

tell use about the cultural and geographic origins of persons who establish a business, as much as they tell us about intended recipients of the products that they provide and the ways that their name-makers want to be remembered and acknowledged, as they seek to create a place that is familiar and recognizable for their families and themselves and create a legacy of belonging in rural southern Florida. (Bletzer 2003:230)

The names Latinos give to their businesses provide important data on the owners and bring uniquely Latino colors and designs to the neighborhood in the process. This is often referred to as the Latinization of a community. These data can also bring an important dimension to the development of Latino small business success indicators, which I will address in chapter 6.

Miyares (2004) uses the term "streetscapes" to help capture the dynamics and color of Latino communities, highlighting how signs provide important information on the community. Latino business signs reflect place names from the home country, cultural artifacts, colors of national flags, and national crests. Signs not only bring color to an otherwise drab urban environment but also serve as visual cues to attract customers.

Bletzer, in an interesting view of Latino-owned businesses in rural southern Florida, finds that the naming of grocery stores and restaurants reflects cultural expressions drawn from the cultural roots of owners and clientele. The business names reflect the "flavor and pride of Latino" identity, or the Latinization of commercial establishments. "The centrality and focal attraction of the neighborhood store within an urbanized area of immigrants . . . is replicated by a country store that creates a similar centrality in a rural area where few sources exist for the purchase of consumable necessities, such as food and household products" (2003:211). Skelly and colleagues (2002) identify tiendas as playing influential and even pivotal social, cultural, and economic roles in Latino communities in rural North Carolina.

The topic of small business naming will be addressed again in the next chapter, with implications for community asset assessment.

SOCIAL INTERACTIONS AND RELATIONSHIPS

Any serious effort to better appreciate the importance of Latino small businesses in urban areas necessitates that we develop a better understanding of the social aspects of how business is conducted in the Latino community. These interactions often form the central element of the uniqueness of Latino social and cultural life and are an essential part of all business transactions.

In essence, these interactions represent the cultural competence of the Latinidad way of doing business.

Alonso's (1979:20) description of a Latino small business in Boston over thirty years ago captures the role of these establishments in the Latino community: "The small corner stores are a fixture in Boston's Hispanic neighborhoods. People go to them not only to shop, but to talk and read the newspapers from their countries. They are a link to a life left behind and a sign of the striving to make a new life here. Most are stamped with the personality of their owner. In many cases they bear his name or the name of the wife or his home town."

Coen, Ross, and Turner describe the importance of tiendas in Latino culture, underscoring the social and economic role they play in these communities:

> Trade stores—small-scale, home-based shops selling daily household necessities—are ubiquitous across low income, urban neighborhoods of developing countries. Surprisingly, while the informal economy literature on marketplaces and small-scale enterprises continues to expand, neighborhood trade stores and their unique dynamics in urban environments remain comparatively overlooked. Through a qualitative case study . . . we reveal the complexity of their significance to the everyday micro-geographies of urban places. Not only are these shops essential outlets for routine wares but also, vis-à-vis a number of more nuanced roles, trade stores play a critical part in configuring the day-to-day survival and opportunities of local residents. (2008:327)

For the purposes of discussion, I have selected only three "nuanced" roles: personalization of the customer, granting of credit and other financial services, and server of the community (*servidor a la comunidad*). These three dimensions of social interactions and relationships capture the Latino style of doing business, which incorporates economics with cultural values in business relations.

1. Personalization of the customer. Personal relationships (*personalismo*) between owner and customer represent one aspect of Latino small business activity. Levitt recognizes this social interaction in her research on Latino businesses in Boston:

> This highly personalized, customer-specific sales strategy, which respondents call *buen trato* (good treatment), includes keeping track of custom-

ers' style or color preferences, inquiring about their health problems, and remembering when they have not been into the store for a long time. . . . A grocery store owner described his customer relations: "Once a Hispanic person starts going to a Hispanic store he becomes your friend for as long as you have that store. . . . Over here, we know the history of most of our customers. The problems that they have. We get invited to all weddings around. We get invited to the baptisms." (1995:131)

Thus, *buen trato* can be conceptualized as a "value-added" dimension to an economic transaction. Consequently, it is easy to see why the closing of a popular Latino business often represents a social as well as an economic setback for the Latino community, as noted in the following quote regarding the closing of a Latino food establishment in Charlotte, North Carolina: "'These places are community centers as much as they are places to get food,' said Tom Hanchett of the Levine Museum of the New South. 'So when you lose one of those, you're losing a grass-roots entrepreneur. But you're also losing a community connection'" (Ordonez 2009). The opening of a Latino small business, in turn, has the potential to be considered a sociocultural addition to a community.

2. Granting of credit and other financial services. Latinos generally are unbanked, as discussed earlier. Thus, provision of credit to credit-worthy customers is an essential aspect of Latino small business activity because of the relatively low economic status of Latino customers in many of the nation's urban communities. Granting of credit is a phenomenon that can be traced back to countries of origin, and getting credit in the United States only represents a continuation of this practice. Mind you, credit is not automatic. If an existing customer recommends a new customer, he or she is vouching for the new person's character and credit worthiness. Granting of credit in turn signifies respect and the fundamental belief that the customer or, if he or she fails, the sponsor will make good on the credit.

The high percentage of Latinos who are unbanked does contribute to this credit squeeze. Checks can be cashed at small businesses without paying a fee. Check cashing takes on added significance when the customer is also willing to settle a debt. Latino small businesses, particularly grocery stores, can be conceptualized as community banks. Furthermore, Latino reluctance to use credit cards and banks has resulted in heavy reliance on cash in a society that increasingly is becoming "cashless" (Jankowski, Rice, and Porter 2007).

It should be noted that in 2007 Bank of America undertook what was considered a controversial initiative to reach out to undocumented Latinos by issuing credit cards to customers without social security numbers or credit histories in an effort to fill the void created by banks refusing to reach out to this population (Jordan and Bauerlein 2007). These credit cards (with a $500 line of credit), however, have high interest rates (variable rate of 21.24% compared with 18.1% nationwide) and require an upfront fee/security deposit ($99). Other banks may follow this path in the future.

3. Servidor a la comunidad. A report by the Hispanic Federation (2002) entitled *Abriendo Caminos: Strengthening Latino Communities Through Giving and Volunteering* captures the potential of Latino-owned small businesses to contribute time, expertise, and funding for community projects. Contributions often go beyond donation of goods and money to include volunteering within the community. This *servidor* or socially responsible role is one that is deeply enmeshed within a cultural tradition of giving and caring.

All too often small business contributions get monetized because of the broader society's emphasis on money. For example, it is not unusual to read about volunteering and see a monetary value on the time given to volunteering. This tendency, I believe, minimizes the human element of volunteering by putting a dollar figure on the activity. Writing a check for $100 has a different significance from contributing ten hours of work on a community project, for example. However, within Latino communities, the contributions represented through good deeds take on greater significance than just giving money to community causes. Needless to say, these two approaches do not have to be mutually exclusive. In fact, when both occur it makes small businesses that much more important in the life and social fabric of the community.

COMMUNITY SERVICE: FUNERALS

The social role Latino small businesses play in their community is multifaceted, particularly in the case of those businesses that are held in high esteem by residents. As initially addressed in the opening chapter, one of the most respected actions a Latino enterprise can take, and one that will certainly garner a stream of loyal Latino customers, is to play a prominent role in helping to bury a community resident. This service captures the essence of social responsibility from a cultural perspective and merges economics with social actions that, to the outside world, may seem out of the ordinary. However, it is culturally symbolic and separates Latino small businesses from businesses owned by white, non-Latino groups (Colon 2005; Thomas 2001).

Few events capture the immediacy of the Latino community more than an untimely death or the death of a prominent member of the community.

The grieving process gets manifested in a wide range of ways, but sending the body of a loved one back to his or her country of origin is often considered the proper thing to do, regardless of a family's economic circumstances, and is a vital part of the grieving process for the family and the community as a whole (Halbfinger 2010). The process can cost several thousand dollars or more but is one that must be undertaken.

Wingett (2006) reports on the costs at La Paz funeral home in Phoenix: "La Paz's low-cost, high volume business model attracts families who don't have a lot to spend. Typical prices range from the 'Economy Burial' package for $1,799 to the 'International Shipout' deal for $1,399 plus airfare. La Paz often refrigerates bodies at no extra charge if families need to raise money through carwashes and donations." Thus, it is not unusual to have a collection made within the community where neighbors, friends, and even strangers donate money to accomplish this final gesture of love and devotion. In cases where the deceased was well-known and respected, the effort to collect money will fall on the family. However, in other cases, two options are available: either cremation or having someone or some institution in the community take on the responsibility to collect donations.

Tellez-Giron (2007:404) views the burial experience through a cultural lens that brings family and community together: "Similar to their family values, Latinos' sense of community is very high. This is particularly true when it comes to helping each other when someone in the community faces a terminal disease. It is a great source of support not only to the patient but particularly for the families. In some communities everybody is part of the dying process, before, during, and after the death. Many of the community members contribute money for the burial expenses."

The rise in cremation among Latinos represents an effort to address the escalating costs (Maderazo 2008). Latino small businesses can and often do play instrumental roles in helping to generate funds to send someone back to his or her country of origin for burial. In 2005 in Massachusetts, 80 percent of the 1,230 Latinos who died that year were sent home for burial, with costs ranging from $4,000 to $6,000 (Farrar 2007).

These costs often necessitate public efforts to obtain funds: "Sometimes it literally takes a village to have a funeral. Friends, neighbors, businesses, and churches will chip in to help pay for the services. In East Boston, for example, Hispanic businesses and restaurants recently put out small cardboard collection boxes to raise money for the funeral of a Guatemalan woman who was killed in a car accident in July" (Farrar 2007:1). As noted in chapter 1, sometimes Latino business owners take on a disproportionate share of the costs in order to provide the funds associated with a funeral and transport of a body.

The mainstream funeral business has started to take notice of the Latino community and the potential of this market. However, the importance of cultural factors has resulted in an increase in the number of Latino-owned funeral homes springing up across the country. Although these institutions constitute a small number when compared with other types of Latin-owned small businesses, they wield considerable influence within the community and have started to increase as the community ages (Wingett 2006; Acosta and Serrano 2008).

INCOME AND WEALTH

Development of a comprehensive understanding of the economic status of Latinos lends itself to a wide variety of ways of looking at their situation (Ibarra and Rodriguez 2005–2006). The conventional way of doing so, however, involves examining the status of Latino workers, households, and small businesses. I touch on each of these perspectives in this book, but addressing the subject of Latino wealth necessitates a change in mindset, as D. Myers notes:

> America has been wallowing in despair since 1973. It's a Peter Pan fallacy where Latinos never change. They stay the same and pile up as newcomers. The rest of society then doesn't see any prospects in that community and doesn't want to invest in it. We need to adopt a "hope model," which is based on facts. It shows us that a different future is unfolding. Immigration is not accelerating. It's holding steady. We have a community of mostly settled immigrants who are great business prospects and who are going to be generating economic benefits for America. They are seen as newcomers, but the truth is they are upwardly mobile and are going to be the economic engine of the future. (Quoted in Grossman 2007:10)

Myers's optimistic tone, however, is moderated by an economic picture of wealth in the nation's African American community. The income gap of African Americans compared with white non-Latinos, for example, has not narrowed much over the more than forty years since Dr. Martin Luther King, Jr., was murdered. Since 1968 the median per capita income narrowed by 3 cents on the dollar. If this were to continue to the point where there was no gap, it would take 537 years to eliminate the gap (Rivera et al. 2009). A flourishing of African American small businesses cannot be expected to overcome this disparity in income. The same can be said for the income gap between Latinos and white non-Latinos.

There is a relationship between business ownership and community well-being, as in the case of Miami (Lowrey 2007). The Latino community is not well-off economically. Nevertheless, it is important to disaggregate data on economic well-being in order to develop a better appreciation of the extent of income and wealth distribution across and within Latino groups.

Net worth (assets minus liabilities) represents an often overlooked perspective and provides important information on household well-being in Latino and other communities of color (Leigh 2006). Robles (2006:246) identifies the key elements that influence net worth: "The data indicate that the net worth of our communities of color is intrinsically tied to educational attainment rates, occupation status, financial market sophistication and participation, home-ownership, and pension participation."

Latino net worth was $534 billion in 2000 (Montemayor and Mendoza 2004). In 2002 Latino households had less than 10 percent ($7,932) of the wealth of white non-Latino households, with $88,651. African American households fared even worse than Latinos, with $5,988 in net worth. There was also disparity within Latino groups. Cubans ($39,787) had the highest household net worth, followed by Mexican Americans ($7,602) and Central and Caribbean households ($2,508) (Kochhar 2004).

Net worth is highly concentrated within the Latino community. Latino households in the top fifth percentile had a net worth of $365 billion, or 49.8 percent of the total net worth of all Latino households. The top next twentieth percentile controlled $31.5 billion, or 42.9 percent. These two groups represented 25 percent of all Latino households and controlled 92.7 percent of total Latino net worth in 2002 (Kochhar 2004). The vast amount of such wealth is accounted for by home values, which dropped significantly during the recession of 2008–2009.

This concentration of wealth among the top twenty-fifth percentile of Latino households reflects formal educational attainment, occupation, and homeownership differences. Forty-five percent of affluent Latino households are concentrated in Chicago, Houston, Los Angeles, Miami, and New York. Miami (10.1%) and Los Angeles (8.5%) account for a significant portion of the affluent households. Chicago, in turn, accounts for 54.4 percent of the Latino middle class earning between $35,000 and $99,999 (*Hispanic.com* 2007).

The Latino middle class is generally overlooked in any discussion of this community, particularly its role in micro-enterprise development (Pachon 2008). Grossman (2007:11) notes that the Latino middle class can no longer be ignored: "Contrary to the image of Latinos as being primarily illegal, poor and uneducated, the reality is that economic mobility does occur. This is a growing Latino middle class and an increasing number of Latino families who are investors, professionals, and represent a dynamic segment of the current and future economy." De la Isla's (2007) observations concerning the neglected Latino middle class capture a prevailing view of this group in the United States:

> It's too bad the current political climate distorts the U.S. population. It's as if we were standing in front of one of those full-length fun-house mirrors that make us look like a cartoon. That's how the current presidential aspirants distort the national portrait. The candidates seem to know the issues. But do they know the public, especially when it comes to the changing demographics and Latinos? Since the 1990s, a convincingly large portion of 44 million Latinos entered the middle-income ranks.

Nevertheless, it is important not to lose sight that the Latino community is still a relatively low-income group and that the four states with the highest concentration of Latinos are also states with high concentrations of those who are severely poor: California (1.9 million), Texas (1.6 million), New York (1.2 million), and Florida (900,000). Furthermore, 26 percent of Latino families in the country have a net worth of zero! Texas has three of the nation's poorest counties (Cameron, Hidalgo, and El Paso), and the Bronx, New York, is the fourth. These areas are home to, on average, 78 percent Latinos (Grossman 2007).

The Latino middle class, like its African American counterpart, has shown signs that its status is precarious and still subject to the economic uncertainty experienced in a major recession:

> African-American and Latino families have more difficulty moving into the middle class, and families that do enter the middle class are less secure and at higher risk than the middle class as a whole: Fewer than one in five Latino families (18 percent) are securely in the middle class. More than twice as many Latino (41 percent) families are in danger of slipping out of the middle class. . . . African-American middle-class families are less secure and at greater risk than the middle class as a whole on four of the five indicators of security and vulnerability. Latino middle-class families are less secure and at greater risk on all five indicators. . . . Assets and housing costs are among the key destabilizing factors Latino and African-American families face: Only 2 percent of African-American and 8 percent of middle-class Latino families have enough net financial assets to meet three-quarters of their essential living expenses for nine months if their source of income disappeared. About 95 percent of African-American and 87 percent of Latino

middle-class families do not have enough net assets to meet three-quarters of their essential living expenses for even three months if their source of income were to disappear. . . . Only 26 percent of African-American and 37 percent of Latino middle-class families spend less than 20 percent of their after-tax income on housing—both are below the national average of 40 percent. (*HispanicBusiness.com* 2009)

The relative youthfulness of the Latino community (not old enough to have acquired wealth), combined with the prospects of higher educational rates as second- and third-generation Latinos enter and graduate from college, is a reason for optimism for this community (Chapa and de la Rosa 2006; Robles 2009.) Lopez (2009) highlights the importance of Latino formal education attainment to social and economic mobility in this country and stresses the need to close the achievement gap in education.

Robles and Cordero-Guzman (2007) emphasize the value of differentiating between Latinos with different formal educational backgrounds, particularly those with college educations, in the startup of small businesses. This perspective holds great promise for Latino and other groups of color in the United States. For example, a study by the Hispanic Scholarship Foundation estimates that a doubling of the college graduate rates of Latinos from 2001 to 2010 would translate into a $1.3 billion increase in the U.S. economy, not to mention its direct impact on Latino communities themselves (Henry 2001).

Latino household wealth is considerably smaller than that of white non-Latinos, with just ten cents on the dollar, making Latinos very vulnerable to economic downturns (Kochhar 2004). Although the overall picture is not bright, there are glimpses of sunshine on the horizon (Armas 2004). First, it is necessary to disaggregate the data on wealth to take into account Latino origins, formal educational level, and occupational status. Breaking down data according to these variables will present a different picture on wealth and income.

HIGH-INCOME LATINOS

Based on the data presented above, it is understandable why low-income, low-wealth Latino households have been the subject of so much national attention. However, high-income, high-wealth Latinos will represent an emerging group with a range of social and economic needs and are a group targeted by businesses. The number of Latino households making $100,000 or more per year and having net worth of more than $500,000 is growing eight times faster than the number of white non-Latinos with similar assets (Fleischer and Suarez 2007; Leder 2007).

How affluent Latino households behave in the marketplace is yet to be fully explored and understood. South, Crowder, and Chavez (2006), for example, in a rare study focused on geographical mobility and spatial assimilation of high-income and English-proficient Latinos, find them to have a higher tendency to be embedded in Anglo contexts (predominantly white, non-Latino communities). Latinos in high-income categories will become attractive customers for certain types of products and services in the early part of this century (Goldman Sachs 2007).

D. Perez stresses that affluence and Latino culture can coexist in the United States:

> Affluence cuts across acculturation, language, or life stage. This person could be an industrialist coming in from Argentina and landing his G4 in Miami. Or it could be the guy walking into the bank in paint-splattered overalls who wants to cash a $400 check. Or the guy who owns five body shops, or the woman who owns a string of beauty salons. They may not look or speak like the affluent, but they are. They may not have a college degree or an MBA, but their business needs are the same. They need access to capital. They need financial advice. They want to preserve and grow their wealth. They want to take care of their kids and provide for their education. They have all the same goals as everyone else, but this audience is not being well-served. (Quoted in Grossman 2007:19)

Reimers summarizes findings from disaggregated data pertaining to Latino economic well-being, presenting a powerful argument for viewing the Latino community from a variety of dimensions in order to better understand their economic situation and propose targeted intervention responses:

> Desegregation reveals that Puerto Ricans and Dominicans are at the bottom on most measures of economic well-being, with Mexicans near and sometimes at the bottom, too. Central Americans are somewhat better off than Mexicans. Furthermore, later generations of every Latino national origin are better off than earlier generations, with most of the improvement occurring between the first and second generation. Regardless of national origins, U.S.-born Hispanics have higher total household incomes than blacks. (2006:321)

It is important to end this section with an acknowledgment that wealth goes beyond monetary acquisition and must extend into cultural factors and considerations. Narrowly defining wealth as financial fails to take into account other forms of wealth. Ramirez takes this point of view about Latino wealth in the following statement "There is no such thing as a poor community, rich in people. Our greatest resources and assets are our families" (2005:6).

PURCHASING POWER

By 2010 people of color will control one quarter of U.S. purchasing power (Cohn 2007). In 2007 African Americans accounted for $845 billion and Latinos for $860 billion in economic power (Miller 2008). One report, although written in 2000 and based on 1998 dollars, projects communities of color as having purchasing power of $6.1 trillion by 2045 (U.S. Department of Commerce 2000). A Philadelphia economic conference organizer notes that these two groups share much in common: "We have similar food, music, dance and history, and we share the struggles we have to face" (Miller 2008:1), Philadelphia's Latino community has grown substantially over the past two decades and in 2001 numbered 129,000, or 8.5 percent of the city's population (Bartelt 2001). The nation's inner cities represent $85 billion in retail purchasing power, or 7 percent of the entire nation's purchasing power, more than the formal retail market of Mexico (McQueen, Weiser, and Burns 2007).

Latino buying power increased by 247 percent from 1990 to 2006 (Turner and Czekalinski 2007) and increased steadily from 2002 and 2008. In 1990 Latino buying power was calculated at $212 billion. In 2003 it was $600 billion, up from $540 billion in 2002. In 2006 it was estimated to be slightly under $800 billion, increasing to $863 billion in 2007 (Selig Center for Economic Growth 2006). In 2008 it stood at $980 billion (*Hispanic Market Weekly* 2009). A billion dollars in purchasing power translates into $1.9 million per minute (Montemayor and Mendoza 2004). Finally, the purchasing power of this community is projected to reach $1.2 trillion dollars in 2011 (Selig Center for Economic Growth 2006) and $1.3 trillion in 2013 (*Hispanic Market Weekly* 2009). This translates into more than 450 percent growth between 1990 and 2011, with non-Latino purchasing power increasing close to 176 percent during the same period. Another estimate has Latino purchasing power increasing by 31 percent from 2009 to 2014 (Best 2009).

These increases constitute several times the overall national rate of consumer purchasing power over the past decade (U.S. Hispanic Chamber of Commerce 2007). Further, as noted earlier in this chapter, the number of Latino households with incomes of at least $100,000 increased by 137 percent between 1990 and 2000, indicating the rise of an economic class with even greater purchasing potential in the early part of the twenty-first century. The Latino middle-class bracket ($35,000 to $99,999), too, witnessed an increase of 40 percent (Cohn 2007).

It is estimated that Latino consumers in the United States will contribute fifty-six years of spending during their lifetime as compared with non-Latinos, owing to their median age of 27 and life expectancy of 83. In 2008, 67 percent of Latinos were under the age of 34 and represented 24 percent of all babies born in this country (Belanger 2009).

Morrison (2006) touches on the youth sector of the Latino market: "After decades of being ignored, urban Latino youths are now regarded in the corporate realm as the 'hottest' and fastest-growing segment of America's consumers. Pegged by market boosters as 'New Generation Latinos,' this highly desirable group consists of predominantly US-born second-, third-, and fourth-generation young adults who consume mostly English-language media and represent over $300 billion in purchasing power." One estimate notes that the 16–24 Latino age group wields economic power of $25 billion (Dougherty 2001).

This purchasing power increase has not been confined to traditional Latino strongholds on the two coasts. In Utah, for example, a state that historically has not enjoyed a large Latino population, Latinos spent $4 billion in 2003 (Burke 2004). In Georgia, another state without a long history of Latino residents, Latinos represented 6 percent of the state's total population in 2004, with an economic purchasing power of $10.9 billion, or a 700 percent increase from $1.3 billion in 1990 (Rodriguez 2004). In 2008 Idaho's Latino community increased its buying power by 11.3 percent from the previous year to $2.3 million (*Latino Business Review* 2009d). North Carolina, too, has seen the economic impact of Latinos, with this group contributing $9 billion to the state's economy (Kasarda and Johnson 2006; Withers 2008).

Population growth and an increase in domestic spending have resulted in an indigenous community effort to meet the daily living needs of this population. In 2002 Lancaster, Pennsylvania, had 517 Latino-owned businesses with receipts totaling $106.3 million, representing a 200 percent increase from 1996 (Agudo 2008). In 2007 Iowa had 1,500 Latino businesses with receipts totaling $288 million: 62 percent were in the retail sector and 20 percent were restaurants (Burros 2008).

Latino small businesses, conventional and informal, have risen in dramatic fashion across a variety of spheres. In 2003 there were approximately two million conventional Latino businesses in the United States, generating $300 billion in business (Martinez 2004). Grocery stores, beauty parlors, barbershops, and restaurants have generally been the focus of attention and studies. However, there is a growing segment of unconventional businesses, such as those focused on the production of documentation for the undocumented, mural painting, personal services, mobile street vending, that scholars and human service professions have generally ignored.

The topic of Latino purchasing power has generally escaped close attention by the general public, and social work, too, is guilty of that. It seems like the nation and helping professions are most comfortable focusing on the needs and challenges confronting this community. Yet Latino economic influence is far from being insignificant both nationally and locally (Schneider 2002; Yago, Zeidman, and Abuyuan 2007).

Dispersal and concentration of Latinos have a direct bearing on their economic influence, as the following statistics highlight. Latino purchasing power in 2008 was estimated to be 9.6 percent of all U.S. purchasing power. At first glance this may appear to be relatively small amount of influence on the national economy (Perkins 2004). However, when examined from a perspective of where Latinos are concentrated geographically, it takes on added significance. For example, in 2003 ten states were responsible for a little over 80 percent of the Latino purchasing power, or $635 billion, with California ($189.1 billion), Texas ($113 billion), Florida ($60.8 billion), and New York ($54.6 billion) accounting for the lion's share of this economic influence (Selig Center for Economic Growth 2006).

Furthermore, Latino concentration in cities within these states, such as Los Angeles, Miami, and New York, which will be addressed later in this chapter, adds to their economic significance from a city, state, and regional perspective. San Diego, for example, is the eleventh largest Latino market in the country. However, if Tijuana's spending or "cross-border consumer base" is included, San Diego ranks as the fourth largest Latino market in the country owing to $3 billion from consumers living in Tijuana but shopping in San Diego (Merritt 2006).

ACCULTURATION

The subject of acculturation has emerged and gained prominence with regard to Latino markets and is no longer the exclusive domain of research related to social problems (Perkins 2004; Valdes 2008). There are numerous definitions of acculturation, but the one by Massey, Zambrana, and Bell (1995:191) lends itself quite well in marketing to Latinos: "a preference for culturally specific food, language, social activities and English language, as well as level of education, place of birth, and number of years in the United States. In essence, the concept has served as a proxy indicator for socioeconomic status, generational status, and place of birth."

Targeting markets based on levels of acculturation has become a central aspect for businesses, small and big, wishing to reach this market (Ayala et al. 2005; Korzenny and Korzenny 2005; Palumbo and Teich 2004). Acculturation is a construct that seeks to capture a generational shift in cultural values and behaviors (Cohn 2007). S. Sosa argues that the convergence of Latino and American values has resulted in a unique transformation of the Latino community: "This acculturation, merging the tradition of the Latino culture with American independence and ambition, is at the core of the Latino middle class and the growing ranks of the wealthy Latino community" (quoted in Grossman 2007:9).

Cultural values and corresponding behaviors can inhibit or enhance indigenous economic inclinations toward small business creation (Frederick 2008; Valdes 2008). However, acculturation can also have an impact on altruistic behavior. Vallejo and Lee (2009) address the subject of Latino acculturation and upward mobility from a different vantage point. Their qualitative study of Mexican "give back" to co-ethnics finds that Mexicans from poor backgrounds who achieved middle-class status displayed a greater propensity to help other, less fortunate Mexicans when compared with those who grew up as part of the middle class.

MARKETING TO LATINOS

"Merchants of death and misery" are not the only corporations targeting the Latino community and using an acculturation construct to do so. As noted in chapter 1, there numerous books and scholarly articles trying to help corporations market to Latinos. Davila (2008), however, raises serious concerns about how advertising is still predicated on stereotypes of Latinos, with very little effort being made to view this community as heterogeneous and complex. Chapter 2 highlighted how this community is getting more complex with each succeeding Latino generation. Inglessis, McGavock, and Korzenny (2009) note that advertising sponsored and produced by Latinos has gained in sophistication and should help counteract negative and simplistic views of Latinos.

The rise in advertising dollars and attention to Latinos seems to be gathering momentum as the recognition of this expanding market is fueled by Census Bureau data and marketing reports of various types. Montemayor and Mendoza, for example, make this comment on Latino purchasing power: "It would be entrepreneurial ignorance—if not totally un-American—to neglect a projected $1 trillion-a-year market" (2004:63). Not surprisingly, major national magazines such as *Newsweek, People, Teen,* and *Vogue* have started Spanish-language editions as a means of reaching the Latino community. The recession of 2008–2009 witnessed advertisers, particularly consumer-product companies and financial-services firms, increasing their advertising dollars targeting Latinos (*Miami-Herald* 2009).

By 2015 this purchasing power is estimated to be $1.3 trillion (*Miami Herald* 2008). The math is overwhelmingly attractive. There is an awareness of the economic force Latinos present in the early part of this century (Sunderland, Taylor, and Denny 2004; Gulina 2007). The nation's top five hundred companies spent $5 billion on Spanish advertising in 2006 (Harris 2007). One estimate of advertising dollars spent targeting Latinos put the increase between 15 and 20 percent during the 1998 to 2003 period (Knowledge @Wharton 2003).

Goldman Sachs (2007) estimates that Latinos will represent 14 percent of aggregate expenditure growth in the United States between 2007 and 2010. In 2005 U.S. companies spent an estimated $3.3 billion on marketing products to Latinos, which represented an increase of 7 percent from the previous year (King 2007). Telecommunication companies such as Univision and the Spanish Broadcasting System have seen their markets increase as the community has grown. Other telecommunication companies have also started to see the Latino market increase, to the point where this market represents a viable segment to focus on (Dougherty 2005).

Other industries, too, have suddenly discovered the Latino market. Goldman Sachs issued two reports providing potential investors with detailed analysis of Latino demographic data, spending patterns, and strategies to invest in "Hispanization" (Kostin 2004; Goldman Sachs 2007). Merrill Lynch and had a 350-person Latino unit that generated $1 billion of new business in 2002 (Bradley and Stuckey 2005).

Proctor and Gamble has a long tradition of marketing to Latinos dating back to the 1960s. However, starting in 2000 it initiated a concentrated effort (*CreativeFortWayne.net* 2004). In 2003 Proctor and Gamble spent $90 million on Latino advertising for twelve products, and it now has a unit with sixty-five bilingual staff with the express purposes of marketing to Latinos (Bradley and Stuckey 2005). One executive noted that "Hispanics are a cornerstone of our growth in North America" (Brennan 2004). State Farm Insurance raised its multicultural outreach by 50 percent from 2007 to 2008 in an effort to expand its insurance business into new markets (Maul 2009). Food

Lion, a regional grocery chain based in Salisbury, North Carolina, converted 59 of its 1,200 supermarkets into Latino stores in an organizational effort to tap the Latino market (Longo 2009).

An estimated $11.2 million was spent specifically on advertisements in Latino magazines in 2002, an increase of 33 percent from the previous year (Jordan 2004). In 2003 General Motors spent $7.7 million in Latino magazine advertisements, or an increase of 166 percent from 2002 (Jordan 2004). Kim, Jolly, and Kim (2007), in a different type of example, identify the presence of Latinos as one of three significant trends in apparel retailing in this country (plus size and aging being the other two). Michelin Tire, too, has seen the potential of this market and developed a program (bilingual point-of-sale, support materials, advertising and public relations) it launched in Miami in 2003 (McCarron 2007).

The dispersal of Latinos to new geographical regions brings with it economic purchasing power that is regionalized. The Southeast, for example, has experienced dramatic increases in Latinos, as noted in chapter 2, with the economic buying power of Latinos in this region increasing by 300 percent, from $24 billion to $79 billion, between 1990 and 2003 (Dougherty 2005).

Pethokoukis (2005) reports on a study that attempted to break the Latino adult market into five categories: (1) New Lifers—foreign-born Latinos who have lived in the United States an average of eight years, with a median annual household income of $40,000; (2) Old Ways—foreign-born individuals who have lived in the United States more than half of their lifetime, with an average age of 54 and a median household income of $47,000; (3) Settled In—those born and raised in the United States, with an average age of 43 and a median annual household income of $68,000 (69%, however, have an annual household income of $100,000); (4) Pioneers—people with an average age of 65 and a median household income of $50,000 (47% of this group live in Albuquerque, Los Angeles, New York, or San Antonio; and (5) Young Americans—75 percent of whom were born in the United States, with an average age of 26 and a median annual household income of $60,000.

COMMUNITY DEVELOPMENT PERSPECTIVES

There are many highways toward community socioeconomic development (Lejano 2006; Rodriguez-Pose and Storper 2006; Pinel 2007; Twelvetrees 2008). Each approach embraces a set of values and principles on how best to achieve community development and the role of community context in such development (Luke 2005). These approaches, in turn, influence how professional roles get conceptualized and carried out on a daily basis, along with all the rewards and tensions associated with any form of community practice, social work–centered or otherwise.

Kirkpatrick (2007) presents two case studies based in Oakland, California, involving two community development corporations, each with a distinctive approach toward achieving their goals. On the surface both appear to achieve success. One embraces a philosophical (market-driven) approach that is antithetical to community social work practice. The other, however, embraces a set of community-oriented and participatory values and approaches that resonate with the social work profession. DeRienzo (2008) also espouses the virtues of a community development model that stresses participatory principles and community decision-making over economic development at—as critics would say—any price.

Kirkpatrick's (2007) findings and conclusions, although limited to a small sample and one urban area of the country, highlight how values influence corresponding professional roles in approaching community development, which may help community social workers address the ambivalence discussed in chapter 1 about engaging in practice to develop and sustain Latino small businesses. The embrace of a set of values that stress principles of participatory democracy and are founded on a social justice perspective provides the moral compass to venture into the for-profit sector yet still maintain the integrity and moral purpose associated with community social work practice (Mendes 2008).

Loza's comments on the increasingly close relationship between nongovernmental institutions and corporations have implications for community economic development practice involving Latino small business development:

> Globalization processes have resulted in greater complexity, interdependence and limited resources. Consequently, no one sector can effectively respond to today's business or wider challenges and opportunities. Nongovernmental organizations and corporations are increasingly engaging each other in recognition that shareholder and societal values are intrinsically linked. For both sectors, these partnerships can create an enabling environment to address social issues and can generate social capital. (2004:297)

Community economic development is not antithetical to community social work practice when values guiding this development resonate with social work values.

LATINO ECONOMIC DEVELOPMENT

Peredo and Chrisman stress the need for a new approach to better understanding community-based enterprises that corresponds to community social work values:

> Theoretical models that separate social, political and environmental factors from the economics dimensions of entrepreneurship cannot account for the failed experiences in business development among very poor populations. In this article, we develop the concept of Community-Based Enterprise (CBE) and argue that it provides a potential strategy for sustainable local development. We maintain that in this emerging form of entrepreneurship, typically rooted in community culture, natural and social capital are integral and inseparable from economic considerations, transforming the community into an entrepreneur and an enterprise. (2004:309)

Progressive community development centers that seek to both enhance community economic goals and enrich the Latino community culturally and politically in the process often have goals that are similar to those found in human service organizations targeting the same community (Mathie and Cunningham 2003). These goals invariably stress participatory democracy, empowerment, cultural pride, and the importance of social capital in enriching the lives of all members of a community and the institutions that serve them, be they economic or social in nature.

Nowak (2007), as highlighted in the introductory chapter, advocates for a place-making vision that systematically integrates business or economic development alongside community cultural investments that increase social and human capital. Quality public space creation, such as building of public plazas, is closely connected to human capital formation and increased meaningful interactions and to relationships between key institutions serving the community and the community itself. Latino small business development, as envisioned in this book, is closely tied to community social and human development.

The following core values of the Minneapolis Latino Development Economic Center (2007) provide an excellent foundation for community social workers who seek to become involved in Latino small business development:

• Promote just, sustainable, and ethical business practices, a healthy, respectful work environment, social responsibility, and economic justice.

- Develop Latino talent, leadership, civic engagement, and political influence.
- Affirm and reflect the strengths of Latino culture and language.
- Nurture free enterprise and the entrepreneurial spirit of our community.
- Listen to and act in the best interests of our membership; contribute our wisdom and experience for the betterment of all members.

Latino small businesses are best appreciated from an ecological viewpoint in order to fully grasp their contributions to a community. Successful enterprises, for example, have been found to attract other ventures to the community and thereby have a synergistic effect—one that needs more study (Hispanic Advocacy and Community Empowerment Through Research 2004).

Unfortunately, there has been a disconnect between Latino small businesses and community development programs targeting small businesses. Hohn's study of three Boston neighborhoods reports the following disconnect:

> In all three neighborhoods, not a single business owner in the study received outside assistance in starting up their business. Not one relied on government programs designed to help small businesses. No one received any kind of business development advising. No one accessed traditional sources of financing. Instead, owners told stories of working two to three jobs, saving every penny, and turning to employers and family members to raise the needed funds to start the enterprise. (2005:23–24)

Gawgy (2006) notes that lack of access to information in Spanish and presented in a culture-specific manner hinders Latino small businesses from benefiting from governmental and private programs that specifically target small business owners of color. For example, something as simple as having a Spanish-speaking, preferably Latino, certified accountant can facilitate the support of Latino businesses (Hispanic Advocacy and Community Empowerment Through Research 2004).

The ability of the Latino community to tap the energy, hope, and competencies of newcomers to the community (both documented and undocumented) has short- and long-term implications for Latino community development. Pages (2005:4) argues strongly for viewing newcomers as assets and providing encouragement and support for their involvement in small business development: "Beyond business basics, the new entrepreneurs merit additional support on equity grounds. A truly inclusive and diverse economy requires a truly inclusive and diverse base of entrepreneurs. These new entrepreneurs bring new ideas and dynamism to their communities. By creating and reinvesting their wealth, these entrepreneurs also help create new economic opportunities for their fellow citizen."

TOURISM

Chhabra and Phillips (2009) note that tourism has long been recognized as a potential strategy for community and economic development. Neighborhoods as places of leisure and businesses such as tourism have been closely tied to the rapid transformation of the manufacturing sector into an information economy, necessitating that low-income and low-wealth communities find viable ways of making this shift (Rath 2006).

This economic potential has only recently started to get attention in a variety of academic disciplines. An economic assessment of downtown Gallup, New Mexico, for example, finds that its potential as a historical district that can attract tourists was generally overlooked in economic development plans (Mitchell 2006). An urban and regional economist (Florida 2002:34) stresses the potential of cultural assets in community economic development: "This milieu provides the underlying eco-system or habitat in which the multidimensional forms of creativity take root and flourish. By supplying lifestyle and cultural institutions like a cutting-edge music scene or vibrant artistic community, for instance, it helps to attract and stimulate those who create in business and technology."

The role and function of Latino small businesses, as emphasized throughout this book, encompasses a wide sphere within the community. Latino small businesses represent a means to help counter the increasing homogeneity of urban covered areas (Carr and Servon 2009). In essence, they bring color and often bright and vibrant shades to urban environments and provide a balance of culture and commerce (Salazar 2005).

Nowak emphasizes the potential of arts and cultural events for generating social capital and economic revenue in newcomer urban communities: "Arts and cultural activities play an important social capital role in immigrant communities. They provide a meeting place for the expression and maintenance of culture, as well as a bridge to cultural integration. . . . In fact, it [Taller Puertoriqueno] became one of the factors that contributed to the revitalization of a commercial corridor in the community" (2007:9).

Stern and Seifert (2007) specifically advance the importance of informal art as a community cultural asset and point to its community economic and social potential. Informal art, as opposed to formal art, captures community activities that are ephemeral and spontaneous and help reinforce the ethnic or cultural identity of a community. Furthermore, this cultural identity brings with it the potential to create economic opportunities where Latino artistic talent can be tapped commercially.

The potential of Latino community development as an art niche has generally not been first and foremost in the minds of community leaders. San Francisco's Mission District, with the assistance of the Precita Eyes Mural Arts Center, has created tours of community murals as a means of presenting the Mission's Latino flavor in a positive light, enhancing cultural assets, and creating an economic vehicle for community development.

The concept of "ethnoscapes" captures the merger of ethnicity, tourism, and community economic development (Shaw, Bagwell, and Karmowska 2004). Young Latino artists in Boyle Heights, Los Angeles, for example, are seeking to establish an arts district that includes galleries, studios, theaters, and cafés. An organization called A.R.T.E.S. (Artists for Revitalizing the East Side) has been established to help achieve this goal (Lopez 2009). One project, Art Squache, seeks to create installations in the windows of small businesses as a means of beautifying the neighborhood. Another project will create banners for streetlights.

Moreno's (2004) analysis of the role of El Museo del Barrio, the Museum of Spanish Harlem, brings to light the potential of cultural institutions playing an economic role in the life of a community. Fainstein and Powers (2005) explore the potential of tourism and New York's ethnic diversity as tools for community economic enhancement. Rath (2008), too, advances the notion of urban ethnic neighborhoods as places for tourism. Blumenthal's (2007) coverage of San Antonio's opening of the Museo Alameda, affiliated with the Smithsonian (MAS), vividly describes the multifaceted social and economic roles the nation's largest Latino museum plays in San Antonio's Latino community.

Getz and Carlson (2005), in turn, argue that tourism-related small businesses are particularly attractive to entrepreneurs where profits often take a secondary role to personal and family needs and preferences. Festivals also have a place in neighborhood tourism and play a role in a community's economic development: "Festivals are emerging worldwide as a growing and vibrant sector of the tourism and leisure industries and are seen to have significant economic, socio-cultural, and political impacts on the destination area and host groups" (Arcodia and Whitford 2007:1).

The emergence of Latino music, art festivals, and even museums as a means of introducing the external community to the Latino community and creating business opportunities for small businesses is not without its critics.

Cohen-Cruz cautions about the possible negative consequences of attracting artists and creating an art zone in Latino communities: "Historically, when artists start settling a low income neighborhood it's a sign that gentrification will follow. Notwithstanding, artists have every right to find a neighborhood they can afford and in which they can work. But they should be mindful of the collateral damage their presence may accelerate. What makes a difference is that artists also contribute" (2007:7). One artist, however, notes that "there is a fine line between development and cultural identity" (J. Lopez 2009).

Blackstock (2005) raises concerns about community-based tourism and the ability of local residents to exercise control over this form of community development once it is established and achieves a measure of success. Davila (2004b) expresses concern about the merger of business and politics and the community disempowerment that invariably is associated with efforts at creating economic/tourism urban zones such as that attempted in Spanish Harlem in New York. Alonso (2007), in turn, argues that tourism in Miami, including places like Little Havana, has not benefited Latino entrepreneurs to the maximum extent possible or beyond very specific geographical boundaries. These concerns reflect the reluctance of community social workers to actively enter into the economic arena, as proposed in this book.

LATIN AMERICAN BUSINESSES IN THE UNITED STATES

Krauss (2007) provides a different perspective on Latino economic power by examining how Latin American companies are establishing enterprises in the United States. Direct foreign investments in the United States from Latin America increased from $8 billion in 1995 to $13.5 billion in 2000 and $30 billion in 2005. Prior to 2000 Mexican companies had virtually no direct investments in this country. By 2005, however, Mexican investments totaled $6 billion from companies such as Grupo Bimbo, a bakery company, and Cemex, the number one supplier of cement and ready-mix concrete in the United States. Southern California, for example, has emerged as a Mexican link to the global economy: "A new economy is emerging that builds on the economic relationship between the countries. Exports and imports between Mexico and the United States have grown rapidly in the last decade, to close to $400 billion annually" (Flanigan 2009:11)

Southern California's role in economic development can best be appreciated against the backdrop of California's role in national economic development. The California State Assembly has estimated that California has the eighth largest economy in the world, with an estimated $1.5 trillion dollar gross state product. Small businesses are responsible for $1.4 billion of the economy and constitute 90 percent of all businesses in the state. These enterprises employ 50 percent of all employees in the state. In 2006 there were 3.6 million small businesses in California (Arambula 2008).

Latin American corporations can view their presence in the United States strategically and help advance the interests of Latino communities, including their small businesses, while conducting business in this country. Corporate philanthropic work can target Latino youth and Latino causes, bringing an enhanced view of Latino businesses to the social world. For example, Orlando's Puerto Rican small business community has a Puerto Rico Business and Community Exchange program with the island as a means of enhancing their business practice skills and increasing business between Puerto Rico and central Florida's Latino community (Stuart 2005).

No less important, Latino-owned businesses are reaching out to the mainstream population. This effort is typified by two Latino small business owners in Tennessee:

> A new Latino grocery in Hermitage looks to expand its customer base beyond the Hispanic market by offering a range of specialties, including cut-to-order meats. "The goal is to introduce the entire community to Latino foods," said Jeff Kearns, owner of El Rodeo on Lebanon Pike. "And what we really want to do is introduce the population to our fresh meat cuts." Alberto Forero, who owns the El Rodeo grocery in Madison, is also working as the head manager of the new store in Hermitage. "All these Hispanic-theme markets tailor to Mexican people," Forero said. "We're trying to educate the customer that even though we're a Hispanic grocery store, that doesn't mean everyone can't buy here." (Humbles 2009)

Latino merchandise brands such as Café Bustelo, a staple in many Puerto Rican homes, have started to branch out into the mainstream and have achieved success in doing so—Café Bustelo's sales have increased by 57 percent to $57 million since 2000 (Sisario 2009). Efforts by this firm have been matched by countless others, such as Goya.

HEALTH INSURANCE COVERAGE

Readers may be surprised by the inclusion of the topic of health insurance coverage in this section and, for that matter, in this book. Concern among small businesses owners who are not able to provide health care for their employees is also a national concern, although it takes on greater prominence in the nation's big cities because of the high concentration of Latinos in these areas.

Gabel and Pickreign (2004) note that lack of employee health insurance coverage is quite common in small businesses. A late 1990s Kaiser Family Foundation study found that half of all uninsured workers in the country were either self-employed or employed in businesses with fewer than twenty-five workers (Oxendine 1999). The vast majority of Latino-owned businesses can be considered "one-person operations," with only 13 percent having any employees (Associated Press 2006). California, probably more than any other state, has started to focus attention on Latino small businesses and provision of health care to employees (Rubio and Arteaga 2000). The California Health-care Foundation (2004), for example, has studied the possibility of these businesses offering health insurance to their employees. It is estimated that there are more than fifty thousand Latino-owned businesses in California. The study finds that there is a lack of knowledge about insurance programs, costs are a primary deterrent, and business owner's have little or no interaction with health care brokers.

California's Latino Issues Forum addressed the need for promoting health access for businesses in communities of color: "Latino and minority small business owners are critical to California's economy. Yet, the barriers they face in maintaining the viability of their businesses often conflict with their ability to provide health insurance for themselves, their families and their employees. Latino and other minority small business owners need additional tools and resources to provide health insurance" (Diaz, Mercer, and Vargas 2007:7).

The Latino Issues Forum, like the California Healthcare Foundation, studied business owners in such communities and found that there is recognition on the part of owners of the value of offering employees health insurance. Furthermore, the study found that affordability and cost containment are intertwined with their own interests, and that level and quality of coverage are important in their deliberations about obtaining health insurance as a business.

Interestingly, there are current efforts on the part of the insurance industry to reach out to Latino small businesses, which are becoming an attractive market because of increased efforts on the part of large corporations to provide their own insurance programs in an effort to cut costs. In New York, for example, Aetna and Empire have actively sought to capture this growing market: "Eager to capture a greater share of the huge, underserved small business market, two of the largest insurers in New York, Empire Blue Cross Blue

Shield and Aetna Inc., are fighting to win over the likes of Mr. Porter. Central to their efforts are fledgling managed care plans for small businesses billed as comprehensive coverage—with benefits like fully covered annual checkups, mammograms and other preventive care—at a relatively modest price" (*Latino Business Review* 2009c).

NATIONAL ECONOMIC VICISSITUDES

As noted in chapter 1, small businesses are a sensitive barometer of national economic swings, up as well as down, and this is particularly the case with Latino small businesses because of their reliance on local customers, many of whom have small incomes and little wealth. Economic downturns are certainly not new to Latino small businesses. A 1981 *New York Times* article entitled "Sales Lagging on Streets of El Barrio" provides a vivid portrait of how Latino small businesses are often the first barometer of a national recession. The description of the toll can easily apply to the latest U.S. economic recession. The economic downturn of 2008–2009 was experienced severely across the nation, with disastrous consequences in Latino communities (Kirchhoff 2008; Kochhar 2008; Associated Press 2009a; Correa 2009).

One example of the impact of the recession is the money being sent from Mexico to help relatives in the United States (Lacey 2009). Some Latino immigrants are returning to their homelands (Matza 2008). The story of Carlos Sanchez from Guatemala provides a face to the toll the recession has taken on Latinos:

> Sanchez still remembers the day he left home. . . . But not as hard as the return trip. When Sanchez, 36, arrived back in Central America recently, after living a third of his life as an illegal immigrant in suburban Washington, he stepped off the flight from Dulles International Airport into a cultural no man's land. He had been an outlaw migrant in one country; now he was a native-born stranger in the other. For years Sanchez had worked all the overtime hours he could handle as a supervisor for a granite counter contractor. . . . Last year, overtime slipped to part time and then almost no time. After months of looking for work, he started looking at airfares. (Hendix 2009)

Another example of the recession's impact involves the decrease in traffic at the Mexico–California border, resulting in a decrease in business among those who sell food and other items at the crossing. "Churro men," small business owners, are facing increasing challenges in making a profit: "The customers that sustained Mauricio for decades don't pass through so much anymore. Now, on a good day, Maurico earns $15. (He sells each bag for $1.50. His profit is $1, his partner who helps make the churros gets 50 cents.) Today it is unlikely he will make that much. After five hours, he has sold only three bags" (Marosi 2009).

Rising credit constraints have also had a dramatic impact on Latino small businesses with bank loans, home equality loans, and credit cards financing their businesses. However, the consequences have not been limited to the United States but are also felt in Latin American and Caribbean countries because the percentage of Latinos sending remittances back home decreased from 73 percent in 2006 to 50 percent in 2008 (Kirchhoff 2008).

The recession has had an impact across all aspects of Latino life and culture for small businesses, as noted by one Latino business owner: "The economy is hitting all of us hard. . . . Nuptials and quinceañeras are going to continue, but families are going to slash their budgets." Quinceañeras (the fifteenth-birthday rite-of-passage celebrations for girls) either are not being held or are taking place on a much smaller scale (*Latino Business Review* 2009c). It is estimated that 400,000 Latina 15-year-olds engage in these celebrations, and traditionally families spend approximately $5,000 per event. Much of this money is spent in local Latino small businesses.

The disappearance of bodegas is but another highly visible consequence of the recession. One New York neighborhood—Broadway from 197th Street to 230th Street—experienced the closing of 137 bodegas, with two or three stores closing every day (Graglia 2009). A study of 927 Latino businesses in New York conducted between November 2008 and January 2009 finds 53 percent in danger of closing (Jonas 2009). More specifically, almost three-quarters of those indicating a danger of closing cited "high rents and unreasonable lease terms," and two-thirds cited "the high costs of doing business" as the primary reasons. Negotiation of fair leases is widely considered one way for Latino small businesses to remain economically viable within their respective communities.

■ ▪ ■ ▪ ■ ▪ ■ ▪ ■

Venturing into the world of small businesses, wealth, and community economic development is one journey most social workers have not dared to take. This chapter has provided but a fragile foundation upon which to examine the economic side of life in the Latino community that rarely sees the light of day, except in the most unusual of sectors. Nevertheless, economics and social development often go hand in hand and provide fertile ground for community social workers.

The economic and social roles of Latino small businesses will only continue to increase in importance in the near future as this population group grows in size. However, as noted earlier, this population is also growing from a diversity perspective, with Mexicans, Puerto Ricans, and Cubans no longer standing out as the three Latino groups in this country. Furthermore, we can no longer view the diverse Latino-owned businesses through a narrow and stereotypical lens.

Latino small businesses and community economic development are complex topics and will continue to be as the population becomes grayer with each succeeded generation. The social work profession, as a result, must make a conscious decision either to embrace this population group, with all the corresponding changes that will result from doing so, or simply to ignore it. The latter would be a grave mistake for the future of the profession. The next chapter offers an asset-focused conceptual paradigm that provides the vehicle through which community social workers can play a significant role in fostering development of small businesses and communities.

PART 2

■ ▪ ■ ▪ ■ ▪ ■ ▪ ■ ▪ ■ ▪ ■ ▪ ■ ▪ ■ ▪ ■ ▪ ■ ▪ ■ ▪ ■ ▪ ■ ▪ ■ ▪ ■ ▪ ■ ▪

COMMUNITY SOCIAL WORK VALUES AND ANALYTICAL FRAMEWORK

Successful community practice cannot be achieved without combining theory and politics. A practice perspective requires social workers to use their analytical abilities to determine the most applicable theories to be applied on the basis of local circumstances and to be able to modify theory to increase its applicability to different community groups. . . . A framework with a dynamic foundation allows practitioners to incorporate the vicissitudes of practice in a manner that still provides them with guidelines for intervention.

—M. Delgado, *Community Social Work Practice in an Urban Context*

5

VALUES, PRINCIPLES, AND ANALYTICAL FRAMEWORK

> The economic condition of inner-cities in the United States is one of the most important issues facing us as a nation. . . . Largely abandoned during an era of industrial restructuring, the inner city is now a frontier of business growth and entrepreneurship. From Harlem in New York to Los Angeles, blighted inner cities have begun to improve.
>
> —K. J. Lacho, D. B. Parker, and M. Carter, "Economics and Initiatives of African-American Churches in Treme"

LATINO SMALL BUSINESSES have a significant presence in the United States, as noted in chapter 4. They defy simple explanations as to their success and role within the community, but the multifaceted role community social workers can play in fostering their development cannot be underestimated.

It would be foolhardy to start a section of a book on community social work practice without first grounding the reader in a set of values and principles related to this form of practice. Values and principles take on greater importance when addressing a much overlooked topic such as fostering the creation and support of Latino-owned small businesses. I hope readers have developed an appreciation and embrace of the potential of small business development and support as part of the social work mission, and that this practice perspective is not antithetical to the values and principles of social workers. Values and principles, in turn, get incorporated into an intervention's analytical framework and guide how they are implemented in carrying out an intervention.

One of the greatest challenges facing health and human services providers seeking to reach the Latino community is how to address present and projected needs without losing sight of valuable cultural and community assets in the process. The ability to identify and mobilize indigenous assets to meet community needs brings with it its share of rewards and challenges. Community social work practitioners, probably more than any other social work practitioners, recognize the presence and importance of community assets and the need to build on them in any form of community intervention, such as small business development. This is not to say that other forms of social work practice cannot tap community assets in interventions. However, this perspective on assets is central to the values, philosophy, and principles associated with community social work practice.

VALUES

The values and principles discussed below are intended to help readers better understand and appreciate how community social work practice has been shaped, and why it is so important to open these forces to public viewing. Readers may wonder why some values either are not listed or are not more prominently articulated. That reaction is perfectly reasonable. This listing represents the vision of just one social worker and is certainly open to dialogue, if not debate. I have no intention of being either comprehensive or detailed; my primary goal is to shine a spotlight so that the roots of practice can be traced back to the values and principles that ground community social work interventions.

A number of key values stand out in shaping how community social work practice is carried out when addressing Latino small businesses. Below and in figure 5.1, four key values are identified that wield considerable influence in how community social work practice involving Latino businesses ventures is conducted on a daily basis. Each of these values can easily stand alone. However, there is a synergistic effect when all of them are present and interacting with one other to create a state of mind or perspective on this phenomenon.

SOCIAL JUSTICE

It is appropriate to start with social and economic justice as a central value of community social work practice because it captures so well how I and countless others view the mission of the profession (Miller 1999). Delgado and Staples (2007), although specifically referring to youth-led community organizing, address the importance of social and economic justice values that inform how social work can envision its mandate for achieving relevance and

significant change in undervalued communities. There are numerous ways to
operationalize social and economic justice, but an embrace of justice signifies
a moral stance against all forms of oppression.

Social and economic justice must represent the cornerstone of community
social work practice: "The basic underlying assumptions . . . are that the social
work profession can be proud of its heritage as the only helping profession
imbued with social justice as its fundamental value and concern and a long
commitment to peace and human rights (Lundy and Van Wormer 2007:728).
Bisman (2004) argues that for social work to have a relevant future, it must
not abandon its moral core but reaffirm its commitment to those who are
undervalued and to the social justice values guiding social workers' mission
in the twenty-first century.

The grounding of community social work practice in social and economic
justice will help ensure that the outcomes of Latino small business initiatives
benefit the community in substantial ways. This explicit focus on justice will
make the profession even more of a target of ultraconservative and reaction-
ary forces because of the threat social justice goals pose for the status quo in
the United States.

SELF-DETERMINATION

Social work and other helping professions always seem to be looking for constructs that help us better understand social interventions and unify various
concepts and constructs. Self-determination, I believe, fits this goal. Self-
determination is often considered the cornerstone of any democratic society

and can occupy a prominent place in values guiding community social work practice.

Although self-determination is often viewed from a psychological or individual viewpoint, this value construct can also be viewed from a sociological-collective perspective, encompassing a community setting. Historically, the value of self-determination has found increasing favor as a way of tapping psychological aspects of individuals, such as autonomy, competence, and connectedness (Patrick et al. 2008). However, the sociology of self-determination lends itself to an ecological interpretation, increasing its significance for social work practice.

The importance of both believing and actually controlling environmental circumstances is much broader than empowerment, although terms such as "empowerment," "connectedness," and "personal growth" often represent key elements of self-determination. This value's attractiveness is enhanced because it can encompass many of social work's values under one roof. The broadening that is achieved through the use of an inclusive construct brings into discussion a social-ecological view of Latino small businesses, allowing for a richer and more in-depth understanding and appreciation of these enterprises.

Community social work practice has either explicated or implicitly embraced the importance of marginalized communities exercising self-determination. Significant progress has occurred to operationalize this value using qualitative rather than conventional quantitative measures. This allows local circumstances to dictate how self-determination is viewed and acted on.

COMMUNITY WELL-BEING

The construct of well-being, like self-determination, is experiencing a tremendous upsurge of interest in scholarly, governmental, and practice spheres (Saunders 2008). Part of the increasing popularity is the result of the use of nonmonetary indicators as measures in research and evaluation. Thus its definition is more influenced by qualitative than quantitative measures, stressing the importance of local or informal knowledge (Hagerty, Vogel, and Moller 2002; Coulton and Korbin 2007). Its grounding within a sociocultural context means that communities must be able to determine what it means and how it can be achieved.

Latino small businesses do not stand alone, as if they were an island surrounded by water. These institutions are embedded in the community they serve. A community that is experiencing high levels of well-being is a community able to support local businesses in a manner that allows them to stay afloat financially. Thus, a community's well-being is integrally tied to a small business's well-being. This ecological perspective is certainly not new to social work and only gets reinforced when viewing small businesses within the broader context of their community.

COMMUNITY CAPACITY RATHER THAN DEFICITS

This value goes hand in hand with the importance of a community having social, cultural, human, and economic capital. Fortunately, community social work is familiar with this value, as evidenced by the extent of practice and scholarship in this area. Yet the critical nature of an asset perspective bears reemphasizing—all communities, regardless of social circumstances, possess strengths and assets that must be recognized and utilized in any form of social intervention.

This value stance goes far beyond creating a psychology that people and communities have assets, although this is certainly an important element. There is a very practical and social side to this value because assets need to be front and center in any intervention design. Latino small businesses and the communities they serve possess immense assets that must be identified and used as central features of community social work practice.

PRACTICE PRINCIPLES

It seems that any book on social work practice, whether or not it is centered on community social work, would be incomplete without a set of practice principles guiding the conceptualization and implementation of this form of practice. This book is certainly no exception. These principles are derived from a variety of sources, including practice, research, and scholarship. Values serve as the fundamental point of influence, along with theory. These values, as addressed in the previous section, must be made explicit for interventions to have any success in creating partnerships between community social workers, community residents and leaders, community-based organizations, and other helping professions.

Elwood's (2006) study of a predominantly Latino community in Chicago illustrates the role community organizations, including Latino small businesses, can play in pursuing neighborhood improvement projects when there is careful attention to spatial politics, community needs, and assets. The community's well-being is closely tied to its institutions in the pursuit of goals that are congruent with neighborhood values and hopes.

The following five principles are significant in themselves but, like values, take on a synergistic effect when viewed and practiced in their totality. These principles have been derived from a variety of scholarly and practice sources, some of which have appeared in my own articles and books on the subject of community social work practice as well as in those by other authors. This does not take away from their importance in guiding community social work practice with Latino small businesses. In fact, it serves to ground this practice within the broader context of the field, further reinforcing our approach to this subject.

Principle 1: All communities, regardless of socioeconomic circumstances, possess inherent assets. McQueen, Weiser, and Burns (2007:5–6) capture this principle quite well in their assessment of entrepreneurial ventures in low-income communities: "Low-income neighborhoods can give rise to successful entrepreneurial ventures. With proper support, residents can seize the opportunity to capitalize on otherwise untapped skills and assets. Many people have skills or experience they could use to increase their income and assets. Entire neighborhoods often have valuable assets that could attract businesses."

The fundamental belief that no community is devoid of assets means that it is incumbent on community social workers to identify and mobilize these assets. They invariably entail economic, social, cultural, and geographic spheres or domains. Local circumstances, however, may shape how these assets get manifested. Our ability to identify assets that are commonly overlooked by other professions will serve us and the community well. This is not a simple feat, particularly when it involves cultural values and traditions that are subtle and not part of the dominant society. Yet values and traditions are an integral part of the lives of countless numbers of marginalized people of color and must surface in any form of intervention.

Principle 2: Communities must play influential roles in the decision-making process pertaining to intervention goals. As already noted in the discussion of the value of self-determination, communities must be at the table throughout all efforts at addressing their needs and hopes. Ultimately owning the decisions that are made helps ensure that outcomes resonate with local community needs and hopes. Participatory democracy necessitates active and meaningful engagement of the community in determining the process and outcomes of social interventions.

Decision-making roles can be built into the process by developing advisory groups composed of Latino small business owners and other key stakeholders in the Latino community. Active efforts to disseminate findings and recommendations further enhance a process that is transparent and open to input from all sectors of the community. The embrace of a community decision-making role also ultimately serves to enhance community leadership capacity.

Principle 3: Communities are the best experts on their conditions and circumstances. This principle often goes against conventional wisdom that only those with formal educational expertise and a lot of initials after their names can be experts. This premise is counter to the core values and principles of community social work practice as envisioned in this and countless other books and articles.

Constructs such as "self-knowledge," "local knowledge," and "informal knowledge" seek to capture this expertise and assist communities in directing their futures (Delgado 2006). Methods that gather this information must be used whenever possible. The information obtained through these constructs helps increase the likelihood that decisions related to the community are made *with* the community rather than for the community.

Principle 4: Latino small businesses must be viewed from a multifaceted perspective that stresses economic/operational, cultural, and social capital dimensions. Latino small business success, which chapter 6 addresses in greater detail, should not and cannot be measured by the proverbial "bottom line" but instead requires broader and more inclusive sociocultural measures. Such a narrow focus defies the community social work preferences for viewing marginalized communities from a social ecological perspective.

A comprehensive and locally determined perspective on Latino small businesses provides a window through which to better understand how these establishments function and how best to support them. The capital (cultural, economic, social, and human) that gets fostered can be expected to reach beyond these businesses to the Latino community at large. Measuring these benefits will prove challenging but necessary.

Principle 5: Sustainable community-focused initiatives in support of Latino small businesses are best achieved through meaningful collaboration. Community social work practice implicitly and explicitly embraces all forms of collaboration in service to the community. Collaboration, however, goes beyond the conventional involvement with other formal service providers. This principle seeks to promote a broader circle of potential collaborators to include informal as well as nontraditional settings.

This inclusive approach helps to increase the likelihood that the entire community owns the results of an intervention from start to finish. Collaboration between formal entities is arduous at best. However, it takes on greater significance and challenges when the collaborating parties may not speak the same language, subscribe to the same ideology, or have a history of working together. Consequently, there is no reservoir of trust to draw on during difficult times. This does not mean, however, that collaborations of the type put forth in this principle are not possible.

IMPORTANCE OF AN ANALYTICAL FRAMEWORK

This section focuses on one of the more popular asset- and needs-focused analytical frameworks found in community social work, which lends itself to fostering and sustaining Latino small businesses (Hyland 2005; Willigen 2005). This focus will be on the use of a community capacity enhancement paradigm (Delgado 2000; Saegert 2006). The potential use of informal and formal Latino small businesses will be stressed as a means of illustrating the use of this method and a largely overlooked community resource.

Taylor and Roberts's assessment of the relationship between theory and practice still holds true more than twenty-five years later:

> Although theoreticians attempt to force practice into discrete categories, most workers seem more eclectic in their approaches to situations. There is reason to believe that they borrow from many different models to deal with a given situation at a particular time and may adopt or utilize quite different models at different times or in various circumstances. . . . It might be assumed also that in the real world, individual workers opt for an eclectic stance and position themselves along a continuum between pure theoretical models according to their values, talents, the expectations of their employers, the nature and sophistication of the groups they are involved with, and the particular goals that they are striving to achieve. (1985:22–23)

Community social work practitioners must reconcile differences between theory and practice because of the highly dynamic nature of community-based practice. Hardcastle, Wenocur, and Power (1997:37) raise this very point: "In fact, the enormous complexity of social work practice means that we seldom find a direct correspondence between theory and practice." Community social work practice, as envisioned in this book, is not highly prescriptive. However, there certainly is a tightrope between description and prescription, and this chapter attempts to straddle these two domains.

ANALYTICAL–INTERACTIONAL DIMENSION

Paradigms must be viewed from two important perspectives if we hope to have them affect a field of practice, as well as help focus research and scholarship on a topic. There is a strong theoretical basis for a paradigm that draws on theories, values, and principles. This analytical part of a paradigm is usually well understood and is available to community social workers through numerous texts, scholarly articles, and lectures.

The latter dimension can be explicit or implicit in nature, which is my preference. The interactional or political side to social paradigms often is either not mentioned or, if mentioned, done so in a passing manner. This aspect is rarely discussed but plays a critical role in bringing a paradigm to life.

However, political considerations of community practice are powerful factors in helping to shape interventions and ultimately determining their degree of success. Terms such as "stakeholders," "powerbrokers," "influence shapers," and "gatekeepers" are but a few examples of terms used to capture this dimension of community-centered practice. Googins, Capoccia, and Kauffman (1983) argue for the importance of interactional forces as an integral part of any discussion pertaining to social interventions. The following five stages, as a result, must be viewed from both theoretical and political perspectives.

STAGES

The identification and mobilization of community assets can be approached from a variety of conceptual perspectives. However, the use of an urban community-enhancement paradigm, which consists of five stages, lends itself well to community social work practice with indigenous institutions such as small businesses (Delgado 2000). This paradigm has its origins in social work values, principles, and practice and has found favor in urban-centered practice because of its emphasis on actively engaging communities of color in shaping all facets of an intervention.

Paradigms, whether deficit- or asset-based, invariably bring with them a developmental-stage perspective that facilitates their implementation. This section identifies and describes these stages, using Latino small businesses as case illustrations whenever possible. The five stages of the community-enhancement paradigm are identification and assessment, mapping, solidification of support, intervention, and evaluation (Delgado 2000). Each stage can consist of multiple steps and is predicated on a set of values that include principles and actions specific to the stage and incorporate both analytical and interactional dimensions.

IDENTIFICATION AND ASSESSMENT

The assessment stage consists of two separate but equally important dimensions. The first dimension of any formal effort to assess is to accomplish the concrete task of identifying the location of Latino small businesses. This step not only involves the actual location of the establishment but also the geographic area surrounding the store or business. Access of an enterprise to foot traffic and public transportation, proximity to other community assets, and historical significance to the community are examples of dimensions that must be actively tapped by an asset assessment. It is relatively easy to focus on the physical structure or the small business itself and miss important nonphysical dimensions that must be an integral part of an asset assessment.

This step may on the surface appear to be straightforward, but it is important to have a clear conceptualization of both formal and informal businesses. Formal businesses may be easier to locate and assess. Informal businesses necessitate a more labor-intensive approach that will involve extensive interviews with key community members who have long histories in the community. The local Chamber of Commerce chapter will not have lists of informal Latino businesses. Informal day-care businesses invariably operate out of apartments or small homes without signs designating their location. Consequently, this stage of the assessment process will in all likelihood consume the greatest amount of time, resources, and energy. Nevertheless, ignoring informal Latino businesses, as noted in chapter 4, will result in an assessment that is incomplete at best.

It is important to venture out and talk with business owners to develop a better understanding of their needs and how best to address them (Richtermeyer 2004). A series of factors or considerations enter into this decision and inform the methodology used to carry out the activity. When communities where English is not the primary language spoken are involved, the assessment and engagement process is enhanced if one is able to converse in the preferred language of the business owner and staff. Fortunately, in the case of Latinos, there is a good likelihood that these individuals are bilingual. Nevertheless, Latinos involved in the informal economy may have weak English-language skills, which invariably play a significant role in forcing them into this sector. This is compounded by the likelihood of being undocumented, further raising a barrier between interviewer and interviewee.

MAPPING

The mapping aspect of an asset assessment is without question the most visual dimension of the entire process, and in many ways the most empowering. Mapping community assets necessitates the development of an actual map that can be seen, held in hand, and shared by a group (Delgado and Humm-Delgado, forthcoming). The act of collectively putting a map together and sharing the stories behind the data is a powerful experience for all of those who get involved—social workers as well as community residents.

Maps have historically been the purview of the elite, representing their goals and biases. Community mapping, as a result, is a participatory experience that places communities in the position of power and decision making as to what information is noteworthy to map. Community asset maps are best conceptualized as visual aids that facilitate the display and analysis of community-generated data in a way that effectively increases a community's understanding of and insights into its resources and abilities (Goldman and Schmatz 2005).

Physically locating and categorizing types of small businesses on a map provide critical information that influences the level and types of interventions that are warranted. Geographical areas with an abundance of Latino small businesses, for example, may not need these establishments as much as areas that may be geographically inaccessible within a community, or where gaps exist in certain types of businesses. Clearly, the strategy for addressing the need for businesses will differ depending on the analysis of these maps.

There are a wide variety of ways to select a primary method for an asset assessment. Delgado and Humm-Delgado (forthcoming), for example, identify seven factors to take into consideration: history of the community undertaking an asset assessment; familiarity of assessment team members with qualitative and quantitative research methods; time that can be devoted to the endeavor; season; funding; time period between the issuing of findings and initiation of an intervention; and level of trust within the community being assessed. Each of these considerations plays an important role in shaping an asset assessment and the data that are generated.

SOLIDIFICATION OF SUPPORT

The value of an intervention enjoying solid support from a community is self-evident, although such an accomplishment may be arduous to achieve. Nevertheless, the desirability of this level of support must not be ignored. This stage of the framework seeks to consolidate interactional support to help ensure minimal community resistance to an intervention. The first two stages help garner the needed support and lay the foundation for the intervention stage and the other stages that follow. Significant buy-in from the Latino community is required in the initial stages.

Gaining community support, or trust, is not relegated to one stage, and once it is achieved one can move onto the next stage. In fact, gaining support is an integral part of all the stages but sufficiently important to warrant a stage onto itself. This stage helps to ensure that support is not taken for granted and provides an opportunity for the community and key stakeholders to come together to explore and decide on the ultimate goals of small business development. It is during this stage that potential differing opinions are aired and discussed and comprises reached.

INTERVENTION

The intervention is the bottom line in most practitioners' view. How these interventions get conceptualized is greatly influenced by the three previous stages. In essence, this stage is only as good as the preceding stages were in setting the requisite foundation. It is during this stage that an intervention design is adopted and implemented. Its shape and the goals it seeks to accomplish would have emerged during the previous stages. Consequently, unless some community tragedy occurs, there will be no surprises as to primary and secondary goals during this stage.

Three possible overarching goals will guide an intervention: (1) to provide support in expanding existing Latino small businesses; (2) to foster development of new businesses to fill existing gaps; or (3) to do both. Chapter 7 outlines a wide range of possible intervention projects that can be initiated to accomplish these goals, on a variety of budgets.

Having flexibility to respond to funding constraints creates opportunities for innovative projects that do not require large expenditure of funds:

> The wonderful aspect of capacity-enhancement interventions is the explicit need to involve as many people as possible, whether they are paid or volunteer their expertise and time. As a result, the lack of disposable funding is not a serious impediment to capacity enhancement. It just means that more time and effort must be devoted to obtaining in-kind donations and that it will take longer to complete a project. (Delgado 2000:53)

This facilitates the development of a track record in this arena and sets the stage for more ambitious undertakings in the future.

Each goal can consist of primary and secondary goals. For example, fostering development of Latino small businesses does not have to be restricted to actually creating businesses. This goal can also include efforts at identifying youths with interest in developing their own businesses, as in the case of Holyoke, Massachusetts, where youths created a mural-painting enterprise.

EVALUATION

The final stage provides practitioners and community participants with an opportunity to undertake a process-and-outcome evaluation of the intervention. This stage, like the preceding stages, must actively involve the community in all facets, from posing of the evaluation questions to collecting data, interpreting findings, making recommendations, and issuing appropriate reports (Delgado 2006). This final stage is just as important as any of the preceding stages and sets the stage for future interventions.

An advisory committee can help address key questions pertaining to evaluation and can serve a coordinating function throughout all stages of the framework. Focus groups and key informant surveys can provide nuanced data, and an advisory group can offer names of potential participants in these efforts. Every effort must be made to enhance community capacity at this stage by engaging community residents to help evaluate the effectiveness of the projects. Latino small businesses and the general Latino community stand to benefit from an evaluation that is culturally grounded.

A culturally grounded evaluation is best accomplished through the selective and strategic use of qualitative and quantitative methods. Fortunately, a mixed-method paradigm has gained in popularity in the last decade or so (Johnson 2004; Morgan 2007) and lends itself to community social work practice that actively seeks participation on the part of the community. In all likelihood, qualitative methods will be front and center in any evaluation effort of Latino small businesses. Quantitative methods can be adjusted to complement qualitative data, as I discuss in chapter 6. However, these quantitative measures must resonate with the community. An advisory committee can help with this determination.

■ ₁■₁■₁■₁■

Community social work interventions predicated on enhancing community capacities have great potential in fostering ethnic and racial small business and community development. Enhancing community capacities resonates with social work and its historic mission to address issues of oppression and social and economic justice in the nation's marginalized communities. These interventions, however, do not exist outside of a set of values and principles.

I sincerely hope that the reader has developed an appreciation for the powerful role that values and principles play in shaping any form of social intervention. However, I believe that they take on even greater importance when new forms of social intervention are being proposed, such as helping to create and support a Latino business venture. These new ventures may be considered bold or even radical in some circles. Nevertheless, community social workers must be prepared to push the envelope in order to maintain relevance in urban marginalized communities.

I also hope that this chapter has ignited interest on the part of the uninitiated in the promise of community capacity enhancement as a paradigm for community social work practice. This paradigm has existed in various forms since the mid- to late 1990s. However, its use has substantially increased during the early part of this millennium as the subject of health disparities has gained prominence and health promotion as an intervention has become the primary vehicle for implementing asset-based paradigms.

6

INDICATORS OF SUCCESS FOR LATINO SMALL BUSINESSES

> Greater Boston contains what is probably the world's largest concentration of academic and research institutions. It is in these institutions . . . that essential components for a high-technology future are being invented and developed. It is a heady environment, rather intimidating to anyone not versed in the scientific disciplines. Only a short drive or even walk from these centers of futuristic fantasy one can find oneself in an altogether different world, which carried associations with America's past rather than its future.
>
> —P. L. Berger

COMMUNITY SOCIAL WORK practice can embrace a capacity-enhancement paradigm to help shape how the profession addresses the emergence and expansion of Latino small businesses. The previous chapter identified the potential of community capacity enhancement to bring together the requisite values and tools to help such enterprises increase their likelihood of success.

Bringing the worlds of research and ethnic small businesses together offers both promise and pitfalls for the social work profession. Berger's observations above about the coexistence of Boston's academic institutions and ethnic small businesses representing the past are quite telling. These two worlds cannot afford to exist as if they are in parallel universes. The role and importance of research and evaluation have grown in the past decade as policy makers and funders have increasingly sought evidence of the success of social interventions. This chapter represents an attempt to build a bridge between these two entities by proposing the establishment of social indicators of Latino small business success.

The search for this evidence is challenging when it comes to the role of communities in facilitating or hindering business development (Coulton 2005; Lynn 2006; Popple and Stepney 2008). Consequently, this chapter addresses both the rewards and challenges of building social indicators that capture the economic, cultural, and social domains, or dimensions, of what constitutes success for Latino small business owners.

These indicators, in turn, serve as a conceptual framework for research on and evaluation of efforts to foster and sustain the development of Latino business ventures. The success measures presented in this chapter acknowledge common barriers endemic to the creation of social indicators. These indicators are purposefully not highly theoretical, thereby lending themselves to use by community social work scholars and practitioners interested in uniting and advancing this field. Furthermore, these domains seek to tap community input in determining success.

SOCIAL INDICATORS

Simply defined, social indicators are statistical measures of a phenomenon gathered by major governmental or quasi-governmental institutions that can be used to inform policy decisions. The emergence of social indicators as a bridge between social science and social policy can probably be traced back to the 1960s in the United States and the work undertaken by Bauer (1966) at the National Aeronautics and Space Administration. Cobb and Rixford's (1998) review of the early history of social indicators raises a fundamental conflict about the nature and purpose of indicators: what is included as an indicator and how social indicators are used to make decisions.

The goals set forth for social indicators have a great deal to do with how they are structured and used. Are the primary purposes of social indicators prescriptive, along with corresponding guidance about what to do, or descriptive, simply highlighting conditions? The answer to this question will dictate how we go about constructing social indicators and therefore is important to how we measure the success or impact of small businesses within and outside the Latino community.

Social indicators have continued to evolve since the 1960s and currently enjoy wide popularity throughout the world. Hagerty, Vogel, and Moller (2002) argue that social indicators are a movement brought together by three guiding principles: (1) expanding social monitoring beyond conventional economic indicators; (2) increasing output in terms of individual living conditions; and (3) making available systematic facts to enhance political debate and social planning. Each of these principles is important, but in combination their potential for shaping public policy and services can be even more significant.

Niemi and McDonald (2004) have chronicled how social indicators have broadened their appeal beyond narrow economic indicators to include fields such as social ecology. Reed, Fraser, and Dougill (2006), in turn, advocate for the use of social indicators to measure progress in sustainable development. Marks, Cargo, and Daniel's charge involving health and social indicators also applies to Latino small business success indicators: "few measures systematically delineate the connections between indicators included in the framework and the domains that they measure and represent. To avoid haphazard selection of indicators and to assure the comprehensiveness and relevance of any given set of indicators, a framework that can accommodate and conceptually classify indicators representing a full range of domains is required" (2007:95–96).

The three domains I have selected for a Latino small business success indicator have already been firmly established in this book (particularly in chapters 3 and 4) and can be used for descriptive or prescriptive purposes, depending on the goals of the Latino community and community social workers.

CRITIQUE OF SOCIAL INDICATORS

A brief critique of social indicators is in order before reviewing the set proposed for measuring Latino small business success. Anyone involved in constructing social indicators will quickly acknowledge that there are competing alternative measures to the ones that ultimately go into the final social indicators (Atkinson et al. 2002). Consequently, the final indicators must be firmly grounded in a highly detailed context that allows examination and possible debate.

Almost thirty years ago Johnston and Carley identified three major challenges in developing social indicators that I believe still prevail today, in various degrees:

> First, there are technical problems relating to social measurement per se; these include indicator specification and construction. Second, a variety of sociopolitical problems, such as possible ideological biases in problem definition, data presentation, and the interpretation of findings, may distort our efforts at societal assessment. Third, a number of communication problems impede the effective presentation of information in social indicators form to both policymakers and the general public. (1981:237)

Klass (2009) identified twelve common statistical fallacies found in social indicators that complement Johnston and Carley's concerns. This critique can also be applied to any indicator selected for determining the success of Latino small businesses:

- cherry picking (biased selection of data)
- instrumentation error (measurement unreliability)
- measurement validity (how well a measurement captures a concept)
- the dominant denominator (misinterpretation due to a function of change in denominator rather than in the numerator)
- reverse causation (relationship between two variables in and of itself does not reveal which might be the cause of the other)
- population mortality (changes and differences in the inclusiveness of the group studied can affect data comparisons) regression artifact (regression artifacts fallacy as the indicator "naturally" regresses to the mean)
- ecological fallacy (drawing false conclusions about individuals from aggregate data)
- the trend is not your friend (determining which trends are speculative and which are not)
- graphical distortion (poorly constructed graphs can distort statistical relationships)
- rate-of-change fallacy (comparing rates of change in two numbers at different levels)
- other confounding effects (another untapped variable may be responsible for the actual change)

Klass's list does not mean that social indicators are fraught with limitations. Having an in-depth knowledge of the substantive area being studied goes a long way toward minimizing errors by providing researchers and practitioners with alternative explanations for potential findings.

COMMUNITY DEVELOPMENT OF SUCCESS INDICATORS

Historically, social indicators have been developed by institutions charged to do so by national and state governments. Hagerty, Vogel, and Moller (2002) note that there are two schools of thought on social indicators—one firmly grounded in official and semiofficial social reporting residing with public institutions, and the other in the independent research tradition in institutes and universities with temporary funding. As a result, social indicators represent a top-down perspective that has the power to determine how an indicator is developed and what elements it consists of. This approach often typifies how policies and programs have been developed in the United States and is largely responsible for the common statistical fallacies Klass identifies.

Indicators rarely take into account the expertise of community residents who are not academics, although that is starting to change: "The majority of 'indicator' initiatives rely on 'expert committees' for proposing the use of currently available indicators, or the development of altogether new measures. Such experts have traditionally been scientists, but are increasingly community members of the affected by the issue being studied" (Marks et al. 2007:94–95). The development of a measure of Latino small business success will necessitate a bottom-up approach stressing participatory democratic principles. Latino small businesses, particularly those in the informal sector, require a nuanced approach and analysis (Zlolniski 2008).

The creation of a classification framework can serve a vital role in bringing together existing indicators as well as new indicators originated by community members. Fraser et al. (2006), for example, stress a community participatory process for developing sustainability indicators that fits well with participatory democratic values espoused in community social work, as noted in chapter 5.

Saunders, Zellman, and Kaye-Blake's (2007) extensive review of the literature on small business performance indicators finds four models for measuring success: business management; organization development; owner personality and business culture; and sector-specific. These models, however, tend to focus on conventional small businesses and as a result miss nuances related to businesses that may be out of the ordinary. They certainly do not apply to informal businesses. Similar limitations exist when factors such as historical, social, and cultural contexts are excluded, resulting in a narrow view of small business success (Marks, Cargo, and Daniel 2007).

The process of arriving at Latino small business indicators is as important as the actual development of universally accepted indicators. Consequently, the domains proposed for Latino small business success indicators are a starting point—an initial framework that will allow the process to begin. Involvement of Latino small business owners and the communities they serve is instrumental in developing success indicators, particularly those that are highly contextualized to take into account local history and circumstances. This may make the process much more labor intensive and therefore expensive. However, fostering democratic participation in the creation of measures necessitates an active and meaningful exchange with owners and their customers.

BROADENING INDICATORS OF SUCCESS

Success indicators, as a result, must be multifaceted and draw upon a range of social, cultural, and human capital dimensions. A specific focus on profits would be too narrow a perspective for measuring small business success, particularly when viewing these establishments within a socially responsible lens. Recent attention in the small business literature has heightened the importance of embeddedness as an overarching concept in better understanding small business performance and contributions to communities (Cooke, Clifton, and Oleaga 2005). This concept stresses the importance of small businesses being in tune with the communities they are based in and seek to serve.

Latino small businesses can fulfill a variety of expressive, instrumental, and informational roles that enhance community well-being. Thus, viewing their success within a narrow capitalistic viewpoint (profits, sales volume, market shares) is too narrow a frame and would not do justice to the richness of these institutions. Further, such a narrow conceptualization would not resonate with community social workers.

Walker and Brown's (2004) study of Australian small business owners found that there needs to be an alternative set of measures for determining success in small businesses. Viewing success from an economic vantage point is usually the preferred approach because of its ease in measuring profit. However, this is too narrow. Lifestyle choices inherent in running a small business also represent legitimate ways of measuring success.

I have identified three domains (operational/economic, cultural, and social) or categories that must form the foundation for any framework of success indicators for Latino small businesses. I am sure there are other domains that should have a prominent place in my list, and there may be some in my list that do not get the attention they may warrant. I am certainly biased. However, the list of indicators that follows represents an initial attempt at developing a measure that incorporates social, cultural, and economic factors.

This measure, it should be noted, needs to be grounded in the context of small business enterprises and Latino community characteristics. Few practitioners, as a result, will be able to apply all the dimensions inherent in this measure. Others will be able to borrow from this measure and add factors that are particularly relevant to their own circumstances. Yet others will use the material presented here as a starting point to develop new and more sophisticated measures of success. Regardless of the decision by practitioners, there is a need to commence grappling with development of comprehensive and culture-specific measures that go beyond conventional measures of success (Bernardez 2005; Cooke, Clifton, and Oleaga 2005; Luken and Stares 2005; Jenkins 2006).

Some of the domains identified for measurement may be considered soft (qualitative) measures; others may be considered hard (quantitative) measures. Regardless of the designation, these domains will require refinement and depth to allow them to capture social, cultural, and economic outcomes.

The outcomes of this process will be shaped by the goals practitioners have for Latino small businesses, and communities must ultimately shape what elements they wish to capture. Community social workers, I believe, are in excellent positions to begin this refinement.

FRAMEWORK AND INDICATORS OF LATINO SMALL BUSINESS SUCCESS

Conducting research in this field brings with it an inherent set of challenges that go far beyond whether a small business is owned by a Latino or some other person of color (Dana 2008). Any discussion of effectiveness of community interventions must take place against the backdrop of current discussions pertaining to evidence-based practice. Ohmer and Korr's (2006) review of the literature on community and evidence-based practice finds relatively few quantitative intervention studies relying on experimental or control groups, raising the need for the field to utilize these forms of studies. However, the complexity of community factors and the range of activities often associated with this form of practice make these types of studies arduous to implement (Minich et al. 2006). Latino small businesses are not simplistic in composition and community orientation.

Furthermore, a focus on these "higher-order" studies reflects a particular bias that may not fit well with the type of work that community social work practitioners often undertake, and this is no small point. Thus, I openly embrace a bias toward qualitative measures based on community input, with an appropriate nod toward relevant quantitative measures when present. Quantitative measures invariably reflect a selection bias on the part of institutions that rarely takes into account the operative reality of life in urban Latino communities.

One of the central arguments for fostering Latino small business development and support is the potential role these community-based institutions can play in the sociocultural fabric of the community. Mirabal's (2009) research on gentrification of San Francisco's heavily Latino Mission District highlights how the disappearance of Latino-owned small businesses serves as a highly visible indicator of a community shift in composition, in this case related to gentrification. Curran (2007) documents how urban gentrification in one community (Williamsburg, Brooklyn) has resulted in small, vibrant, and varied manufacturing businesses owned by immigrants being displaced as business rents increase. Thus, the presence or absence of Latino small businesses can serve as a social indicator of a community ascending or descending in viability.

Operational/ Economic Success

1. Duration of existence

2. Profitability

3. Number of employees (relatives and non-relatives)

4. Core customer base

5. Owner-customer Latino-origin congruence

Cultural Capital Success

1. Engagement in Community Cultural Events
   A. *Sponsorship*
   B. *Collections for funerals/scholarships/ disasters in countries of origin*
   C. *Support of community sports team*

2. Beautification or Latinization of neighborhood

3. Transnational connectedness

Social Capital Success

1. Participation on agency boards, advisory committees, task forces, and coalitions

2. Membership in and creation of business associations

3. Mentorship and support for community economic development

4. Foster care parenting/ mentoring/volunteering

6.1 LATINO SMALL BUSINESS SUCCESS INDICATORS

Figure 6.1 provides a brief snapshot of key domains and factors that can constitute elements of social indicators that are culturally grounded and attempt to view Latino small businesses from a multifaceted viewpoint that helps identify the complexity of these institutions within Latino communities.

OPERATIONAL/ECONOMIC SUCCESS

The measure of a Latino small business success indicator I have come up with is limited to three dimensions. Contrary to what might be expected in the dominant society, economic success is but one aspect of any indicator. Nevertheless, an economic or operational domain is very much in order as one of the dimensions owing to the high rate of Latino small business failures.

DURATION OF EXISTENCE

Residential stability is often a key indicator of Latinos developing cultural and economic organizations that serve their needs (Borges-Mendez 2006). Thus, permanent settlement in a geographical area such as barrios or Latino-specific neighborhoods provides Latino small business owners with a critical demographic and historical foundation upon which to develop and expand their ventures.

Integrating years of existence into any small business success indicator seems logical. Delgado (2007), for example, finds longevity of small business to be positively correlated with an expanded range of social service provision and a more evolved view of social responsibility toward the Latino community. A Latino community with numerous well-established small businesses is a community that enjoys a high degree of stability.

The longer a business has survived, the less energy, time, and resources are going into survival, and the easier it is for owners to focus on provision of a range of socially responsible services that go beyond the selling of a product or service. The survival rates of Latino small businesses, as already noted, are lower than for other groups, making the early phases (two years and under) a particularly important period in development. This period, as a result, necessitates that Latino small business owners focus their attention on startup concerns.

Once this initial critical period is over, owners are able to more fully develop their socially responsible roles. This does not mean that they do not practice socially responsible roles during the startup phase; however, it does mean that these generous acts take on secondary importance during the initial phase and cannot be operationalized to the same extent as later on in a small business's development.

PROFITABILITY

It would be impossible to develop a social indicator of Latino small business success without paying attention to the financial bottom line. In fact, there probably are no small business success indicators in general that ignore profits. The ability to sustain the well-being of the owner and his or her family stands as a testament to this indicator.

However, it is also important to attempt to measure how much money is generated in the community by having the business operational in the neighborhood. As noted in chapter 4, small business financial activities must be viewed from a multiplier (1.55) perspective within the community. The extent to which these establishments have supplies that are locally owned, pay rent to Latino landlords, employ local residents, and so on represents a dimension of profitability that must be captured to fully appreciate the economic and operational impact of Latino small businesses.

NUMBER OF EMPLOYEES

The ability of Latino small businesses to employ local residents—relatives and nonrelatives—brings an economic dimension to any discussion of Latino small business success that has implications for community economic development. Employment does not have to be full time. In fact, when hired, employees tend to be part time. Development of a measure that capture hours, number of employees, and pay (formal or informal employment) helps capture a more realistic dimension of this domain.

As already addressed, the majority of Latino small businesses tend to employ but a handful of employees. Consequently, this measure is not going to have great variation. Nevertheless, when employees are part of the operation, there is a community-wide impact if they are also residents of the community. The addition of a temporal perspective that captures small business developmental cycles and the number of employees in those cycles is very useful in viewing these establishments in a more comprehensive fashion.

CORE CUSTOMER BASE

This measure seeks to capture the percentage of customers that have been with the business over an extended period of time. The degree to which core customers are a significant part of a business's clientele reflects well on the business–customer relationship and can be a proxy for a range of other social-related measures covered in the section below on social capital success.

The greater the stable customer base, the more it is assumed to reflect satisfied customers. These customers, in turn, are probably the best marketing tool a Latino small business can enjoy because they will spread the word to new residents. It is important to keep in mind that Latino small businesses rarely undertake conventional marketing or advertising campaigns. There are few media outlets when compared with the dominant society. Consequently, satisfied customers are probably the most cost-effective and efficient way of branding.

OWNER–CUSTOMER LATINO-ORIGIN CONGRUENCE

To what extent is the small business serving the needs of the entire Latino community, and is it specifically Latino-origin? The customer base should ideally reflect the composition of the community the business serves whenever possible. This achievement may be related to developmental stage, with initial startup targeting the same Latino-origin group as the owner. However, as the business evolves or matures, the country-of-origin base of customers can be expected to expand to include other Latino and non-Latino groups, making the business more of a community institution than a limited business venture.

When Latino businesses reach out to a customer base beyond their own country of origin, they have the potential to build bridges between different sectors of the community and improve interethnic community relationships. Unfortunately, few institutions are in a position to do so in inner-city communities that are highly segregated or fragmented. Any social indicator that can capture this dimension can prove extremely fruitful in developing a better understanding of how to minimize intergroup tensions.

CULTURAL CAPITAL SUCCESS

Cultural capital has not received the same attention as its social and human capital counterparts. However, as culture increases in significance as a construct that has viability for community capacity enhancement or development, this will change. Cultural capital seeks to capture and build on cultural assets (Delgado 2007) and mobilize them to strengthen community bonds. Cultural capital, unlike social capital, which stresses connectedness and relationships irrespective of ethnic and racial backgrounds of residents, specifically taps values, traditions, and beliefs.

SPONSORSHIP OF CULTURAL EVENTS

The sponsorship of community social and festive events by Latino small businesses enjoys a long cultural tradition. The degree of support these businesses provide, as evidenced by the number of sponsorships and the time, energy, and financial contributions made, represents the dimension of engagement in community events. Furthermore, the length of time that a business has sponsored these events brings a complementary dimension that builds on duration of existence.

Any social indicator seeking to capture this dimension of Latino small business success must also tap the nature and importance of these sponsorships. Do the sponsorship events bring together the entire Latino community or are they focused on a subgroup? Obviously, the greater the audience impact of the event, the better from a success perspective or indicator. Community leaders, for example, would not seek business sponsorship if it would tarnish the event—for example, if liquor companies seek to sponsor events such as "Semana Latina," a patron saint festival, or Independence Day in the owner's country of origin.

COLLECTIONS FOR FUNERALS, SCHOLARSHIPS, AND DISASTERS

The nature and extent of a small business's role in collecting funds for community events represents a natural extension of a socially responsible role in the community. Consequently, it stands to reason that any measure of Latino small business success must capture this dimension in a manner that is culturally affirming. Latino small businesses often are called on to serve as fiscal conduits for a variety of community needs. Some, like scholarships, are uplifting; others, such as funerals, may not be. Regardless of the nature of these events, businesses become the catalyst or community focal point for collecting needed funds.

As detailed in chapter 4, collecting funds to help defray the costs of funerals is a highly visible and compassionate measure that can be captured in an index of small business success. An extension of this measure can also include the extent to which these establishments play critical roles in helping to fund various types of scholarships for community residents. A measure can be developed that takes into account the actual dollars collected or contributed. Although such a measure lends itself to quantification, it misses the qualitative aspects of this type of activity or gesture.

Finally, Latino small businesses are often called into action to help collect funds and goods to address natural disasters in their countries of origin. Hurricanes and earthquakes are two natural disasters that almost yearly can be counted on to occur in these areas, and it would not be unusual to see a prominent Latino small business coordinating relief efforts within a community. These types of businesses, as a result, hold great influence within their respective communities and fulfill critical socially responsible roles.

SUPPORT OF COMMUNITY SPORTS TEAMS

Sponsorship of community sports teams, most notably baseball, softball, and soccer, is often accomplished through the lending of a business's name for jerseys and financial support. The teams, as a result, are expected to represent the establishment in a positive manner because the small business owners' reputation is tied to their performance and behavior. Soccer in the United States caters to the best players that can afford to play the game, not necessarily the best players (Rhoden 2009). Sports leagues with small business sponsors help Latino players join and play with minimal or no regard to ability to pay.

Support of these activities, incidentally can go beyond the conventional types of teams. I visited a chess team in a San Antonio Latino community that was based in a drug prevention program but enjoyed the sponsorship of various Latino small businesses. This chess team competed across the state of Texas.

Sports leagues provide forums for the entire Latino community to come together and celebrate in a community-wide fashion: "On weekdays, the men are janitors, landscapers, farmhands, and factory workers across the region. Most Sundays from spring through fall they seek exercise, camaraderie, competition, and bonds of ethnic identity in the sport many knew in their homelands as *futbol*" (Matza 2009). These community venues, in turn, provide Latino small businesses with an opportunity for good publicity. Often these sporting events attract local Latino media as well as English-focused media, thereby broadening Latino small businesses' exposure beyond the confines of the community itself. These events also provide businesses with an opportunity to sell their products "where league-authorized vendors do a lively business in Latino comfort food: refried beans, sugary Mexican soft drinks, and homemade, wagon-wheel shaped crisps of fried dough called chicharrines" (Matza 2009). A cultural capital social indicator, as a result, must capture the synergistic effect of sports league sponsorship and the businesses these events support.

BEAUTIFICATION OR LATINIZATION OF NEIGHBORHOODS

The beautification or Latinization of the neighborhood is a qualitative measure of success that holds great potential for how Latino owners can successfully transform their neighborhoods. Assuming the role of art critic is certainly not one that I expect community social workers to embrace with enthusiasm. The qualitative element known as beautification clearly poses challenges in its development of a social indicator.

As noted in several sections of this book, Latino small business naming goes beyond an actual business name and can be viewed from an artistic perspective that takes into account the nature and color of the signs. Some businesses go so far as to commission murals to be painted on the outside walls of their establishments. In one instance in Holyoke, Massachusetts, a business commissioned local youth to paint a mural on one of the exterior walls. The mural grew so popular that other local businesses also commissioned murals. Thus, an entire neighborhood experienced beautification. The experience became a win–win for the small businesses, the community, and the youths who painted the murals.

Another often overlooked aspect of beautification can be the food served in communities where sports leagues enjoy popularity. Local business efforts to spruce up parks and playing fields, which are often in less than optimum condition, also benefit the community as well as being good for local businesses (Matza 2009). The greening of a Latino community that results from sports leagues and teams is a direct benefit to and by Latino small businesses.

Beautification takes on greater prominence when local residents can weigh in on the physical conditions of the neighborhood and how Latino small businesses have successfully Latinized their surroundings through various projects with artistic underpinnings. Each community needs to express itself in determining how beautification is to be conceptualized.

TRANSNATIONAL CONNECTEDNESS

The transnational nature of the Latino community necessitates that a measure be developed to help capture this aspect. To what extent do Latino businesses serve as a bridge between life in the United States and in the country of origin of people who patronize these establishments? The answer to this question brings a dimension to such businesses that rarely has been acknowledged, with the exception of literature that views these establishments from a nontraditional perspective.

The connectedness of establishments with countries of origin facilitates the exchange of information between customers and residents and serves as a means for mutual support group in instances where there is great sorrow pertaining to events back home or particular challenges in making an adjustment to life in the United States. Some Latino establishments, such as beauty parlors, barbershops, grocery stores, record stores, and restaurants, may have magazines and newspapers from back home for customers to read while they shop for goods or receive personal services.

SOCIAL CAPITAL SUCCESS

Readers may argue that social networks must play a prominent part in any Latino small business indicator of success, and I could not agree more. As noted in chapter 3, the nature and extent of social networks cannot be ignored in any serious discussion of social indicators of Latino small business success. Another perspective on social networks (social capital) is the degree of integration into the neighborhood. This measure, however, must be carefully weighed and calibrated because social networks can be both facilitating and hindering forces.

Egbert, for example, finds that social networks have the potential to seriously hinder ethnic small business development, particularly during the critical startup phase: "Social networks include social obligations and responsibilities, and the resources may be detracted from the enterprise in order to meet the profile obligations of an owner. Requests for money from members of the entrepreneur's family, former schoolmates, neighbors, or friends are common examples" (2009:38). Social networks, however, are often the primary source of startup capital for Latinos and other groups of color.

PARTICIPATION ON BOARDS, COMMITTEES, TASK FORCES, AND COALITIONS

Latino small business owners often bring leadership skills that generally get overlooked when there is any discussion of community leaders. Their involvement in leadership roles on agency boards, advisory committees, and task forces, for example, reflects their social capital success. They have been recognized as bringing an authentic voice to deliberations on these committees. Consequently, community social workers must be attuned to how these small business owners are being integrated into the human service fabric of a community.

Data related to membership in, roles in, and longevity on various committees, for example, bring an element to social capital that must not be ignored in any effort to measure the success of Latino small businesses. These measures, however, must not focus exclusively on formal participation but must endeavor to include community efforts such as those involving concerned citizens.

MEMBERSHIP IN AND CREATION OF BUSINESS ASSOCIATIONS

As initially noted in chapter 1 and will be addressed in greater detail in the next chapter, the creation and expansion of Latino business associations represents a developmental stage in the maturity of the Latino community. Data related to the history and composition of such associations can provide important insight into determining the success of Latino small businesses. The exact nature of the data, however, will be determined by local circumstances since these associations can have multiple goals.

Associations often provide a conduit for bringing together disparate sectors of the Latino small business sector to have their voices heard in city and state governmental circles. These forums can also be places where small businesses can pool resources and talents in helping other Latino small businesses get started or provide a political base for Latinos with political aspirations, offering training and consultation on various aspects of small business development, a forum for social events, and so on.

MENTORSHIP AND SUPPORT FOR COMMUNITY
ECONOMIC DEVELOPMENT

Assisting other Latinos in opening their own small businesses is an undertaking with profound implications for the economic development of the Latino community. Latino small business owners are in a propitious position to help other Latino startup firms, and any efforts to assist others must be captured by any success indicator. This broadening of success to others highlights how social capital can encompass multiple players and levels.

In all likelihood, mentoring and support for other Latino small businesses will be undertaken in an informal manner rather than as a systematized effort as part of a Latino small business association, although it can certainly occur within this forum or structure. Development of an understanding of the nature and extent of mentoring and support brings depth to any social indicator and serves to do justice to these small businesses and the economic role they can play in the community.

Encouragement and support of small businesses may occur within the market these businesses cater to or in other markets. The motivation for these acts may be socially responsible or may even be self-serving by bringing more businesses into the community. An understanding of when and how these acts occur will provide needed information on how to structure formal activities to encourage small business development.

FOSTER CARE PARENTING/MENTORING/VOLUNTEERING

Latino small business owners can generate social capital success by making their community presence felt in a variety of ways that may be less visible, such as being foster parents or serving as class parents for their children in school or participating in school-based committees of various kinds.

One Latino restaurant in Holyoke, Massachusetts, exemplifies this social indicator. The co-owners of the business are also foster parents to several Latino children. In addition, they play an active role in supporting various social service causes through donations, volunteering, and getting information out to the community. They donate to local events as a means of showing support for the cause to the larger community.

NEED FOR FUTURE RESEARCH

Martinelli highlights the importance of research in helping to answer fundamental questions about ethnic and racial small businesses: "Entrepreneurship cannot be fully understood without making reference to the socio-cultural and politico-institutional context in which it arises and develops. The entrepreneur is an innovator who combines and transforms the factors of production (labor, land and capital, but also knowledge and social capital) in order to produce value-added goods and services to be sold in a more competitive market, within a given context" (2006:53).

It is appropriate to end this chapter with a call for future research undertaken in collaboration between community social work scholars and practitioners. This partnership, when undertaken with active participation of communities, will bring to the fore results that have meaning to the ultimate beneficiaries of the research and scholarship, namely, the community itself.

Irazabal and Farhat note that Latino-focused scholarship and research has simply not caught up with the rapid increase in the Latino population:

"Understanding the Latino urban experience and developing plans to better respond to both the needs of Latino communities and their integration within society is not only relevant, but also urgently necessary" (2008:207). Community social work is in a unique position to address this growing gap and to do so in an imaginative manner that not only creates economic opportunities but also engages in place making in the community, which goes far beyond just creating small businesses for the sake of creating economic opportunities.

Community social workers are in a position to develop case studies that integrate theory, research, and findings and bring the worlds of academia and practice together. I have historically taken the view that case studies fulfill important functions in the advancement of theory, paradigms, and research. Case studies are not the "poor cousins" of quantitative data. I do not share in the thinking that social workers must strive to emulate the medical profession in conducting the highest form of research, which invariably will be trials. Research on communities of color rarely seeks to uncover assets and strengths and instead has a fascination with deficits and needs. This is not to say that these communities do not have needs and problems. However, their strengths and assets have historically allowed urban communities of color not only to survive incredible trials and tribulations, but also to thrive and make important contributions to the wider community and society.

Community social work practice in Latino economic development necessitates that careful attention be paid to documenting both the process and the outcomes of interventions. This does not mean that we cannot search for creative ways of documenting success at the same time as we are encouraging participatory democracy in pursuit of community economic and social development.

There is a place for social indicators in the documentation of success, but they must be carefully grounded in social, economic, and cultural contexts to give them the needed meaning to accurately describe and prescribe strategies for enhancing urban Latino small businesses. Social indicators are not a panacea and should be used to buttress data derived from other sources. Otherwise, they cannot fully capture the dynamics behind the success of any racial and ethnic group in this country in creating small businesses.

Some of the social indicators, as noted, may resonate with readers and others may simply not make any sense. Regardless of where one stands on the social domains and the elements they comprise, the field is sufficiently open to welcome other domains and elements that might better reflect the operative reality of Latino small businesses. I challenge readers to be creative and propose other measures that better capture small business creation and expansion. The development of such measures will not be easy, but it will be very rewarding.

Social workers' involvement in the development of these measures is but one way they can make a significant contribution to the Latino community. In the final chapter I identify seven distinct areas where we can exert our influence and a host of ways to tap people's knowledge and skills related to enhancing community capacity.

7

IMPLICATIONS FOR THE
SOCIAL WORK PROFESSION

> In my opinion, social work educators are becoming more con-
> cerned with research funding and teaching students how to
> change the client than with social justice and actions for the rights
> of Latino immigrants and the poor. Unfortunately, we risk teach-
> ing students to become like elites, only concerned with their own
> class interests and being social control agents, but not learning
> how to advocate for the under classes such as the immigrant poor.
>
> —R. M. Salcido, "Latino Population Growth, Characteristics, and
> Language Capacities"

THE ROLE OF community social work practitioners and scholars is not to
support the status quo and make undervalued people adjust better to their
socioeconomic circumstances. As noted in chapter 6, our knowledge of communities can come together with our knowledge of research to create culturally and community-based measures of success that will aid in obtaining
financial support for Latino small business ventures.

Community social work is clearly about bridging divides and creating innovative practice that builds upon a community's assets and hopes. Some
social workers may see Salcido's assessment above as extreme. Nevertheless,
it is a call to action to the field to revisit the origins of the profession and envision a role that is based on social justice, and one that seeks to identify and
tap indigenous community assets.

This chapter examines implications for community social work practice
from two perspectives: (1) how community social workers can assist in the
creation and support of racial and ethnic small businesses; and (2) how community social workers can benefit from development of a relationship with
ethnic and racial small businesses in creating conditions to facilitate community social, economic, and cultural development. These perspectives are

closely tied to each other. However, each addresses a particular aspect of social work practice.

This chapter also provides concrete examples, including challenges, for involving small business owners in planning and programming for Latinos, and for developing associations and coalitions that foster development and sustenance of Latino small businesses and relationships between these establishments and health and human service organizations. Social workers must possess a keen understanding of what motivates someone to enter the world of small business development. The decision to enter this arena is influenced by motivation and experience: "Starting a business is a process requiring a great deal of self-awareness and conscious work on the self. To become self-employed means that the individual departs from the established model of the 'normal' work relationship of salaried work and enters a work field in which he/she is not only responsible for the creative and conscious development of new, everyday routines, but also takes on the burden of responsibility for the maintenance of the job itself" (Kontos 2003:190).

The following goals of community social work practice are representative of this type of involvement: (1) developing a social and economic environment that is supportive of small businesses; (2) generating community and organizational support for small businesses; (3) participating in fund-raising efforts to support community economic undertakings; (4) assessing the needs of small businesses and generating reports and recommendations on their findings; and (5) assisting Latino small businesses in negotiating governmental bureaucracies and access to credit.

COMMUNITY SOCIAL WORK SUPPORT

I hope that readers have developed a sense of the multiple ways that community social workers can help to establish and maintain Latino small businesses. The following six activities represent but a small sampling of the range of ways that we can engage the Latino community in bringing to fruition the potential of small businesses to alter the social, economic, and political makeup of this growing community across the United States.

TECHNOLOGY/GOING GREEN

There are a variety of supports that can be developed to help small businesses owned by Latinos and other groups of color. The increased importance of technology can be felt throughout all spheres of life in this country. However, the gap between Latinos and the white, non-Latino community is probably greatest when it comes to technical information systems. Thus it is appropriate to begin with this topic.

Qureshi and York (2008) argue that information technology is essential for ethnic small businesses to thrive and create economic, social, and human development. The use of computers to increase performance is one area that is open to progress, particularly in the case of owners who have grown up without access to computers (Lerman et al. 2004). Computers can be used for a multitude of business-related tasks, such as tracking inventory, accounting, and storing information on customers, to increase the profit margin and free owners to facilitate greater community involvement.

The development of websites also holds much promise for Latino enterprises. Latinos are one of the fastest growing segments on the Internet, exceeding the U.S. online population growth by 50 percent. In February 2009 almost twenty million Latinos accessed the Internet, a 6 percent increase over the previous year (TechWeb 2009). Much of this increase has been from groups who historically had very low rates of Internet usage, such as newcomers, those with limited formal education, and those with annual household incomes of under $30,000 (Pew Hispanic Center 2009l).

Smith (2009:8) goes so far as to say that the recent recession has spurred on Latino Internet users: "There is a silver lining in this dark cloud [recession]. Hispanic media and Hispanic consumers are becoming more active online. The Internet seemed to be a hard sell in the Hispanic community for some time, but that has changed as many news organizations find it a more cost-efficient way to maintain presence.".

A 2008 estimate has the Latino community representing 11 percent of the total U.S. Internet market, with Latino users tending to be younger than overall Internet users (Wayne 2009). A high percentage of 18–34-year-olds reflects a tendency to use community and entertainment sites. Members of this age-group are attractive to business because of their earning power. There are indications that Latino small businesses are turning to the Internet to advertise. In 2002 it was estimated that 2.3 million Hispanic small businesses had an Internet presence (Korgaonkar, Silverblatt, and Becerra 2004).

Ethnic and racial businesses that use the latest computer technology have greater revenues and employment growth compared with businesses that do not (Community Development Technologies Center 2002b). One study of ethnic small businesses in the Los Angeles region found that they have been slower than majority-owned small businesses to embrace the Internet to boost productivity and increase their market reach (*Los Angles Times* 2009).

The "go green" movement is another area where Latino small businesses can benefit. Community social workers can initiate and broker efforts to help Latino small businesses become more environmentally conscious, with benefits that extend far beyond the business owner and the community. Increasing energy efficiency, for example, has a direct impact on profits by reducing the costs of doing business. Social workers can facilitate this movement by acting as brokers between Latino small business owners and the appropriate governmental agency. In 2008 Microsoft launched a Spanish version of *Office Accounting 2008* to assist Latino small businesses, evidence that major corporations understand how Latino population growth can dovetail with the movement to save energy.

There is much room for creativity in fostering the use of technology and enhancing green opportunities for Latino businesses. Huppe et al. (2006), for example, describe the use of an "enviroclub" as a vehicle for helping small businesses prevent pollution and save operating costs in the process, which has applicability for Latino small businesses. Similar efforts can be made in other arenas with particular significance to Latino small businesses and their communities.

DEVELOPMENT OF BUSINESS ASSOCIATIONS

Latinos coming together to form associations, whether of a business nature or other types, are not a new phenomenon. Zabin and Rabadan (1998), for example, recognize the importance of Mexican hometown associations in the United States and find that these organizations play active and meaningful social, economic, and political roles both in Los Angeles's Latino community and in their respective towns of origin, including development and support of local small businesses. Davis, Renzulli, and Aldrich (2006) find significant social and economic value in small businesses participation in voluntary associations as a means of reducing owner isolation, broadening their community influence, expanding markets, and exchanging new ideas.

Latino small business associations are often overlooked in the professional literature, and as a result they are poorly understood for their potential to create community economic development and as vehicles for addressing a range of community social and economic injustice issues. These associations are manifested in a variety of ways (nature of small businesses,

Latino backgrounds, geographical area covered) by taking into account local circumstances.

At first an association may consist of relatively few members owing to the small size of the Latino community and the businesses that support it. However, as the community increases in size, so does the potential for Latino small business associations to grow in size and influence. Community social workers are in a good position to facilitate the creation of these associations and in the process help politically transform the community.

The business and social roles and functions of Latino business associations have not received the attention they warrant in the literature, with rare exceptions. Farr (1994), for example, provides an excellent historical account of the birth of Philadelphia's Spanish Merchant Association and the forces that led to its creation in 1969 and its evolution over the next two decades. The growth of the Latino community in Philadelphia played a tremendous role in helping to create a social, economic, and political environment that fostered the need for Latino small businesses to be developed and sustained. The Spanish Merchant Association, in turn, showed how a coalition of small businesses could come together with a common purpose and goals that provide not only economic but also social and political benefits to this growing community.

Latino small business associations can be found in various forms, as evidenced by the Latino Farmers Cooperative of Louisiana. This association is unique because of its emphasis on agriculture. The projects it sponsors reflect this realm of interest and priority: community gardens, poultry production, cow-share clubs, cheese-making workshops, hydroponics, farmers' markets, and small-scale fishing. The cooperative also has a project, the Farmers Incubator Project, that seeks to build capacity for a new generation of Latino farmers. Technical assistance and training are typical ways in which it reaches out to the Latino farming community.

Creating Latino small business associations can have many benefits, from offering health insurance as a collective (see next section) to purchasing products on a wholesale basis. The benefits can also easily extend into the political arena by creating an additional voice for the community to speak out on social justice issues. Latinos are sometimes discriminated against simply for being Latino. Historically, Latino small businesses have generally not benefited from political advocacy: "While Latino political engagement has increased over the past decade, Latinos have not done so as much in advocating for its business community. . . . The lack of time and resources, as well as the lack of access to business associations . . . may be factors in the current state of Latino business people's civic engagement" (*Latino Business Review* 2009).

ASSISTANCE IN BROKERING HEALTH INSURANCE

As addressed in chapter 4, Latino small business owners invariably have not accessed health insurance programs for themselves, their families, or their employees who are not relatives. Barriers such as cost and lack of information have been identified as significant. Latino owners recognize the need for and importance of health insurance for themselves and their employees; consequently, attitudinal barriers to the value of health insurance are not a concern. Access to quality, affordable health insurance is, however, a serious issue.

Health insurance companies are making efforts to reach out to the Latino sector but have had limited success. A poor understanding of how best to reach the community is often mentioned as one of the primary reasons for the lack of success. Community social workers are in excellent positions to help initiate or broker initiatives to bring Latino small businesses to the table with public officials and insurance providers. This brokering role is one that social workers have historically undertaken. Their knowledge of communities can be an important asset in bringing interested parties together.

CONNECTING LATINO BUSINESSES TO INFORMATION AND TECHNICAL SUPPORT

The theme of disconnect between Latino small businesses and the organizations and programs established to help small business, and in many cases those targeting "minority" businesses, opens up an arena for community social workers to help broker these services. Interestingly, social brokering has been a role associated with the profession since its origins in the nineteenth century, and it is one that has increased significantly in the twenty-first century. In similar fashion to the brokering of health insurance, there are abundant resources that have been established specifically to help small business development in general and businesses of color in particular. However, there is a set of barriers that has limited these resources from reaching Latino small businesses. This disconnect is probably the result of a convergence of lack of knowledge on how to reach these small firms and a lack of bilingual/bicultural capability.

As noted throughout this book, universities are starting to assume a greater role in helping Latino small businesses through access to faculty with expertise on small businesses, students who can conduct research in support of Latinos, and resources such as workshops and conferences specifically tailored to reach Latinos. The role of lawyers in assisting Latino small business development has generally been overlooked, but law schools have established clinics with a goal of supporting these endeavors (Jones 2007–2008).

Social work schools, however, are generally absent from these collaborative ventures between universities and Latino businesses. These schools can establish field placements in community development corporations and other nonprofits with the specific intent of broadening technical assistance and services for small businesses.

Ormachea and Langer (2009) advocate the use of a broad strategy for delivery of legal services to immigrant small businesses. This approach has implications for other professional services, such as accounting, information technology, and community social work technical support. Local graduate professional schools can become part of a clearinghouse where immigrant small businesses can turn for assistance. Centralizing these services facilitates delivery and publicity.

FOSTERING SPONSORSHIP OF COMMUNITY EVENTS

Community social work practice and Latino festivals, galas, and parades go well together. Interestingly, if I had said community social work involvement in health or housing fairs, it would not raise an eyebrow. However, involvement in festivals, galas, and parades invariably does. These venues are excellent ways in which social workers can use their organizing skills to create a positive view of the Latino community as well as provide an avenue for expression of Latino pride and contributions to the broader Latino community. Latino small businesses can help create places and spaces of resistant cultural meaning in society (Campbell 2007).

Latino small business involvement in sponsoring community festivals, galas, and parades seems to be one of the most prominent ways these institutions encourage Latinidad, or ethnic pride, on a broad community scale (Garcia and Rua 2007). Latino festival sponsorship, unlike the sponsorship of sports teams, has a broad appeal that can encompass all age-groups and genders. Nowak (2007:9) reinforces the role and importance of civic cultural celebrations: "Public cultural activities play an important social capital role in immigrant communities. They provide a meeting place for the expression and maintenance of culture, as well as a bridge to cultural integration." Halter (1995:172) does so also: "In addition to providing space for social interactions, some of the entrepreneurs help organize community entertainment, such as dances, concerts, fashion shows, and beauty contests, or political events, such as marches, rallies, and speakers. They sometimes sponsor these activities with the hope that it will increase their visibility and prestige."

Latino festivals fulfill a variety of important functions within and outside the Latino community. Probably most important, they provide the community an opportunity to come together and celebrate its accomplishments. Further, they convey to the outside world their presence and accomplishments through pageants, music, dancing, and honoring of outstanding members of the community. Veronis notes that the sponsorship of festivals and parades, such as Toronto's Canadian Hispanic Day Parade (CHDP), serves to increase Latino small business visibility: "One of the aims of the CHDP is to provide Latin American businesses with opportunities to promote themselves by sponsoring the event through various sponsorship packages" (2005:1659).

Another perspective on Latino small businesses that actively sponsor and support Latino festivals and events is to view them as some form of tradition-bearing organization, although this is not the mission usually associated with such organizations. Tradition-bearing organizations have an explicit mission is preserve and protect traditions within a community (Dobransky 2007). The transformation of public space and public events such as festivals and parades serve to either preserve or disse minate a community's history. These types of celebrations effectively conserve an interpretation of a community's past and also shape its current cultural self-image (Momen 2007). Latino small businesses, in turn, have a venue through which to sponsor a high-profile community event, through donations, volunteering, and acting as a possible catalyst for increasing Latino community social capital: "The sponsorship of these businesses is for the community as a whole, not only for the parade. By having all the businesses, they are giving support to the community; they give support to the businesses themselves; and the businesses give support to the community by contributing through their sponsorship" (Veronis 2005:1664).

SOCIAL RESEARCH

Research in support of Latino small businesses can take many different forms. Robles and Cordero-Guzman issue a research charge that community social workers can assist in meeting: "Research that continues to uncover the facets of the social and community links between the micro-entrepreneurs and self-employed sector with the economic realities of community revitalization, gentrification, sustainable urbanism, transnational migration, ethnic biculturalism, and the permeable boundaries of the ethnic enclave would provide us with a deeper understanding of the role of the smallest entrepreneur in Latino communities" (2007:193).

Social action research, in turn, represents an arena with tremendous potential for social work involvement. Efforts such as those undertaken by the

Greenling Institute to research, rank, and report banking practices toward small businesses of color involve important social action strategies and tactics that are very familiar to social work (Gonzalez-Rivera 2008).

The continued development of social indicators of Latino small business success that actively incorporate both qualitative and quantitative measures is but one example of how research can both inform practice and aid the community in the process. These measures of success, as already noted, must be grounded in the sociocultural context of the Latino community. Community social workers can ensure that is the case.

IDENTIFYING POTENTIAL COMMUNITY BUSINESS OWNERS

The concept of community leader can certainly resonate in community social work practice. This concept has generally been limited to those individuals who display characteristics and perspectives that bring communities together and mobilize them to achieve social change. The concept of community leader can also be applied to those persons who dream of owning their own businesses within the community. McQueen, Weiser, and Brody (2007:5) make this very point: "All communities harbor would-be-CEOs with dreams of running their own companies. Nonprofits that want to nurture those ambitions are learning how to identify the best prospects and support them—frequently in ways that are out of the ordinary."

Identifying and brokering training and consultation opportunities for these individuals is a role that social workers can play in fostering Latino small business development (Lichtenstein and Lyons 2006). These individuals may well be active in the informal market and, with the necessary support, can move over to the formal market, with all the benefits inherent in such a move for themselves, families, and the broader community. Developing internships or mentoring programs that help future business owners is certainly a viable and important role that community social workers can assume with minimal difficulty. This role takes on even greater prominence if these partnerships involve young Latinos with aspirations of owning their own businesses.

After closely analyzing the key cross-cutting themes in both the literature and the case illustrations that have been presented throughout this book, one cannot help but marvel at the dynamic and influential nature of small businesses in urban communities of color and the role these establishments have and will continue to play in the Latino community.

I have provided a list of ways in which social workers can engage in Latino economic development through the fostering of small businesses. The implications of community social work practice with Latino small businesses, however, go far beyond this one sector and can result in enriching the profession and the community in the process. Involvement represents a win–win for the profession and the community and furthers social work's historic mission to intervene in marginalized communities through the embrace of an assets perspective.

Community social workers' understanding of, knowledge of, and access to the Latino community puts them in an excellent position to support the creation and expansion of Latino small businesses and in the process enrich the community in countless ways. This support is not restricted to practitioners but must also involve schools of social work and universities reaching out to these small businesses owners. Nevertheless, as noted in the epilogue, social work involvement in Latino small business development will not come without social and political challenges for the profession.

EPILOGUE

It is also important that we engage in a vigorous debate regarding policies that will foster a more entrepreneurial environment for all Americans and that we bring people together as a networking hub to stimulate the flow of ideas and actions.

—R. D. Strom, "Fostering Research on Minority Entrepreneurship"

I MUST BE honest: I love epilogues. An epilogue can serve many different purposes. However, I like to view epilogues as a way of bringing to light themes and issues that were not resolved in the course of writing a book but are too important not to identify before turning the last page.

The previous chapter provided a variety of ways that community social workers can envision their role in the economic and social development of Latino small businesses and the community they serve. However, undertaking this charge brings with it a set of challenges that cannot be ignored. The need for healthy discourse and debate on the subject, as encouraged in Strom's quote above, serves many different purposes—some directly related to the subject at hand and its implications for community social work practice in an expanded social and economic arena.

The questions and statements that follow are not meant to be provocative. Rather, they are intended to stimulate thought and discourse. Of course, they will also stimulate debate. Nevertheless, community social work practice or any other profession that eschews debate is either unimportant or in the waning days of its relevancy.

ARE LATINO SMALL BUSINESSES A PANACEA?

I would love to say yes, yes, yes! However, the honest answer is no, no, no. Latino small businesses, formal or informal, are certainly not the answer to all the stressors and the consequences of oppression associated with urban living in the United States for Latinos or any other group of color. Yet they have to be part of any thinking about how to provide avenues for economic advancement in this country.

Not all Latinos are interested in running their own businesses, and in that way they are no different from any other racial and ethnic group. Running a business necessitates a great deal of motivation and willingness to sacrifice and invest in an establishment that primarily serves as a means of economic survival. Owning a Latino small business, particularly one that is successful, also requires a willingness to assume socially responsible roles that go beyond that of a proprietor to one of *servidor*, or someone who is willing to serve the community, thus demanding commitment, motivation, and skills that transcend the ability to make a profit.

WHAT DOES THE FUTURE HOLD FOR URBAN LATINOS?

No one can answer this question without psychic powers or the ability to look into a crystal ball. Unfortunately, I do not have those powers, nor do I own a crystal ball. Nevertheless, I need to answer this question, and I do so with great hopes. There is little question that the country is becoming Latinized beyond cities such as Los Angeles, Miami, and New York. The proliferation of books focused specifically on dispersal of Latinos into suburbia and rural sectors of the country attests to this movement.

The dispersal patterns are particularly strong, as noted in chapter 2, and there is no immediate stop on the horizon. These patterns have shifted the Latino community from a regional to a national force, enhancing the national social, economic, and political significance of this community. Furthermore, the economic fortunes of the country have a direct association with migration from and to Latin American countries. Positive economic times translate into increased immigration; slow economic times result in return migration. Nevertheless, each of these waves results in a net gain of Latinos in this country.

A reshifting of views on the Latino community from one that is deficit-driven to one that stresses assets such as stability and economic growth is very much in order, with Latino-owned businesses playing the role of a community economic engine that is worthy of investment (Hayes-Bautista 2004a). The globalization of the world's economy will only serve to strengthen Latinos and the Spanish language in the United States. As noted earlier, the Spanish language has slowly shifted from a deficit to an asset when placed in an economic framework.

The social work profession has made important strides in embracing strengths, resiliency, and asset constructs. Including small businesses in these paradigms is a natural extension of this perspective and better positions the profession to make important contributions to this area of practice.

IS COMMUNITY SOCIAL WORK UP TO THE CHALLENGE?

All helping professions should be expected to confront challenges in these difficult times, particularly if social change is central to their mission. It would certainly be a sad state of affairs to write this book and secretly worry about whether community social workers are up to the task of translating many of its key concepts into reality. I am not in the habit of devoting years of my life to a task that has absolutely no chance of succeeding. Thus, the answer to the challenge is an unqualified yes.

The importance of community as a setting for practice and the embrace of social and economic justice make the community social work profession the one with the most potential to achieve the goals set out in this book. This does not mean, however, that other helping professions cannot make important contributions, and community social workers must actively seek to work with them whenever possible. Interdisciplinary collaboration involving Latino small businesses helps ensure a more comprehensive understanding of their role in Latino communities. Nevertheless, I firmly believe that community social work as a field has the best potential to deliver on the entire package stressed in this book.

If I had to identify one aspect of this social intervention that will prove the most challenging, it would be a bias that social workers may have about entering the business world and economic sphere of community life. This concern about enterprises, profits, and capitalism's casualties is noteworthy. Most of us in the field have eschewed the economic machines that have devastated neighborhoods and the livelihoods of millions of people. In fact, we spend most of our time, both professionally and outside of professional practice, addressing these consequences. Nevertheless, the business side of this intervention necessitates that we become more versed in the concepts, language, and literature of economics and business.

However, it is my sincere hope that this book has presented small enterprises in a way that is not monolithic, developing an understanding that not all for-profit enterprises are alike. Exploitation of people is not central to the philosophy of Latino small business owners, who in all likelihood live alongside the people they serve. Thus they have a vested interest in being well regarded and in turn seek the well-being of their customers and the community they serve. Broadening our understanding and appreciation of small businesses will allow the profession to justify intervening in this realm.

ARE EVIDENCE-BASED PRACTICE AND LATINO SMALL BUSINESSES MUTUALLY EXCLUSIVE?

As in any discussion of innovative social work practice, questions about "does it work" loom large here. Mind you, there are no community social workers, practitioners or scholars, who would simply say, "Trust me, it works." This approach, if it ever existed, is no longer prevalent in today's quest for evidence and tight funding.

As noted in chapter 6, community social work practice must contend with the murky world of "community context" in order to bring to fruition the promise of evidence-based practice. The challenge of controlling and measuring the impact of Latino small businesses will no doubt call for creative approaches to identifying evidence. These approaches must stress participatory democratic principles of involving small business owners in helping to construct measures that effectively tap the multifaceted role their establishments play in the life of their community. They also require venturing out into the broader community to get its perspective on these establishments and their importance.

The politics of evidence-based practice are usually not openly discussed when results are reported to funders and to scholarly audiences. Yet there is an implicit understanding that evaluation of an intervention is not done without confronting and surmounting numerous organizational and community factors and considerations. In essence, invariably ethical dilemmas are encountered and addressed—sometimes successfully, and other times not.

IS THE UNITED STATES REALLY BECOMING LATINIZED?

One must question whether the projections, or threats, of the United States becoming a "mini-Latin American country," with all the negative symbols that usually are associated with this grouping of nations, are valid. The proliferation of books on marketing to Latinos certainly gives the impression that it is only a question of time before the United States adopts Spanish as the second official language. But this view of the Latino "explosion" is much too narrow and further reinforces the vision of Latinos as consumers rather than as citizens.

Language is often considered the first marker in the shift of a community, and the question of how Spanish is viewed in the United States represents an excellent starting point. Garcia and Mason (2008) analyze the role of Spanish and how it has gradually undergone a transformation from a language associated with poverty and stigma to one with considerable economic value. The dominant society in this country has historically viewed Spanish negatively, as a language of the conquered and colonized, associated with poor, uneducated immigrants, and highly racialized. The English-as-the-official-language movement captures the historical view that Spanish is a threat to American society and the principles on which it was founded. Arizona's recent legislation against "illegal" immigrants represents but the latest efforts at scapegoating undocumented Latinos (Archibold 2010a–d; Nagourney 2010).

However, if business owners and politicians wish to engage the Latino community, there must be a rethinking of how to categorize this language as an asset rather than a liability. Further, the embrace of Spanish will effectively ground the country within the Southern Hemisphere, not to mention Spain. Many people would argue that Miami is essentially the capital of this region, and that city may indeed have more in common with its southern neighbors than the rest of the country does. Los Angeles, I would argue, has slowly moved into the status of capital of Mexico and Central America.

Obviously, the use of Spanish in a trivialized manner through advertising jingles or slogans is not what I envision. Use of Spanish that is superficial and disrespectful of the culture will backfire on the product or service being advertised.

SMALL BUSINESSES AS THE CENTER OF THE LATINO UNIVERSE

Readers can rightly question how a small business that may not employ anyone outside of the owner's family can be such an important institution in the life of a community. These establishments may not be the center of the

Latino universe, but they certainly have a prominent place in the major star constellation.

As this book has attested to, these institutions are clearly much more than economic enterprises, and that is what makes them so important. They can influence the whole array of social, cultural, and economic capital in the nation's urban Latino communities. I have mentioned instances where a Latino small business with a wide following was forced to close and the wide-ranging consequences of such a move. The death of a Latino business has meant the death of a star, so to speak.

The Latino community would never be the same if these establishments simply disappeared. In fact, it is hard to imagine a Latino community being served exclusively by dominant groups. On the other hand, imagine what the community would look like if all its material needs were met by Latino establishments. The political, social, cultural, and economic consequences of such a state would have profound implications.

Social workers are well equipped to identify and assess community assets, and the profession has certainly progressed in this area the past two decades. However, social workers must also plan interventions that effectively enhance or foster development of urban communities, Latino or otherwise.

MAKING PUBLIC SPACE MEANINGFUL AND HOSPITABLE

I am not talking about the hospitality industry when I make reference to making public space meaningful and hospitable. Too often discussions of economic development take on a tone and substance that are totally devoid of a human, or social capital, dimension. In many ways, that is probably one of the great fears social workers have about venturing into the economic domain when discussions on community development take place.

The creation of places (settings) and opportunities (spaces) that effectively foster community connectedness is probably one of the most significant goals that community social workers can strive to achieve. Latinos small businesses can help connect community residents in ways that go far beyond making culturally relevant products and services. The sponsorship of community events such as festivals and sporting events, for example, serves multiple community-centered goals. Opportunities for the community to come together in affirmation of cultural identity always serve to portray the Latino community in a positive light to a broader community that may harbor feelings of fear and dislike toward Latinos. In these instances, internal community goals match well with external community goals.

ARE THERE ANY LIMITS OR BARRIERS TO COMMUNITY SOCIAL WORK?

This question will result in considerable debate. If the answer is no, then community social work is best conceptualized as an expanding universe that is still picking up speed and will not contract anytime in our lifetime. If the answer is yes, are we selling this field short? Yes, we are: there are actually no limits to what this field can and should accomplish.

Not envisioning limits essentially equates with a license to be creative and bold. These qualities mirror those of Latino small businesses. These institutions have often managed to do wonderful things in the community with minimal support from government or other official entities. Social workers, too, must be prepared to make do with minimal support. This does not mean, however, that our ventures are not significant regarding goals and outcomes. It does, however, free us from the strings that are attached to funding sources.

CAN WE FOSTER LATINO SMALL BUSINESS DEVELOPMENT WITHOUT RUINING THEIR CHEMISTRY?

It is fitting to end this book with this provocative question. Latino small businesses can benefit from community social work intervention. But at what expense? These enterprises have existed in various forms as long as Latinos have been present in the United States, and in some cases even before colonization by the English. Thus, the development of initiatives that build on cultural values and traditions and do not undermine the social fabric of the community can be expected to help fulfill our mission as a profession.

Ethnic and racial small businesses that are resource-constrained have no choice but to be creative and exploit physical, social, or institutional opportunities that other, more resource-rich firms neglect or are unable to see (Baker and Nelson 2005). This refusal to embrace limitations is often a characteristic one sees in undocumented Latinos who have overcome incredible odds to make it to this country. These survival skills must not be undermined in any intervention.

Our ability as social workers to socially navigate the terrain of the community in a manner that is affirming and respectful bodes well for our relevance in the United States of the twenty-first century. The demographic patterns are distinctive and clear. We can position our profession on the cusp of this demographic tsunami. We cannot stop this tidal wave but are in a position to ride it if we act accordingly.

This epilogue has provided me with an opportunity to showcase key issues and cross-cutting themes found throughout the book and assist readers in drawing their own conclusions about how community social workers can play an influential role in fostering the development of racial and ethnic small businesses. I have not purposefully chosen these themes to create controversy, although that is usually inherent in any discussion of Latinos in this country. The subject of fostering Latino community economic development through the support of small business ventures is certainly open for debate within and outside of the profession. This debate should be welcomed because it will signal the beginning of an exciting era in social work and, more specifically, in community social work practice. The outcome of the debate will reverberate within and across other professions, improving them in the process.

REFERENCES

Acosta, D., & M. Serrano. (2008). *End-of-life issues for Hispanics/Latinos.* Seattle: University of Washington School of Medicine. http://faculty.washington.edu/daacosta/HHP/module8/content.html (accessed May 19, 2009).

Acs, Z. J., & K. Kallas. (2007). State of literature on small- to medium-sized enterprises and entrepreneurship in low-income communities. *Milken Institute Series on Financial Innovation and Economic Growth* 7:21–45.

Adams, A., & J. Armstrong. (2005, December 17). Lodi Hispanics see emerging leadership. *Lodinews.com.* http://www.lodinews.com/articles/2005/12/17/news/l_hispanics_051214.txt (accessed May 14, 2009).

Agudo, L. (2008, December 1). *Minority entrepreneurship helps boost economic development.* Kutztown, Penn.: Kutztown University Latino Business Resource Center.

Aja, A. (2006). The Intra-immigrant dilemma. *New Politics: A Journal of Socialist Thought* 10:1–8.

Alberts, H. (2006). Geographical boundaries of the Cuban enclave economy in Miami. In *Landscapes of the ethnic economy*, ed. D. H. Kaplan & W. Li, 35–47.

Alderslade, J., J. Talmage, J. & Y. Freeman. (2006). *Measuring the informal economy—one neighborhood at a time.* Washington, D.C.: Brookings Institution.

Allen, J. (2002). The Tortilla-Mercedes divide in Los Angeles. *Political Geography* 21:701–9.

Alliance for a Better Community. (2008). *Policy brief: Recommendations for banking in Los Angeles' Latino market.* Los Angeles: Alliance for a Better Community.

Alonso, G. (2007). Selling Miami: Tourism production and immigrant neighborhoods in the capital of Latin America. In *Tourism, ethnic diversity and the city*, ed. J. Rath, 164–80. New York: Routledge.

Alonso, R. (1979, February 21). They keep stamp of individualism: Hispanic neighborhood stores. *Boston Globe*, 20.

Alvarez, A. M. (2009). Latino small business: A big present, a bigger future. In Cisneros & Rosales 2009, 71–82.

Alzenman, N.C. (2008, November 28). For immigrants, a ripple effect; tough times trickle down through newcomers' networks. *Washington Post*, A1.

Ambruster-Sandoval, R., C. B. Munoz, & E. Reese. (2008). Race, class, and revolution: Reflections on Edna Bomacich's career and the struggle for social justice. *Critical Sociology* 34:323–37.

Amoruso, C. (2005, August 26). L.A.'s Black-Brown divisions deepen: Is there hope for change? *IMDiversity.com.*

Ansley, F., & J. Shefner, eds. (2009). *Global connections and local receptions: New Latino immigration to the Southeastern United States.* Knoxville: University of Tennessee Press.

Aponte, R. (2001). Latinos in Indiana: Growth, distribution, and implications. *Julian Samora Research Institute Statistical Brief* 14:1–10.

Arambula, J. (2006, July 26). *Microenterproses: The engine of regional economy.* Sacramento: Assembly Committee on Jobs, Economic Development, and the Economy.

———. (2008, June 26). *Memorandum: Small business issues.* Sacramento: Assembly Committee on Jobs, Economic Development, and the Economy.

Aranda, E. (2009). Puerto Rican migration and settlement in South Florida. In *Caribbean migration to Western Europe and the United States*, ed. M. Cervantes-Rodriguez, R. Grosfoguel, & E. H. Mielants, 111–30. Philadelphia: Temple University Press.

Archibold, R. C. (2006, May 2). Immigrants take to the U.S. streets in show of strength. *New York Times*, 1.

———. (2010a, April 20). Immigration bill reflects a firebrand's impact. *New York Times*, A12.

———. (2010b, April 25). Arizona enacts stringent law on immigration: A debate flares anew. *New York Times*, A1, A9.

———. (2010c, April 26). Arizona's new immigration law widens the chasm between sides. *New York Times*, A13.

———. (2010d, April 27). In wake of immigration law, calls for an economic boycott of Arizona. *New York Times*, A13.

Arcodia, C., & M. Whitford. (2007). Festival attendance and the development of social capital. *Journal of Convention & Exhibition Management* 8:1–18.

Armas, G. C. (2004, October 18). Wealth gap in the U.S. widens. *Miami Herald*, 1.

Arreola, D. D., ed. (2004). *Hispanic spaces, Latino places: Community and cultural diversity in contemporary America*. Austin: University of Texas Press.

Associated Press. (2006). Hispanic-owned business growth rapid. *Foxnews.com*. http://www.foxnews.com (accessed May 9, 2009).

———. (2009a, March 24). Blacks, Latinos hit by layoffs; jobless rate rises fast for minorities. *Boston Globe*, 6.

———. (2009b, May 14). Less immigration slows Asian, Hispanic growth: Officials push back estimates on when minorities will become the majority. http://www.msnbc.msn.com/id/30732546/ (accessed May 14, 2009).

Asthana, A. (2006, August 27). Hispanic exodus from Calif. Reshapes makeup of other cities. *Washington Post*, 1.

Astrachan, J. H., & M. C. Shanker. (2007). Family business' contributions to the U.S. economy: A closer look. In *Handbook on research on family business*, ed. Z. Poutziouris, K. X. Smyrnois, & S. B. Klein, 56–66. Northampton, Mass.: Edward Elger.

Atkinson, T., B. Cantillon, E. Marlier, & B. Nolan. (2002). *Social indicators: The EU and social inclusion*. Oxford: University of Oxford Press.

Audretsch, D. B. (2002). The dynamic role of small firms: Evidence from the U.S. *Small Business Economics* 18:13–40.

Aviles, M. D., R. Ventura, G. Yago, & B. Zeidman. (2004). *The Isabel Project: Closing the Latino capital parity and procurement gap*. San Francisco: Latino Foundation.

Ayala, G. X., K. Mueller, E. Lopez-Madurga, N. R. Campbell, & J. P. Elder. (2005). Restaurant and food shopping selections among Latino women in Southern California. *Journal of the American Dietetic Association* 105:38–45.

Badillo, D. A. (2004). Mexicans and suburban parish communities. *Journal of Urban History* 31:23–46.

———. (2006). In search of Mexican American urban history: Redefining politics and culture. *Journal of Urban History* 31:908–17.

Baker, T., & R. E. Nelson. (2005). Creating something from nothing: Resource construction through entrepreneurial bricolage. *Administrative Science* 50:329–66.

Balch Institute for Ethnic Studies. (2004). *Latino Philadelphia: Our journeys, our communities: A community profile*. Philadelphia: Historical Society of Pennsylvania.

Banderas News (2006, June). Latinos launch bank to meet growing wealth needs. http://www.banderasnews.com/0606/nz-latinobank.htu (accessed May 9, 2009).

Baraya, A. R., M. C. Budden, & L. M. Escobar. (2008). Strategically enhancing business capacities and social development in the Hispanic community. *Journal of Business and Economics Research* 6:67–71.

Barcus, H. R. (2007). The emergence of new Hispanic settlement patterns in Appalachia. *Professional Geographer* 59:298–315.

Bares, S. L. (2007). An intra-ethnic analysis of social affiliations among Latinos in the United States. *Journal of Poverty* 11:107–33.

Barone, M. (2007, May 8). The realignment of America: The native-born are leaving "hip" cities for the heartland. *Wall Street Journal*, 1.

Barrera, M. L. (2008). Back to business: Giving small businesses a voice. *Hispanic Enterprise.* http://hispaniconline.com/HE/2008_ol/Features-HispCommerce .html (accessed March 26, 2009).

Barreto, M. A., & G. R. Sanchez. (2009). Black–brown relations in the New South: Results from the Latino National Survey**.** Paper presented at the National Conference on Latino Politics, Power & Policy, Brown University, Providence, R.I.

Barrios, J. J. (2005). *The unbanked Latino: Expanding banking access for Latinos in Massachusetts***.** Boston: Massachusetts General Court.

Bartelt, D. W. (2001). *Latino Philadelphia: A report of the Latino Workforce Development Taskforce.* Philadelphia: Temple University.

Barth, J. R., G. Yago, & B. Zeidman. (2006). *Barriers to entrepreneurship in emerging domestic markets: Analysis and recommendations.* Santa Monica, Calif.: Milken Institute.

Bates, T. (1989). Small business viability in the urban ghetto. *Journal of Regional Science* 29:625–43.

———. (1997). *Race, self employment & upward mobility: An illusive American dream.* Washington, D.C.: Woodrow Wilson Center Press.

———. (2005). Analysis of young, small firms that have closed: Delineating successful from unsuccessful closures. *Journal of Business Venturing* 20:343–58.

———. (2006). The urban development potential of Black-owned businesses. *Journal of the American Planning Association* 72:227–37.

Bates, T., & W. D. Bradford. (2007). *Venture capital investment in minority businesses***.** http://economics.sbs.ohio-state.edu/jmcb/05217/05217.pdf (accessed June 29, 2009).

Bates, T., W. E. Jackson, & J. H. Johnson. (2007). Advancing research on minority entrepreneurship. *Annals of the American Academy of Political and Social Science* 613:10–17.

Bates, T., & Robb, A. (2008). Analysis of young neighborhood firms serving urban minority clients. *Journal of Economics and Business* 60:139–48.

Bauer, R. A., ed. (1966). *Social indicators*. Cambridge: MIT Press.

Bauzon, K. (2007). Adaptation and identity formation in the Cuban-American community: Reflections and considerations. *Kasarinlan Philippine Journal of Third World Studies* 22:85–116.

Baxamusa, M. H. (2008). Empowering communities through deliberation: The model of community benefits agreement. *Journal of Planning Education and Research* 2:261–76.

Baycon-Levent, T., E. Masurel, & P. Nijkamp. (2006). Gender differences in ethnic entrepreneurship. *International Journal of Entrepreneurship and Innovation Management* 6:173–90.

Bean, J. J. (2000). "Burn, Baby, Burn": Small business in the urban riots of the 1960s. *Independent Review* 2:165–88.

Beck, T., & A. Demiguc-Kunt. (2006). Small and medium-size enterprises: Access to finance as a growth constraint. *Journal of Banking & Finance* 30:2931–43.

Behnke, A. (2008). Expanding the Latino market niche: Developing capacity and meeting critical needs. *Journal of Extension* 46:1–11.

Belanger, M. (2009, August 12). Hispanic consumers a cure for recession blues? *Progressive Grocer.* http://www.lexisnexis.com (accessed September 8, 2009).

Benedict, A., & R. B. Kent. (2004). The cultural landscape of a Puerto Rican neighborhood in Cleveland, Ohio. In Arreola 2004, 187–205.

Benioff, R. (2008). *Profiles of engagement: Public markets as engines for urban revitalization.* Los Angeles: Center for Community Partnerships, University of California, Los Angeles.

Benitez, C. (2007). *Latinization: How Latino culture is transforming the U.S.* Ithaca: Paramount Books.

Berger, P. L. (1995). Forward. In Halter 1995a, vii–ix.

Bernard, A. B., & M. J. Slaughter. (2004). *The life cycle of a minority-owned business: Implications for the American economy.* Washington, D.C.: Minority Business Development Agency.

Bernardez, M. (2005). Achieving business success by developing clients and community: Lessons for leading companies, emerging economies and a nine year case study. *Performance Improvement Quarterly* 18:37–55.

Bernhardt, A., H. Boushey, L. Dresser, & C. Tilly. (2008). *An introduction to the "Gloves-Off" economy.* Los Angeles: Institute for Research on Labor and Employment, University of California, Los Angeles.

Besser, T. L. (2000). The importance of community values in small business strategy formation: Evidence from rural Iowa. *Journal of Small Business* 38:68–74.

Best, K. (2009, May 21). Hispanic business booms: Commercial interests respond to rapid growth of Latin population. *Florida Today*, 3.

Bibb, E., M. Fisberg, J. Harold, & E. Layburn. (2004). *The blended value glossary.* Palo Alto, Calif.: Stanford University School of Business.

Bisman, C. (2004). Social work values: Then moral code of the profession. *British Journal of Social Work* 34:109–23.

Blackburn, R., & M. Ram. (2006). Fix or fixation? The contributions and limitations of entrepreneurship and small firms to combating social exclusion. *Entrepreneurship and Regional Development* 18:73–89.

Blackford, M. G. (2003). *A history of small business in America.* Second edition. Chapel Hill: University of North Carolina Press.

Blackstock, K. (2005). A critical look at community based tourism. *Community Development Journal* 40, 1:39–49.

Blakely, E. J., & T. K. Bradshaw. (2002). *Planning local economic development: Theory and practice,* Third edition. Thousand Oaks, Calif.: Sage.

Blanchard, L., B. Zhao, & J. Yinger. (2007). Do lenders discriminate against minority and women entrepreneurs? *Journal of Urban Economics* 63:467–97.

Blanchflower, D. G. (2009). Minority self-employment in the United States and the impact of affirmative action programs. *Annals of Finance* 5:361–96.

Bletzer, K. V. (2003). Latino naming practices of small-town businesses in rural southern Florida. *Ethnology* 42:209–35.

Block, D. (2008). The increasing presence of Spanish-speaking Latinos in London: An emergent community? *Journal of Language, Identity and Education* 7: 5–21.

Blum, A. S. (2004). Cleaning the revolutionary household: Domestic servants and public welfare in Mexico City, 1900–1935. *Journal of Women's History* 15:67–90.

Blumenthal, R. (2007, April 14). Museum honors Hispanic culture: Celebrating a prize for San Antonio. *New York Times*, A9.

Bogan, V., & W. Darity. (2008). Culture and entrepreneurship: African American and immigrant self-employment in the United States. *Journal of Socio-Economics* 37:1999–2019.

Bolin, T. (2006). *The economic and fiscal impacts of immigration.* Berkeley: Institute for Research on Labor and Employment, University of California.

Bonacich, E. (2004). Asian and Latinos in the Los Angeles garment industry: An exploration of the relationship between capitalism and racial oppression. In *Immigration and entrepreneurship: Culture, capital, and ethnic networks,* ed. I. Light & Bhachu, 51–74. New Brunswick, N.J.: Transaction Publishers.

Booth, H. (2006). Demographic forecasting: 1980 to 2005 in review. *International Journal of Forecasting* 22:547–81.

Borer, M. J. (2006). The location of culture: The urban culturalist perspective. *City & Community* 5:173–97.

Borges-Martinez, R. (2006, November). CBOs and non-profits in policy intermediation in new Latino settlements: The cases of Holyoke and Lawrence, Massachusetts. Paper presented at the ARNOVA Conference, Chicago.

Borges-Mendez, R. (2006). *Latino business owners in East Boston.* Boston: Mauricio Gaston Institute for Latino Community Development and Public Policy, University of Massachusetts, Boston.

———. (2007). The Latinization of Lawrence: Migration, settlement, and incorporation of Latinos in a small town of Massachusetts. In Montero-Sieburth & Melendez 2007a, 228–53.

Borjas, G. J., ed. (2007). *The immigrant to the United States.* Chicago: University of Chicago Press.

Bradford, N. (2005). *Place-based public policy: Towards a new urban and community agenda for Canada.* Ottawa: Canadian Policy Research Networks.

Bradley, III, D. B., & L. Stuckey, L. (2005). Impact and effect of Hispanic growth on small business and entrepreneurial development. *International Journal of Entrepreneurship* 9:1–18.

Brennan, P. (2004, March 15). America becoming a Hispanic nation. *Newsmax.com.* http://www.archive.newsmax.com/archives/articles/204/3/14/105948.shtml (accessed April 19, 2009).

Brettell, C. B. (2008). "Big D": Incorporating new immigrants in a sunbelt suburban metropolis. In Singer, Hardwick, Brettell 2008, 53–86.

Brettell, C. B., & K. E. Alstatt. (2007). The agency of immigrant entrepreneurs: Biographies of the self-employed in ethnic and occupational niches of the urban labor market. *Journal of Anthropological Research* 63:383–97.

Brookings Institution. (2009, May 1). *Politics, policy and the 2010 Decennial Census.* Washington, D.C.: Brookings Institution.

Brugmann, J., & C. K. Prahalad. (2007, February). Cocreating business's new social compact. *Harvard Business Review,* 1–12.

Brush, C., D. Monti, A. Ryan, & A. M. Gannon. (2007). Building ventures through civic capitalism. *Annals of the Academy of American Political and Social Sciences* 613:155–77.

Bryce, H. J. (2006). Nonprofits as social capital and agents in the public policy process: Toward a new paradigm. *Nonprofit and Voluntary Sector Quarterly* 35:311–18.

Bucks, B. K., A. B. Kennickell, & K. B. Moore. (2006). Recent changes in the U.S. family finances: Evidence from the 2001 and 2004 Survey of Consumer Finances. *Federal Reserve Bulletin.* Washington, D.C.: Board of Governance of the Federal Reserve System.

Buddle, R. (2006). *Mexican and Central American L.A. garment workers.* Berlin: Lit Verlag.

Burke, J. (2002, September 13). Hispanic women lead in minority ownership. *Bankrate.com.* http://www.bankrate.com/brm/news/biz/thumb/20020913a.asp (accessed January 23, 2009).

———. (2004, November 30). Banks focus more on accommodating Latino customers: Some are gearing whole branches specifically to Spanish-speaking people. *Salt Lake (Utah) Tribune,* E1.

Burns, D. (2009, March 31). Latino businesses help resurrect Iowa's rural downtowns. *Hispanic Trending.* http://juantornoe.blogs.com/hispanictrending/hispanic_owned_companies/index.html (accessed May 1, 2009).

Burros, D. (2008, October 15). ISU expert: Latino businesses crucial for Iowa's downtowns. *Iowa Independent,* 1.

Business Week. (2005, January 17). Tapping a market that is hot, hot, hot: Wealth is soaring among fast-growing Hispanics—yet 56% have no bank accounts. http://www.businessweek.com/magazine/content/05_03/b3916046_mz011.htm (accessed April 26, 2009).

Business Wire. (2008, May 19). Hispanic purchasing power: Projections to 2015—report available now. http://www.allbusiness.com/population-demographics/demographic-groups/10511476-html (accessed April 18, 2009).

Bustillo, M. (2007, July 16). Taco trucks in New Orleans hit by legislative crunch. *Boston Globe,* A2.

Caldwell, A. A. (2005, August 11). Non-whites now majority in Texas. *Boston Globe,* A25.

California Department of Finance. (2007). *Population characteristics by race, ethnicity, gender and age for Caifornia. and its counties.* Sacramento: Department of Finance.

California Health Care Foundation. (2004).Latino small business: A promising opportunity to insure more Californians. *Small Business Health Insurance Issues* 2:1–2.

Camarillo, A. M. (2007). Cities of color: The new racial frontiers in California's minority-majority cities. *Pacific Historical Review,* 76:1–28.

Camayd-Freixas, Y., & G. Karush. (2006). *Latinos in New Hampshire.* Manchester: Community Economic Development Press, University of Southern New Hampshire.

Camayd-Freixas, Y., G. Karush, & N. Lejter. (2006). Latinos in New Hampshire: Enclaves, diasporas, and an emerging middle class. In Torres 2006, 171–86.

Campbell, H. (2007). Chicano life. *Journal of Consumer Culture* 5:207–33.

Campbell, W. S. (2008). Lessons in resilience: Undocumented Mexican women in South Carolina. *Affilia* 23, 3:231–41.

Capps, R., E. Henderson, J. D. Kasarda, J. H. Johnson, S. J. Appold, D. L. Croney, D. J. Hernandez, & M. E. Fix. (2007). *A profile of immigrants in Arkansas.* Washington, D.C.: Urban Institute.

Card, D., & E. G. Lewis. (2005). *The diffusion of Mexican immigration during the 1990s: Explanations and impacts.* Cambridge, Mass.: National Bureau of Economic Research.

Carey, Jr., D., & R. Atkinson. (2009). *Latino voices in New England.* Albany: State University of New York Press.

Carr, J. H., & L. J. Servon. (2009). Vernacular culture and urban economic development: Thinking outside the (big) box. *Journal of the American Planning Association* 75:28–40.

Carvagal, M. J. (2004). Measuring economic discrimination of Hispanic-owned architecture and engineering firms in South Florida. *Hispanic Journal of Behavioral Sciences* 26:79–101.

Caskey, J. (1994). *Fringe banking: Check-cashing outlets, pawnshops, and the poor.* New York: Russell Sage Foundation.

Caskey, J., C. R. Duran, & T. M. Solo. (2006). The urban unbanked in Mexico and the United States. *World Bank Policy Research Working Paper* 3885.

Cava, A., & D. Mayer. (2007). Integrative social contract theory and urban propensity initiatives. *Journal of Business Ethics* 72:263–78.

Cavalluzzo, K.S., L. C. Cavalluzzo, & J. D. Wolken. (2002). Competition, small business financing, and discrimination: Evidence from a new survey. *Journal of Business* 79:641–80.

Cavalluzzo, K. S., & J. D. Wolken. (2005). Small business loan turndowns, personal wealth, and discrimination. *Journal of Business* 78:2153–78.

Cave, D. (2009, December 24). Recession slows population rise across Sun Belt: Fewer quit Northeast. *New York Times*, A1, A15.

Censky, A. (2007, November 14). Study: Latino economic power increasing. *Arizona Republic*, 1.

Center for Continuing Study of the California Economy. (2005). *2005 California Regional Economics Project.* Palo Alto, Calif.: Center for Continuing Study of the California Economy.

Center for Sustaining Agriculture & Natural Resources (CSANR). (2005). Small farms: The heart of Washington agriculture. *CSANR Technical Report.* Pullman: Washington State University.

Cervantes-Rodriguez, A. M. (2006). Nicaraguans in Miami-Dade County: Immigration, incorporation, and transnational enterprise. *Latino Studies* 4:232–57.

Chaganti, R., & P. C. Greene. (2002). A study of entrepreneurs' ethnic involvement and business characteristics. *Journal of Small Business Management* 40:126–43.

Chapa, J., & B. de la Rosa. (2006). The problematic pipeline: Demographic trends and Latino participation in graduate sciences, technology, engineering, and mathematics programs. *Journal of Hispanic Higher Education* 5:203–21.

Chavez, L. R. (2008). *The Latino threat: Constructing immigrants, citizens, and the nation*. Palo Alto, Calif.: Stanford University Press.

Chayes, M. (2009, April 16). Cops: Thefts targeting Hispanics. *Newsday* (New York), A18.

Chhabra, D., & R. Phillips. (2009). Tourism-based development. In Phillips & Pittman 2009, 236–48.

Chinchilla, N. S., & N. Hamilton. (2001). Doing business: Central American enterprises in Los Angeles. In Lopez-Garza & Diaz 2001, 188–214.

Chinyelu, M. (1999). *Harlem ain't nothin' but a third world country: The global economy, empowerment zones and the colonial status of Africans in America*. New York: Mustard Seed Press.

Chun, S-C. (2007). The "other Hispanics"—What are their national origins? *Hispanic Journal of Behavioral Sciences* 29:133–55.

Churchill, N. C., & V. L. Lewis. (2004). The five stages of small business growth. In *Small businesses: Critical perspectives*, ed. S. D. Staff, 2:291–308. New York: Routledge.

Cisneros, H. (2009, April 8). Latinos and the law of large numbers. *Latino News and Opinion*. http://www.pontealdia.com/columnists/latinos-and-the-law-of-large-numbers.html (accessed May 13, 2009).

Cisneros, H., & J. Rosales, eds. (2009). *Latinos and the nation's future*. Houston: Arte Publico Press, University of Houston.

Cobb, C. W., & C. Rixford. (1998). *Lessons learned from the history of social indicators*. San Francisco: Redefining Progress.

Coen, S. E., N. A. Ross, & S. Turner. (2008). "Without tiendas it's a dead neighborhood": The socio-economic importance of small trade stores in Cuchabamba, Bolivia. *Cities* 25:327–39.

Coetzer, A., & M. Perry. (2008). Factors influencing employee learning in small business. *Education + Training* 50:648–60.

Cohen-Cruz, J. (2007). *Between the edge and the root: Action Lab in Hunts Point*. http://www.communityarts.net/readingroom/archivefiles/2006/07/between_theedg_1.php (accessed May 26, 2009).

Cohn, I. (2007). *Hispanics in the United States*. New York: United Nations ECLAC.

Cohn, M., & K. McDonough. (2007). Information start-ups need to succeed. *Business Information Review* 24:193–203.

Coleman, S. (2005). Is there a liquidity crisis for small, black-owned firms? *Journal of Developmental Entrepreneurship* 10:29–47.

Colon, M. (2005). Hospice and Latinos: A review of the literature. *Journal of Social Work in End-Of-Life & Palliative Care* 1:27–43.

Community Development Technologies Center. (2002a). *Minority women enterprises: Going to scale.* Los Angeles: Community Development Technologies Center.

———. (2002b). *Minority business enterprises: Gaining the technical advantage.* Los Angeles: Community Development Technologies Center.

Congressional Report. (2005, September 15). *New communities and opportunities: Perspectives on emerging Latino populations.* Washington, D.C.: United States Senate.

Conrad, C. A., J. Whitehead, Mason, & J. Stewart, eds. (2005). *African-Americans in the U.S. economy.* Lanham, Md.: Rowman & Littlefield.

Conte, C. (2008, July 28). Small business in U.S. history. *America.gov.* http://www.america.gov (accessed December 6, 2008).

Conti, K. (2003, November 9). Latinos find haven in New Hampshire: Residents drawn by affordable housing, jobs. *Boston Globe*, 1.

Contreras, A. R. (2004). Epilogue: Latinos at the portal of the 21st century. *Education and Urban Society* 36:223–34.

Contu, N. E. (2004). *Latinos and Latinas in the South: A report prepared for the Southern Arts Foundation.* Atlanta.

Cooke, D. K. (2005). African-American business ownership: Strengths in numbers, but where. *Journal of Applied Business Research* 21:37–44.

Cooke, P., N. Clifton, & M. Oleaga. (2005). Social capital, firm embeddedness and regional development. *Regional Studies: The Journal of the Regional Studies Association* 39:1065–77.

Corburn, J., & R. Bhatia. (2007). Health impact assessment in San Francisco: Incorporating the social determinants of health into environmental planning. *Journal of Environmental Planning and Management* 50:323–41.

Cordero-Guzman, H. (2005). Community-based organizations and migration in New York City. *Journal of Ethnic and Migration Studies* 31:889–909.

Corraiejo, J. C. (2009, April 20). Small minority-owned businesses a path to new "Main Street." *Entrepreneur.* http://www.entrepreneur.com/tradejournals (accessed September 8, 2009).

Correa, C. (2009, May 7). Down economy hurting Latino business owners. *OzarksFirst.com* http://ozarksfirst.com.

Coulton, C. (2005). The place of community in social work practice research: Conceptual and methodological developments. *Social Work Research* 29:73–86.

Coulton, C. J., & J. E. Korbin. (2007). Indicators of child well-being through a neighborhood lens. *Social Indicator Research* 84:349–61.

Cravey, A. J. (2005). Desire, work and transnational identity. *Ethnography* 6: 357–83.

CreativeFortWayne.net (2004, March 9). Hispanic nation. http://www.creative fortwayne.net/archives/000163.php (accessed April 20, 2009).

Credit Union League of Connecticut. (2008). *Connecticut Credit Unions: Serving the Hispanic Market*. Wallingford, CT: Credit Union League of Connecticut.

Crockett, R.O. (2004, March 15). Why are Latinos leading Blacks in the job market? *Business Week*, 70.

Crow, B. (2004, March 15). Hispanic nation: Is America ready? *Business Week*, 58–62, 66, 68, 70.

Cruz, A. R. (2005). Taquerias, laundromats, and Protestant churches: Landmarks of Hispanic barrios in Denton, Texas. *Urban Anthropology* 34:281–303.

Curran, W. (2007). "From the frying pan to the oven": Gentrification and the experience of industrial displacement in Williamsburg, Brooklyn. *Urban Studies* 44:1427–40.

Curran,W., & S. Hanson. (2005). Getting globalized: Urban policy and industrial displacement in Williamsburg, Brooklyn. *Urban Geography* 26:461–82.

Dalla, R. L., & A. Christensen. (2005). Latino immigrants describe residence in rural midwestern meatpacking communities: A longitudinal assessment of social and economic change. *Hispanic Journal of Behavioral Sciences* 27: 23–42.

Dana, L. (2008). *Handbook of research on ethnic minority entrepreneurship*. Northampton, Mass.: Edward Elgar.

Danes, S. M., J. Lee, K. Stafford, & R.K.Z. Heck. (2008). The effects of ethnicity, families and culture on entrepreneurial experience: An extension of sustainable family business theory. *Journal of Developmental Entrepreneurship* 13:229–68.

Datel, R., & D. Dingemans. (2006). Immigrant space and place in suburban Sacramento. In Furuseth & Smith 2006, 171–99.

Davies-Netzley, S. A. (1999). *Exploring Latina entrepreneurship*. Irvine: Center for Research on Latinos in a Global Society, University of California, Irvine.

Davila, A. (2001). Latinos inc.: *The marketing and making of a people*. Berkeley: University of California Press.

———. (2004a). *Barrio dreams: Puerto Ricans, Latinos, and the neoliberal city*. Berkeley: University of California Press.

———. (2004b). Empowered culture? New York City's empowerment zone and the selling of El Barrio. *Annals of the American Academy of Political and Social Science* 594:49–64.

———. (2008). *Latino spin: Public image and the whitewashing of race*. New York: New York University Press.

Davis, A. E., L. A. Renzulli, & H. E. Aldrich. (2006). Mixing or matching? The influence of voluntary associations on the occupational diversity and density of small business owners' networks. *Work and Occupations* 33:47–72.

Davis, D., T. M. Deaton, D. Boyle, & J-A. Schick, eds. (2009). *Voices from the Nueva Frontera: Latino immigration in Dalton, Georgia.* Knoxville: University of Tennessee Press.

Davis, H. L. (2006, September 6). Asian Latinos: The new face of America? http://www.gather.com (accessed May 12, 2009).

Davis, M. (2000). *Magical urbanism:Latinos reinvent the US big city.* New York: Verso.

Davis, R. (2008). The heard voice: The emergence of the Hispanic across the Mid-West, 1971–1985. *Journal of Latino-Latin American Studies* 3:4–15.

DeBaise, C. (2006, November 22). Hispanic entrepreneurs succeed in fertile Latino market. *Small Business.com.* http://www.smsmallbiz.com/marketing/ (accessed September 21, 2009).

Defilippis, J., R. Fisher, & E. Shragge. (2006). Neither romance nor regulation: Re-evaluating community. *International Journal of Urban and Regional Research* 30, 3:673–89.

De Haan, L., & A. Zoomers. (2005). Exploring the frontiers of livelihoods research. *Development & Change* 36, 1:24–47.

De la Garza, R., & L. SeSipio. (2006). *New dimensions of Latino participation.* Los Angeles: Thomas Rivera Policy Institute Symposium, University of California.

De la Isla, J. (2007, August 9). Commentary: Candidates need to recognize Latino middle class. *Huntington News.* http://www.huntingtonnews.net/columns/070809-shns-columnsmiddleclass.html (accessed October 9, 2009).

Delapa, R. M., J. A. Mayer, J. Candekaria, N. Hammond, S. Peplinski, C. DeMoor, G. Talavera, & J. Elder. (1990). Food purchase patterns in a Latino community: Project Salsa. *Journal of Nutrition Education* 22:133–36.

Delgado, E. (2005). Incorporating the untapped: The case of Memphis Tennessee. *Urban and Regional Planning Economic Development Handbook.* http://www.umich.edu/-econdeu/informaleconomyus/ (accessed May 6, 2009).

Delgado, E. A., & M. E. Canabal. (2006). Factors associated with negative spillover from job to home among Latinos in the United States. *Journal of Family and Economic Issues* 27:92–112.

Delgado, M. (1996). Puerto Rican food establishments as social service organizations: Results of an asset assessment. *Journal of Community Practice* 3:57–70.

———. (1997). Role of Latina-owned beauty parlors in a Latino community. *Social Work* 42:445–53.

———. (1998a). *Social work practice in nontraditional settings.* New York: Oxford University Press.

———. (1998b). Latina-owned businesses: Community resources for the prevention field. *Journal of Primary Prevention* 18:447–60.

———. (1999). *Social work practice in nontraditional urban settings.* New York: Oxford University Press.

———. (2000). *Community social work practice in an urban context: The potential of a capacity enhancement paradigm.* New York: Oxford University Press.

———. (2003). *Death at an early age and the urban scene: The case for memorial murals and community healing.* Westport, Conn.: Praeger.

———. (2004). *Social youth entrepreneurship: The potential for youth and community transformation* Westport, Conn.: Praeger.

———. (2006). *Designs and methods for youth-led research.* Thousand Oaks, Calif.: Sage.

———. (2007). *Social work practice with Latinos: A cultural assets paradigm.* New York: Oxford University Press.

———. (2008). Urban social work practice. In. *Encyclopedia of Social Work*, ed. T. Mizrahi & L. E. Davis, 251–57. New York: Oxford University Press.

———. (forthcoming). *Ex-Inmates of color and community re-entry: The potential of small businesses aiding the re-entry process.* Boulder, Colo.: Lynne Rienner.

Delgado, M., & K. Barton. (1998). Murals in Latino communities: Social indicators of community strengths. *Social Work* 43:346–56.

Delgado, M., & D. Humm-Delgado. (forthcoming). *Asset assessments and community social work practice.* New York: Oxford University Press.

Delgado, M., L. K. Jones, & M. Rohani. (2005). *Social work practice with immigrant and refugee youth in the United States.* Boston: Allyn & Bacon.

Delgado, M., & J. Santiago. (1998). Botanical shops in a Puerto Rican/Dominican community in New England: Implications for health and human services. *Social Work* 43:183–86.

Delgado, M., & L. Staples. (2008). *Youth-led community organizing: Theory and action.* New York: Oxford University Press.

Delgado, M., & H. Zhou. (2008). *Youth-led health promotion in urban communities: A capacity-enhancement perspective.* Lanham, Md: Rowman & Littlefield.

Democratic Policy Committee. (2005, September 15). *New communities and opportunities: Perspectives on emerging Latino populations.* Washington, D.C.: United States Senate.

———. (2008, April 22). *Hispanic small businesses: Diversity, economic growth, and job creation in America.* Washington, D.C.: United States Senate.

DePalma, A. (2005a, May 26). Fifteen years on the bottom rung: Mexican immigrants and the specter of an enduring underclass. *New York Times*, A1, A16–A17.

———. (2005b, May 27). Who has work? He who finds busboys: Employment agency heeds call for Mexican kitchen help in New York. *New York Times*, A20.

DeRienzo, H. (2008). *The concept of community: Lessons from the Bronx*. Milan: IPOC di Piero Condemi.

Diaz, D. R. (2005). *Barrio urbanism: Chicanos, planning, and American cities*. New York: Routledge.

Diaz, S., S. O. Mercer, & N. E. Vargas. (2007). *Healthy investments: Promoting health access for Latino & minority small businesses*. Los Angeles: Latino Issues Forum.

Diaz-Briquets, S. (2004). The evolution and characteristics of Cuban-owned firms in the United States. *Cuban Studies* 35:87–104.

Diaz Mcconnell, E., & F. Miraftab. (2008). Sundown town to "Mexican Town": Old-timers and newcomers in small town America. Paper presented at the Population Association of America Conference, New Orleans.

Dickerson, M. (2002, April 3). Latino job seekers find "Born in USA" not enough. *Los Angeles Times*, A-1.

Dobransky, K. (2007). City folk: Survival strategies of tradition-bearing organizations. *Poetics* 35:239–61.

Dolnick, S. (2009, October 20). For African immigrants, Bronx culture clash turns violent. *New York Times*, A23.

Donato, K. M., M. Stainback, & C. L. Bankston III. (2005). The economic incorporation of Mexican immigrants in Southern Louisiana: A tale of two cities. In Zuniga & Hernandez-Leon 2005, 76–100.

Donato, K. M., C. Tolbert, A. Nucci, & Y. Kawano. (2008). Changing faces, changing places: The emergence of the nonmetropolitan immigrant gateways. In Massey 2008, 75–98.

Dougherty, S. (2005). Riding the rising wave of Hispanic buying power. *EconSouth*, Spring, 1–3.

Dougherty, T. (2001). Hispanic purchasing power takes off. *Hispanic Magazine*, June, 23–24.

Dreier, C. (2006). Katrina on power in America. *Urban Affairs Review* 41:528–49.

Dresser, L. (2008). Cleaning and caring in the home: Shared problems? Shared possibilities? Madison: Center on Wisconsin's Strategy.

Drever, A. I. (2008). New Orleans: An emerging Latino destination. *Journal of Cultural Geography* 25:287–303.

Du, S., S. Sen, & C. B. Bhattacharya. (2008). Exploring the social and business returns of a corporate oral health initiative aimed at disadvantaged Hispanic families. *Journal of Consumer Research* 35:483–94.

Duany, J., & F. V. Matos-Rodriguez. (2006). Puerto Ricans in Orlando and central Florida. http://hispanicchamber.net/net/images/pdf/puerto_ricans-orl.pdf (accessed March 29, 2009).

Duncan, B., V. J. Hotz, & S. J. Trejo. (2006). Hispanics in the U.S. labor market. In Tienda & Mitchell 2006, 228–90.

Duneier, M. (1999). *SIDEWALK*. New York: Farrar, Straus & Giroux.

Dunn, T. J., A. M. Aragones, & G. Shivers (2005). Recent Mexican migration in the rural Delmarva Peninsula: Human rights versus citizenship rights in a local context. In Zuniga & Hernandez-Leon 2005, 155–83.

Durand, J., D. S. Massey, & C. Capoferro, C. (2005). The new geography of Mexican immigration. In Zuniga & Hernandez-Leon 2005, 1–20.

Durand, J., E. Telles, & J. Flashman. (2006). The demographic foundation of the Latino population. In Tienda & Mitchell 2006, 66–99.

Dymski, G. A., & R. E. Weems, R.E. (2005). Black-owned banks: Past and present. In Conrad et al. 2005, 246–51.

Dymski, G., L. Wei, C. Aldana, & H-H. Ahn. (2010). Ethnobanking in the USA: From antidiscrimination vehicles to transnational entities. *International Journal of Globalisation* 4, 2:163–91.

Eckholm, E. (2007, May 25). In market, hopes for health and urban renewal. *New York Times*, A12.

Economist. (2007, June 16). Ethnic towns: Chinatown times ten. *Economist*, 16.

Edgecomb, E. L., & M. M. Armington. (2003). *The informal economy: Latino enterprises at the margins.* Washington, D.C.: Aspen Institute.

Edwards, K., & M. Ram. (2006). Surviving on the margins of the economy: Working relationships in small, low-wage firms. *Journal of Management Studies* 43, 4: 895–916.

Egan, T. (2005, March 24). Vibrant cities find one thing missing: Children. *New York Times*, 16.

Egbert, H. (2009). Business success through social networks? A comment on social networks and business success. *American Journal of Economics and Sociology* 68:665–72.

El Nasser, H. (2005, February 15). "New urbanism" embraces Latinos. *USA Today*, 1.

———. (2008, June 30). Latino growth stimulates local economy: Jump in Hispanic energies economy in Kansas county. *USA Today*, 1.

Ellin, N. (2006). *Integral urbanism*. New York: Routledge.

Elwood, S. (2006). Beyond cooptation or resistance: Urban spatial politics, community organizations, and GIS-based spatial narratives. *Annals of the American Geographers* 96:323–41.

Esmalloffice.com. (2007). Hispanic Entrepreneurs. http://www.esmalloffice.com (accessed April 20, 2009).

Entman, R. M. (2006). *Young men of color in the media: Images and impacts.* Washington, D.C.: Joint Center for Political and Economic Studies.

Erick, P. C., E. P. C. Chang, E. Memili, J. J. Chrisman, F. W. Kellermanns, & J. H. Chua. (2009). Family social capital, venture preparedness, and start-up decisions. *Family Business Review* 22, 3:279–92.

Estabrook, M., Y. Sakano, S. Tubb, D. Varela, & R. Williams. (2005). *Grocery stores and social capital: A study of seven Cincinnati neighborhoods.* Cincinnati: University of Cincinnati.

Estrada, W. D. (2006). *Los Angeles' Olvera Street.* Portsmouth, N.H.: Arcadia.

Fainstein, S. S., & J. C. Powers. (2005). *Tourism and New York's ethnic diversity.* Cambridge: Harvard School of Design.

Fairlie, R. W. (2004). Recent trends in ethnic and racial business ownership. *Small Business Economics* 23:203–18.

———. (2007). Entrepreneurship among disadvantaged groups: Women, minorities and the less educated. *The Life Cycles of Entrepreneurial Ventures* 3: 437–75.

———. (2008). Estimating the contribution of immigrant business owners to the U.S. economy. Washington, D.C.: Small Business Administration.

Fairlie, R. W., & A. Robb. (2004). *Families, human capital, and small business: evidence from the characteristics of business owners' survey.* IZA Discussion Paper no. 1296; Yale University Economic Growth Center Discussion Paper no. 871.

Fairle, R. W., & C. Woodruff. (2007). *Mexican-American entrepreneurship.* Kansas City, Ks.: Kauffman Foundation.

Falconi, J. L., & J. A. Mazzotti, eds. (2007). *The other Latinos: Central and South Americans in the United States.* Cambridge: Harvard University Press.

Farr, G. E. (1994, April). *Spanish Merchants Association of Philadelphia.* http://www .hsp.org/collections/Balch%20manuscript_guide/html/spanishmerchants.html (accessed May 20, 2009).

Farrar, L. (2007, August 19). It can take a village to send Hispanics to final home. *Boston Globe*, 1.

Faura, J. (2006). *Hispanic marketing grows up: Exploring perceptions and facing realities.* New York: Paramount Books.

Fennelly, K. (2005). Latinos, Africans and, Asians in the North Star state: Immigrant communities in Minnesota. In *Beyond the gateway: Immigrants in a chang-*

ing America: Migration and refugee studies, ed. E. M. Gozdziak & S. F. Martin, 111–36. Lanham, Md: Lexington Books.

———. (2008). Prejudice toward immigrants in the Midwest. In Massey (2008), 151–78.

Fennelly, K., & M. Orfield. (2008). Impediments to integration of immigrants: A case study in the Twin Cities. In Singer, Bretelle, Hardwick 2008, 200–25.

Ferguson, K. M., & N. Islam. (2008). Conceptualizing outcomes with street-living young adults. *Qualitative Social Work* 7:217–37.

Ferguson, K. M., & B. Xie. (2008). Feasibility study of the social enterprise intervention with homeless youth. *Research on Social Work Practice* 18:5–19.

Fernandez, M. (2007a, May11). Latin food at Yankee Stadium. Now, how about that! *New York Times*, A21.

———. (2007b, September 14). Cash to get by is still pawnshop's stock in trade. *New York Times*, A1, A18.

Feuer, A. (2003, September 6). Ethnic chasm in El Barrio: Changes pit Mexicans against Puerto Ricans. *New York Times*, A10.

Filkins, D. (2001, April 1). From Mexico, with faith: Four nuns serve in a place of need. *New York Times*, 25.

Fischer, M. J., & M. Tienda. (2006). Redrawing spatial color lines: Hispanic metropolitan dispersal, segregation, and economic opportunity. In Tienda & Mitchell 2006, 100–37.

Flanigan, J. (2006, March 16). Exploding Latino market becomes attractive to banks. *New York Times*, A24.

———. (2009, June 18). Thriving on Mexican-American market. *New York Times*, 11.

Fleischer, F., & E. Suraez. (2007). *The changing face of Hispanic middle-class and affluent.* Denver: Cohn Marketing.

Florida, R. (2002). *The rise if the creative class . . . and how it's transforming work, leisure, community, and everyday life.* New York: Basic Books.

Foner, N., ed. (2001). *New immigrants in New York.* New York: Columbia University Press.

Fonseca, M., J. George, M. Girgis, M. Langer, A. Mont, S. Robinson, & M. Sriram. (2009). *Improving the use of asset-building financial services by Latino immigrants in Langley Park, Maryland.* College Park, Md.: Digital Repository, University of Maryland.

Fraser, E.D.G., A. J. Dougill, M. S. Reed, & P. McAlpine. (2006). Bottom up and top down: Analysis of participatory processes for sustainability indicator identification as a pathway to community empowerment and sustainable environmental management. *Journal of Environmental Management* 78:114–27.

Frederick, H. H. (2008). Introduction to special issue on indigenous entrepreneurships. *Journal of Enterprising Communities: People and Places in the Global Economy* 2:185–91.

Fretty, P., & S. P. Rhodes. (2005). *"A piece of the pie."* Denver: Outskirts Press.

Frey, N. (2009a, March 20). *Bursting "migration bubble" favors coastal metros, urban cores.* Washington, D.C.: Brookings Institution.

———. (2009b, March). *Getting current: Recent demographic trends in metropolitan America.* Washington, D.C.: Brookings Institution.

Fried, B. (2009). *A new kind of market economics: Three ambitious projects launch low-income entrepreneurs on the road to success.* New York: Project for Public Spaces.

Frosch, D. (2009, February 2). Paying taxes, and fearing deportation. *New York Times*, A9.

Fry, R. (2008). *Latino settlement in the new century.* Washington, D.C.: Pew Hispanic Center.

———. (2009). *Latino children: A majority are U.S.-born offspring of immigrants.* Washington, D.C.: Pew Hispanic Center.

Fry, R., & F. Gonzalez. (2008). *One-in-five and growing fast: A profile of Hispanic public school students.* Washington, D.C.: Pew Hispanic Center.

Furuseth, O. J. (2005). Change in rural North Carolina: The new Latino presence. In *Rural change and sustainability: Agriculture, the environment and communities*, ed. S. J. Essex, A. W. Gilig, R. Yarwood, J. Smithers, & R. Wilson, 281–94. Wallingford, UK: CBI Publishing International.

———. (2010). A new rural North Carolina: Latino place-making and community engagement. In *The next rural economics: Constructing rural place in global economies*, ed. G. Halseth, S. Markey, & D. Bruce, 45–58. Wallingford, UK: CAB International.

Furuseth, O. J., & H. A. Smith, eds. (2006). *Latinos in the new South.* Surrey, England: Ashgate.

Gabel, J. R., & J. D. Pickreign. (2004, April). Risky business: When mom and pop buy health insurance for their employees. *Issue Brief*, 1–8.

Gaines, J. (2008, January). Looming boom: Texas through 2030. *Texas Economy*, 1–6.

Galbraith, C. S, C. L. Rodriguez, & C. H. Stiles. (2007). Social capital as a club good: The case of ethnic communities and entrepreneurship. *Journal of Enterprising Communities: People and Places in the Global Economy* 1:38–53.

Galbraith, C. S, C. H. Stiles, & C. L. Rodriguez. (2003). Patterns of trade in ethnic enclaves: A study of Arab and Hispanic small businesses. *Journal of Small Business and Entrepreneurship* 16:1–12.

Galperin, B. L. (2007). Cuban-American entrepreneurs in Tampa, Florida: An evolutionary perspective. *International Journal of Business and Globalisation* 1:222–40.

Galst, L. (2008, March 8). Banks springing up to serve the underserved. *New York Times*, B6.

Garcia, G. (2004). *The new mainstream: How the multicultural consumer is transforming American business*. New York: HarperCollins.

Garcia, J. A. (2003). *Latino politics in America: Community, culture, and interests*. Lanham, Md.: Rowman & Littlefield.

Garcia, J. L. (2006). *Promoting sustainable agriculture among Latino farmers*. http://agebb.missouri.edu/sustain/lac/sustainaglatino.pdf (accessed May 21, 2009).

Garcia, L., & M. Rua. (2007). Processing Latinidad: Mapping Latino urban landscapes through Chicago ethnic festivals. *Latino Studies* 5:317–39.

Garcia, O., & L. Mason. (2008). Where in the world is US Spanish. In *Language and poverty*, ed. W. Harbert, S. McConnell-Ginet, & A. Miller, 78–101. Bristol, UK: Multilingual Matters.

Garcia, S. (2006). Banks slow to cater to Latino business customers. *San Fernando Valley Business Journal*, 2.

Gates, C. A. (1938). The social worker in the service of the small loan business. *Annals of the American Academy of Political and Social Science* 196:221–24.

Gawgy, K. (2006, April 4). Agencies reach, but still miss some Latino businesses. *Gazette.net*. http://www.gazette.net (accessed May 9, 2009).

Gay, C. (2006). The effects of economic disparity of Black attitudes towards Latinos. *American Journal of Political Science* 50:982–97.

George, S. (2007). *Little Havana, Florida*. Portsmouth, N.H.: Arcadia.

Georgarakos, D., & K. Tatsiramos. (2009). Entrepreneurship and survival dynamics of immigrants to the U.S. and their descendents. *Labour Economics* 16:161–70.

Gerson, D. (2006, March 22). New York leads nation in growth rate of Hispanic-owned business. *New York Sun*, 1.

Getz, D., & J. Carlson. (2005). Family business in tourism: State of the art. *Annals of Tourism Research* 32:237–58.

Giese, G., & D. Snyder. (2009). An outlook on the growing Hispanic market segment and the absence abilities of the U.S. banking industry to effectively penetrate the Hispanic market segment. *Journal of Business and Economic Research* 7:103–11.

Gillium, J. C. (2009, March 31). Minority, mostly Hispanic, flock to suburban schools. *USA Today*, 1.

Glasser, R. (2006). Mofongo meets mango: Dominicans reconfigure Latino Waterbury. In Torres 2006, 103–24.

Goldman, K. D., & K. J. Schmatz. (2005). "Accentuate the positive": Using an asset-mapping tool as part of a community-health needs assessment. *Health Promotion Practice* 6, 2:125–28.

Goldman Sachs. (2007). *US Hispanization: Long/short strategies.* New York: Goldman Sachs.

Gonzalez, D. (2009, April 26). A family divided by 2 words, legal and illegal. *New York Times*, 1, 20–21.

Gonzalez-Rivera, C. (2008, December 9). *Report-card ranks best and worst small business lending to minorities.* Berkeley, Calif.: Greenling Institute.

Goodman, S. (2008, May 13). A tenuous prosperity lost: Hispanics, who benefited from expansion, are hit hard by slump. *New York Times*, C1–C4.

Googins, B., V. Capoccia, & N. Kaufman. (1983) "Interactional Dimensions of Planning: A Framework for Practice," *Social Work* 28:273–78.

Grady, S. M. (2007). Understanding differences. *Nevada's Silver and Blue*, 31–32.

Graglia, D. (2009). From coast to coast, Latino small business owners at risk. *FT2W*. http://feetin2worlds.wordpress.com/2009/02/16/from-coast-to coast-la (accessed April 3, 2009).

Grainer, M. (2006). *Hispanic entrepreneurship: A comparison of two Georgia communities.* Atlanta: Georgia Institute of Technology.

Green, G. P., & A. Haines. (2008). *Asset building and community development.* Second edition. Thousand Oaks, Calif.: Sage.

Green, M. B., & R. B. McNaughton. (2008). The rise and fall of specialized small business investment: Taking the taxi to oblivion. In Dana 2008, 289–308.

Greene, G., & M. M. Owen. (2004). Race and ethnicity. In *Handbook of entrepreneurial dynamics: The process of business creation*, ed. W. B. Gartner, K. G. Shaver, N. M. Carter, & D. Reynolds, 26–38. Thousand Oaks, Calif.: Sage.

Greenhouse, S. (2005, September 6). Union organizers at poultry plants in South find newly sympathetic ears. *New York Times*, A15.

———. (2007a, April 15). At Asian restaurants where delivery is a mainstay, workers sue over wages. *New York Times*, 24.

———. (2007b, August 19). At nail salons, beauty can have a distinctly unglamorous side. *New York Times*, A22.

Grenier, G. J., L. Perez, S. C. Chun, & H. Gladwin. (2007). There are Cubans, there are Cubans, and there are Cubans: Ideology diversity among Cuban Americans in Miami. In Montero-Sieburth & Melendez 2007, 93–111.

Greve, A., & J. W. Salaff. (2005). Social network approach to understand the ethnic economy: A theoretical discourse. *GeoJournal* 64:7–16.

Grey, M. A. (2006). Obstacles and opportunities: Latino-owned small businesses in Iowa. *Journal of Latino-Latin American Studies* 2:1–23.

Grey, M. A., N. M. Rodriguez, & A. Conrad. (2004). *Immigrant and refugee small business development in Northeast Iowa.* Cedar Falls: University of Northern Iowa.

Grey, M. A., & A. C. Woodrick. (2005). "Latinos have revitalized our community": Mexican migration and Anglo responses in Marshalltown, Iowa. In Zuniga & Hernandez-Leon 2005, 133–54.

Grier, S., & S. K. Kumanyika. (2008). The context for choice: Health implications of targeted food and beverage marketing to African Americans. *American Journal of Public Health* 98:1616–29.

Griffith, D. C. (2005). Rural industry and Mexican immigration and settlement in North Carolina. In Zuniga & Hernandez-Leon 2005, 50–75.

Grimaldi, P. (2009, May 15). Latino small business owners banking on unity for empowerment. *DomesticBank.com.* http://www.domestic.com/en/news_2html (accessed May 15, 2009).

Gross, J. S. (2005). Business improvement districts in New York City's low-income and high-income neighborhoods. *Economic Development Quarterly* 19:174–89.

Grossman, L. P. (2007). *Increasing wealth in the Latino community: A TRPI Conference Summary Report.* Los Angeles: Tomas Rivera Policy Institute, University of Southern California.

Grow, B. (2004, March 15). Hispanic nation. *Business Week*, 59–62, 66, 68, 70.

Gruidl, J., & D. M. Markley. (2009). Entrepreneurship as a community development strategy. In Phillips & Pittman 2009, 220–35.

Guerra, A. M. (2007). Innovative library programs for the Hispanic population: Opportunities for the public library administrator. In *Advances in library administration and organization*, ed. E. D. Garten, D. W. Williams, & J. M. Nyce, 24:249–318. San Diego: JAI Press.

Gulina, M. (2007, March 20). *Moving the needle—VCs focus on the Hispanic demographics.* New York: Young Venture Capital Society.

Gutierrez, R. A., ed. (2009). *Mexicans in California: Transformations and challenges.* Urbana: University of Illinois Press.

Gutierrez, V. F., S. Wallace, & X. Castaneda. (2004). Demographic profile of Mexican immigrants in the United States. *Health Policy Fact Sheet.* UCLA Center for Health Policy Research.

Hacker, G. A., R. Collins, & M. Jacobson. (1987). *Marketing booze to Blacks.* Washington, D.C.: Center for Science in the Public Interest.

Hagan, J., & S. L. Phillips. (2008). Border blunders: The unanticipated human and economic costs of the U.S. approach to immigration control. *Criminology & Public Policy* 7:79–96.

Hagerty, M., J. Vogel, & V. Moller. (2002). Introduction. *Social Indicators Research* 58:1–8.

Halbfinger, D. M. (2010, February 1). Brooklyn fire victims mourned in two countries. *New York Times*, A12–A13.

Halkias, D. (2007). *Characteristics and business profile of immigrant owned small firms: The case of Albanian immigrants in Greece.* San Diego: Center for Comparative Immigrant Studies, University of California, San Diego.

Halter, M., ed. (1995). *New migrants in the marketplace: Boston's ethnic entrepreneurs.* Amherst: University of Massachusetts Press.

———. (2000). *Shopping for identity: The marketing of ethnicity.* New York: Schocken.

Hammann, E-M., A. Habisch, & H. Pechlaner, H. (2009). Values that create value: Socially responsible business practices in SMEs—empirical evidence from German companies. *Business Ethics: A European Review* 18:37–51.

Hammel, L., & G. Denhart. (2007). *Growing local value: How to build business partnerships that strengthen your community.* San Francisco: Berrett-Koehler.

Hamilton, N., & N. S. Chinchilla. (2001). *Seeking community in a global city: Guatemalans and Salvadorans in Los Angeles.* Philadelphia: Temple University Press.

Hardcastle, D. A., S. Wenocur, & P. R. Powers. (1997). *Community practice: Theories and skills for social workers.* New York: Oxford University Press.

Harris, I. C. (2009). Ethnicity effects on the family business entrepreneurial process. *Family Business Review* 22, 3:293–96.

Harris, P. (2007, November 4). Viva la revolution!: For decades, Hispanics have existed mainly in the shadows of the American dream. *Observer* (England), 26.

Harvey, D. (2000). *Spaces of hope.* Berkeley: University of California Press.

Harvey, J., & D. Lionais. (2004). Depleted communities and community based entrepreneurship: Revaluing space through place. *Entrepreneurship & Regional Development: An International Journal* 16:217–33.

Haverluk, T. W., & L. D. Trautman. (2008). The changing geography of US Hispanics from 1990–2006: A shift to the South and Midwest. *Journal of Geography* 107:87–101.

Hayes-Bautista, D. E. (2004a). Community action research with Census data: The Latino Coalition for a New Los Angeles, 1992–1993. In *Latino social policy: A participatory research model*, ed. J. Mora & D. R. Diaz, 229–44. New York: Haworth Press.

———. (2004b). *La nueva California: Latinos in the Golden State.* Berkeley: University of California Press.

Hendix, S. (2009, July 12). Outlaws in the U.S., strangers at home; downturn strands illegal Latino immigrants between cultures. *Washington Post*, A1.

Henry, T. (2001, May 23). Latino students get help. *USA Today*, A3.

Hernandez, D. M. (2002). Latino demographic growth: Gone today, here tomorrow. *American Quarterly* 54:129–37.

Hernandez, D. (2006). Quite crisis: A community history of Latinos in Cambridge, Massachusetts. In Torres 2006, 149–70.

Hernandez, S. A., & C. M. Newman. (2006). Minding our business: A model of service-learning in entrepreneurship education. *Journal of Entrepreneurship Education* 9:53–59.

Hirschman, C. (2005). Immigration and the American century. *Demography* 12:595–620.

Hirschman, C., & D. S. Massey, (2008). Places and peoples: The new American mosaic. In Massey 2008, 1–21.

Hispanic Advocacy & Community Empowerment Through Research. (2004). *The economic impact of Latino entrepreneurship in Richmond*. Minneapolis: Hispanic Advocacy & Community Empowerment Through Research.

Hispanic Business & Entrepreneurship. (2007). *Contacto Business News*. http://www.contactomagazine.com/biznews/hispanicbizdata0307.htm (accessed May 2, 2009).

HispanicBusiness.com. (2009, October 9). Many African-American and Latino families in danger of falling out of middle class, according to new report. *HispanicBusiness.com*. http://www.hispanicbusiness.com/news/2009/7/28/many_africanamerican _and_Latino_families_in.htm (accessed October 9, 2009).

Hispanic.com. (2007). Hispanic statistics and research. http://hispanic.com (accessed April 15, 2009).

Hispanic Federation. (2002). *Abriendo caminos: Strengthening Latino communities through giving and volunteering*. New York: Author.

Hispanic Market Weekly. (2008, July 7). Banking on the dollars: A special report on financial services in the U.S. Hispanic market. *Hispanic Market Weekly*, 1–11.

Hispanic Market Weekly. (2009, March 2). Latino buying power in growth mode. Author, p.1.

Hoffman, W. (2004, June 11). Interest growing in local Hispanic bank. *Dallas Business Journal*. http://www.bizjournals.com/dallas/stories/2004/06/14/stories4.html (accessed May 9, 2009).

Hohn, M. (2005). Immigrant entrepreneurs: A key to Boston's neighborhood revitalization. *Communities & Banking*, Summer, 20–27.

Holguin, J., E. Gamboa, & F. Hoy. (2007). Challenges and opportunities for Hispanic entrepreneurs in the United States. In Dana 2008, 195–211.

Holvino, E. (2008). Latinos y Latinas in the workplace: How much progress have we made? *CDO Insights* 2:1–13.

Hondagneu-Sotelo, P. (2001). *Domestica: Immigrant workers cleaning and caring in the shadows of affluence*. Berkeley: University of California Press.

Howard, P. H., & B. Fulfrost. (2008). *The density of retail food outlets in the Central coast region of California: Association with income and Latino ethnic composition*. Santa Cruz: Center for Agroecology & Sustainable Food Systems, University of California, Santa Cruz.

Hoy, F. (2008). Hispanic entrepreneurship in the United States. In Dana 2008, 177–94.

Huck, P., S. L. W. Rhine, P. Bond, & R. Townsend. (1999). Small business finance in two Chicago minority neighborhoods. *Economic Perspectives, Federal Reserve Bank of Chicago*, 48–59.

Hudson, M. (1996). *Merchants of misery: How corporate America profits from poverty*. Monroe, Me.: Common Courage Press.

Huerta, A. (2007). Looking beyond "mow, blow and go": A case study of Mexican immigrant gardeners in Los Angeles. *Berkeley Planning Journal* 20:1-19.

Hum, T. (2001). The promises and dilemmas of immigrant ethnic economies. In Lopez-Garza & Diaz 2001, 77–101.

———. (2005). Immigration grows to half of New York's labor force. *Regional Labor Review*, Spring, 20–24.

Humbles, A. (2009, September 16). Latino businesses in Tennessee grow. *Latino Business Review*. http://latinobusinessreview.blogspot.com/2009/09/latinos-businesses-in-tennessee-grow.html (accessed September 19, 2009).

Humphreys, J. M. (2006). The multicultural economy 2006. *Georgia Business and Economic Conditions* 66:1–15.

Huppe, F., R. Turgeon, T. Ryan, & C. Vanasse. (2006). Fostering pollution prevention in small business: The Enviroclub initiative. *Journal of Cleaned Production* 14:563–71.

Hutchinson, B. O. (2005). Black capitalism: Self-help or self-delusion. In Conrad et al. 2005, 271–80.

Hyland, A., M. J. Travers, K. M. Cummings, J. Bauer, T. Alford, & W. F. Wieczorek. (2003). Demographics and tobacco outlet density. *American Journal of Public Health* 93:1794.

Hyland, S. E., ed. (2005). *Community building in the twenty-first century*. Santa Fe: School of American Research Press.

Ibarra, B., & E. Rodriguez. (2005–2006). Closing the wealth gap: Eliminating structural barriers to building assets in the Latino community. *Harvard Journal of Hispanic Policy* 18, 1:25–38.

Ibarra, N. (2007, April 16). Survey: Hispanics claim largest piece of minority-business pie. *Hispanic Business*. http://www.hispanicbusiness.com/news/newsbyid.asp?id=61704 (accessed April 19, 2007).

Iber, J., & A. DeLeon. (2005). *Hispanics in the American West.* Santa Barbara: ABC-CLIO.

Illinois Coalition for Immigrant and Refugee Rights. (2009). *The political and economic power of immigrants, Latinos, and Asians in Illinois.* Chicago: Illinois Coalition for Immigrant and Refugee Rights.

Immigration Policy Center. (2009, February 20). *New Americans in the silver state: The political and economic power of immigrants, Latinos, and Asians in Nevada.* Washington, D.C.: Immigration Policy Center.

Inagarni, S., D. A. Cohen, B. K. Finch, & S. M. Asch. (2006). You are where you shop: Grocery store locations, weight, and neighborhoods. *American Journal of Preventive Medicine* 31:10–17.

Inglessis, M., H. McGavock, & F. Korzenny. (2009). Hispanic TV advertising, where did all the mariachis go? *Journal of Spanish Language Media* 2:3–154.

Institute for Health Policy Studies. (2002). *Fact sheet on Latino youth: Population.* San Francisco: Center for Reproductive Health Research and Policy.

Irazabal, C., & R. Farhat. (2008). Latino communities in the United States: Place-making in the pre–World War II, postwar, and contemporary city. *Journal of Planning Literature* 22:207–28.

Irwin, M., & I. Sharkova. (1998). Social capital of local communities. *Metroscope,* 13–19,

Iwata, E. (2008, August 6). Private equity says "hola" to Latino firms. *USA Today*, A.6.

Jankowski, C., T. Rice, & R. D. Porter. (2007). Against the tide—currency use among Latin American immigrants in Chicago. *Economic Perspectives* 31:2–21.

Jenkins, H. (2006). Small business champions for corporate social responsibility. *Journal of Business Ethics* 67:241–56.

Jensen-Campbell, C. (2005). *Today's Hispanic consumer.* http://www.usdm.net (accessed April 21, 2009).

Johnson, B. (2004). *An unlikely fit: Will the undocumented apply for a temporary status.* Washington, D.C.: Immigration Policy Center.

Johnson, H., & R. Sengupta. (2009). *Closing the gap: Meeting California's need for college graduates*. Sacramento: Public Policy Institute of California.

Johnson, J. H., G. C. Burthey, & K. Ghorm. (2008). Economic globalization and the Future of Black America. *Journal of Black Studies* 38:883–99.

Johnson, K. M., & D. T. Lichter. (2008a). *Population growth in new Hispanic destinations.* Carsey Institute, University of New Hampshire, 8, 1–5.

———. (2008b). *Hispanic natural increase: A growing source of population growth in urban and rural America.* http://paa2008.princeton.edu (accessed April 16, 2009).

Johnson, R. B. (2004). Mixed methods research: A research paradigm whose time has come. *Educational Researcher* 33:14–26.

Johnston, D. F., & M. J. Carley. (1981). Social measurement and social indicators. *Annals of the American Academy of Political and Social Sciences* 453:237–53.

Johnstone, H., & D. Lionais. (2004). Depleted communities and community business entrepreneurship: Resolving space through place. *Entrepreneurship and Regional Development* 16, 3:217–33.

Jonas, J. (2009, March 30). Small business: Suffering in good times and bad. *Gotham Gazette: New York City News and Policy.* http://www.gothamgazette .com/article/fea/20009030/202/2873 (accessed April 4, 2009).

Jones, N. (2007). *Keeping count: An assessment of the data on Washington's Latino-owned businesses.* Seattle: Daniel J. Evans School of Public Affairs, University of Washington.

Jones, R. C. (2008). The ambiguous role of suburbanization and immigration in ethnic segregation: The case of San Antonio. *Urban Geography* 29:196–223.

Jones, S. (2005, August 4). Spanish-spiced hip-hop. *USA Today*, 4.

Jones, S. R. (2007–2008). Supporting urban entrepreneurs: Law, policy, and the role of lawyers in small business development. *New England Law Review* 30:71–78.

Jones, T., & M. Ram. (2007). Re-embeddening the ethnic business agenda. *Work, Employment & Society* 21:439–57.

Jordan, B. (2007). *Social work and well-being.* London: Russell House.

Jordan, M. (2004, March 3). Hispanic magazines gain ad dollars. *Wall Street Journal*, 12.

Jordan, M., & V. Bauerlein. (2007, February 13). Bank of America casts wider net for Hispanics. *Wall Street Journal*, 1.

Juffer, J. (2009). Compassion and rage: The face of the immigrant. *South Atlantic Quarterly* 108:219–35.

Kandel, W., & J. Cromartie. (2004). *New patterns of Hispanic settlement in rural America.* Washington, D.C.: United States Department of Agriculture.

Kandel, W., & E. A. Parrado. (2004). Hispanics in the American South and the transformation of the poultry industry. In Arreola 2004, 255–76.

———. (2005). Restructuring of the U.S. meat processing industry and new Hispanic migrant destinations. *Population and Development Review* 31:447–71.

Kaplan, D. H., & W. Li. (2006). *Landscapes of the ethnic economy.* Lanham, Md.: Rowman & Littlefield.

Kasarda, J. D., & J. H. Johnson. (2006). *The economic impact of the Hispanic population on the state of North Carolina.* Chapel Hill: University of North Carolina.

Kasinitz, P., J. H. Mollenkopf, & M. C. Waters, eds. (2004). *Becoming New Yorkers: Ethnographies of the new second generation.* New York: Russell Sage Foundation.

Kaufmann, M. (2007). Immigration and the future of black power in the U.S. cities. *Du Bois Review: Social Science and Research on Race* 4:79–96.

Kay, A. (2006). Social capital, the social economy and community development. *Community Development Journal* 41:160–73.

Kayitsinga, J., L. Post, & F. Villarruel. (2007). *Latino population trends and projections*. East Lansing: Julian Samora Research Institute, Michigan State University.

Kelderhouse, E. R. (2009, May 9). Banking Latino immigrants. *Hispanic Bank Marketing*, 1–3.

Kessner, J. L. (2007). *Racial and ethnic conflict in South Florida: Hurricane Andrew and the housing crisis*. Middletown, Conn.: Wesleyan University.

Kilen, M. (2009, September 13). Latinos take up farming in Iowa. *Des Moines Register*, 3.

Kilgannon, C. (2004). In Queens Park, graying ghosts of soccer's past. *New York Times*, A1, A15.

———. (2007, September 15). The hustlers and surgeons of fender dents. *New York Times*, B9.

Kim, D.Y. (2004). Leaving the ethnic economy: The rapid integration of second-Generation Korean Americans in New York. In Kasinitz, Mollenkopf, & Waters 2004, 154–88.

Kim, H-Y., L. Jolly, & Y-K. Kim. (2007). Future forces transforming apparel retailing in the United States. *Clothing and Textiles Research Journal* 25:307–22.

Kim, H., H. E. Aldrich, & L. A. Keister. (2006). Access (not) denied: The impact of financial, human, and cultural capital on entrepreneurial entry in the United States. *Small Business Economics* 27:5–22.

King, K. (2007, October 1). Hispanic entrepreneurship, buying power on the rise. *CNN.com.* http://www.CNN.com (accessed 4-9-09).

Kirchhoff, S. (2008, May 15). Slow economy hits Hispanics hard; housing bust feeds big rise in unemployment. *USA Today*, 4B.

Kirkpatrick, L. O. (2007). The two "logics" of community development: Neighborhoods, markets, and Community Development Corporations. *Politics & Society* 35:329–59.

Kirton, G. (2009). Career plans and aspirations of recent black and minority ethnic business graduates. *Work, Employment and Society* 23:12–29.

Klass, G. (2009). Just plain data analysis: Common statistical fallacies in analyses of social indicator data. Illinois State University.

Klein, S. A. (2008, March 31). The rise of Hispanics; What a great demographic shift means for Chicago's economy, business climate and the rapidly changing face of political power. *Crain's Chicago Business*, 84.

Kleiner, A. M., & J. J. Green. (2008). Expanding the marketing opportunities and sustainable production potential for minority and limited-resource agricultural producers in Louisiana and Mississippi. *Southern Rural Sociology* 23:149–69.

Klim, K., & N. Gresham-Jones. (2001). What can bankers do to better service the Latino community? *Community Development*, Summer, 1–2.

Klotkin, J. N., & D. Friedman. (1993, February 1). The Los Angeles riots: Causes, myths, and solutions. *Progressive Policy Institute*, 1–5.

Knowledge@Wharton. (2003, August 13). Hable Espanol?: Your company will soon have to do that. *Knowledge@Wharton.* http://knowledge.wharton.upenn .edu (accessed April 20, 2009).

Kochhar, R. (2004). *The wealth of Hispanic households: 1996 to 2002.* Washington, D.C.: Pew Hispanic Center.

———. (2008). *Latino labor report, 2008: Construction reverses job growth for Latinos.* Washington, D.C.: Pew Hispanic Center.

Kochhar, R., R. Suro, & S. Tafoya. (2005). *The New Latino South: The context and consequences of rapid population growth.* Washington, D.C.: Pew Hispanic Center.

Koehler, G., & V. Koehler-Jones. (2006). *Training California's new workforce for 21st century nanotechnology, MEMS, and advanced manufacturing jobs.* Workplace Learning Institute, Economic and Workforce Development, California Community Colleges.

Kollinger, P., & M. Minniti. (2006). Not for lack of trying: American entrepreneurship in Black and White. *Small Business Economics* 27:59–79.

Kontos, M. (2003). Considering the concept of entrepreneurial resources in ethnic business: Motivation as a biographer resource? *International Review of Sociology* 13:183–204.

Korgaonkar, P., R. Silverblatt, & E. Becerra. (2004). Hispanics and patronage preferences for shopping from the Internet. *Journal of Computer-Mediated Communication* 9:1–13.

Korsching, P. R., & J. C. Allen. (2004). Locality based entrepreneurship: A strategy for community economic vitality. *Community Development Journal* 39: 385–400.

Korzenny, F., & B. Korzenny. (2005). *Hispanic marketing: A cultural perspective.* Oxford: Elsevier Butterworth-Heinemann.

Kostek, J. (2009, August 9). A Dominican family's Latin food business success Dominican family is a main ingredient in successful Latin food businesses. *Tribuna* (Danbury, Conn.), 2.

Kostin, D. J. (2004). *Hispanization of the U.S.: The growing influence of the Hispanic and Latino communities in the United States economy.* New York: Goldman Sachs.

Kostrzewa, J. (2008, April 13). Carcieri, Latinos at an impasse. *Providence Journal.* http://www.projo.com/business/ (accessed September 8, 2009).

Kotkin, J. (2010). Movers & shakers: How immigrants are reviving neighborhoods given up for dead. In *Urban society: Fourteenth Edition,* ed. M. A. Levine, 23–32. Boston: McGraw Hill Higher Education.

Kraft, R. A. (2008, March 31). *Immigration agents arrest 49 during raids of Dallas night clubs.* Dallas: Kraft & Associates. http://www.immigration-law-answers-blog.com/2008/03/articles/deportation-detention/im . . . (accessed June 22, 2009).

Krauss, C. (2007, May 2). Latin American companies make big gains north of the border. *New York Times,* C1.

Kuznets, S. (1971). Notes on the pattern of U.S. economic growth. In *The reinterpretation of American economic history,* ed. R. W. Fogel & S. L. Engerman, 17–24. New York: Harper & Row.

Kyeyoung, P. (2004). Confronting the liquor industry in Los Angeles. *International Journal of Sociology & Social Policy* 24:103–36.

Lacey, M. (2009, November 16). Money starts to trickle north as Mexicans help out relatives. *New York Times,* A1, A3.

Lacho, K. J., D. B. Bradley, & M. Cusack. (2006). Business nonprofits: Helping small businesses in New Orleans survive Katrina. *Entrepreneurial Executive* 11:55–68.

Lacho, K. J., T. Parker, & K. Carter. (2005). Economics and initiatives of African-American churches in Treme: The oldest African-American neighborhood in the United States. *Journal of Economics and Economic Education Research* 6:83–106.

Landa, V. (2007, April 22). The secret behind the growing number of Latino entrepreneurs. *San Antonio Express-News,* 3H.

Lange, L. (2007, January 27). Life in Miami's colorful Little Havana stills centers on Castro. *Daily Item* (Sunbury, Penn.), C2.

Larson-Xu, A. (2008). Neighborhood based organization: Latinos and the community at large: A case study of Walla Walla, Washington. http://walatinos.org/images/Larson%20finalreport.pdf (accessed May 22, 2009).

Laskett, J. H. M. (2006, March 27). Playing catch-up: The labor movement in Los Angeles and San Francisco, 1985–2005. *Los Angeles Times,* A9.

Latino Business Review. (2009a, July 19). Latino businesses to shape economy. http://latinobusinessreview.blogspot.com/2009/07/latino-businesses-to-shape-economy.html (accessed September 8, 2009).

———. (2009b). Latinas prove construction industry not just for boys. http://latinobusinessreview.blogsport.com/2009/09/latinas-prove-construction-industry-not.html (accessed September 19, 2009).

———. (2009c, January 29). Hispanic small business owners being helped by insurers. http://latinobusinessreview.blogspot.com/2009/01/hispanic-small-business-owners-being.html (accessed September 18, 2009).

———. (2009d, July 24). Hispanic purchasing power grows in Idaho. http://latino businessreview.blogspot.com/2009/07/hispanic-purchasing-power-grows-in .html (accessed September 19, 2009).

Latino Economic Development Center (2007). *Annual report.* Minneapolis: Latino Economic Development Center.

Lavin, M. (2005). Supermarket access and consumer well-being: The case of Pathmark in Harlem. *International Journal of Retail & Distribution Management* 33:388–98.

Laws, M. B., J. Whitman, D. M. Bowser, & L. Krech. (2002). Tobacco availability and point of sale marketing in demographically contrasting districts of Massachusetts. *Tobacco Control* 11:ii71–ii73.

Le, C. N. (2007). Asian small businesses. *Asian Nation: The Landscape of Asian America"* http://www.asian-nation.org/small-business.shtml (accessed May 16, 2007).

Leach, M. A., & F. D. Bean. (2008). The structure and dynamics of Mexican migration to new destinations in the United States. In Massey 2008, 51–74.

League of United American Citizens. (2003). *LULAC outlines a vision of American as Hispanic population grows.* Washington, D.C.: League of United American Citizens.

Leder, G. (2007, December 1). The new Hispanic wealth: The success of Latin American business owners and professionals mean opportunities for advisors. *On the Wall Street.* http://www.accessmylibrary.com (accessed April 25, 2009).

Lee, J. (2002). From civil relations to racial conflict: Merchant–customer interactions in urban America. *American Sociological Review* 67:77–98.

Lee, T. (2008). Immigration and the link from racial identity to group politics. *Annual Review of Political Science* 11:457–78.

Lee, Y., & K. Park. (2008). Negotiating hybridity: Transnationalism reconstruction of migrant subjectivity in Koreatown, Los Angeles. *Journal of Cultural Geography* 25:245–62.

Leigh, W. A. (2006). Wealth measurement: Issues for people of color in the United States. In Nembhard & Chiteji 2006, 23–66.

Lejano, R. P. (2006). Community and economic development: Seeking common ground in discourse and in practice. *Urban Studies* 43:1469–89.

Lepoutre, J., & A. Heene. (2006). Investigating the impact of firm size on small business social responsibility: A critical review. *Journal of Business Ethics* 67:257–73.

Lerman, R. I., C. Ratcliffe, H. Salzman, D. Wissoker, & J. Gaudet. (2004). *Can expanding the use of computers improve the performance of small minority-and women-owned enterprisers?* Washington, D.C.: Urban Institute.

Levitt, P. (1997). The social aspects of small-business development: The case of Puerto Rican and Dominican entrepreneurs in Boston. In *Latino poverty and economic development in Massachusetts*, ed. E. Melendez & M. Uriate, 143–58. Boston: University of Massachusetts Press.

Lewis, H. (2009). From Mexico to Iowa: New immigrant farmers' pathways and potentials. *Community Development* 40, 2:139–53.

Leyshon, A., R. Lee, & C. C. Williams, eds. (2003). *Alternative economic spaces.* London: Sage.

Li, W., et al. (2006). How ethnic banks matter: Banking and community economic development in Los Angeles. In Kaplan & Li 2006, 113–34.

Liberto, J. (2009, August 19). Latinos flock to New Orleans. *CNNMoney.com.* http://money.com/2009/08/19/news/economy/New_Orleans_Hispanics/index.htm (accessed September 8, 2009).

Lichtenstein, G. A., & T. G. Lyons. (2006). Managing the community's pipeline of entrepreneurs and enterprises: A new way of thinking about business assets. *Economic Development Quarterly* 20:277–386.

Light, I. (2007). The informal economy buffer, migration chains, and poverty intolerance. *City & Community* 6:245–48.

Light, I., & C. Rosenstein. (1995). *Race, ethnicity, and entrepreneurship in urban America.* New York: Aldine de Gruyter.

Llana, S. M. (2009, September 25). For Mexicans seeking to cross the US border, it's not just about jobs anymore. *Christian Science Monitor*, 6.

Lobo, A. P., R. O. Flores, & J. J. Salvo. (2002). The impact of Hispanic growth on the racial/ethnic composition of New York City neighborhoods. *Urban Affairs Review* 37:703–27.

Lofstrom, M. (2010). *Entrepreneurship among California's low-skilled workers.* San Francisco: Public Policy Institute of California.

Lofstrom, M., & T. Bates. (2009). Latina entrepreneurship. *Small Business Economics* 33, 4:427–39.

Lofstrom, M., & C. Wang. (2007). Mexican-Hispanic self-employment entry: The role of business start-up constraints. *Annals of the American Academy of Political and Social Sciences* 613:32–48.

Longo, D. (2009, August 17). Innovation key to meeting needs of Latino shoppers. *Progressive Grocer.* http://www.lexisnexis.com (accessed September 8, 2009).

Lopez, E., E. Ramirez, & R. I. Rochin. (1999). *Latino economic development in California.* Sacramento: California Research Bureau.

Lopez, I. H. (2005). Race on the 2010 census: Hispanics & the shrinking white majority. *Daedalus* 134:42–52.

Lopez, J. (2009, August 29). Eastside dreams: Young Latinos want to create an arts district of their very own in Boyle Heights. *Los Angeles Times*, D1.

Lopez, M. H. (2009). *Latinos and education: Explaining the attainment gap.* Washington, D.C.: Pew Hispanic Center.

Lopez-Garza, M. (2001). A study of the informal economy and Latina/o immigrants in Greater Los Angeles. In Lopez-Garza & Diaz 2001, 141–68.

Lopez-Garza, M., & D. R. Diaz, eds., *Asian and Latino immigrants in a restructuring economy: The metamorphosis of Southern California.* Palo Alto: Stanford University Press.

Los Angeles Times. (2009, September 8). Business is "robust" for small L.A. county firms. http://www.latimes.com (accessed September 8, 2009).

Losby, J. L., J. F. Else, M. E. Kingslow, E. L. Edgcomb, E. T. Malm, & V. Kao. (2002). *Informal economy literature review.* Washington, D.C.: Aspen Institute.

Low, S. M. (2000). *On the plaza: The politics of public space and culture.* Austin: University of Texas Press.

Lowrey, Y. (2004). *Dynamics of minorities-owned employer establishments, 1997–2001.* Washington, D.C.: Small Business Administration Office of Advocacy.

———. (2007). *Minorities in business: A demographic review of minority business ownership.* Washington, D.C.: Small Business Administration Office of Advocacy.

Loza, J. (2004). Business–community partnerships: The case for community organization capacity building. *Journal of Business Ethics* 53:297–311.

Luke, D. A. (2005). Getting the big picture in community science: Methods that capture context. *American Journal of Community Psychology* 35:185–200.

Luken, R., & R. Stares. (2005). Small business responsibility in developing countries: A threat or an opportunity? *Business Strategy and the Environment* 14:38–53.

Lundy, C., & K. Van Wormer. (2007). Social and economic justice, human rights, and peace. *International Social Work* 50:727–39.

Luthens, F., S. M. Norman, & S. M. Jensen. (2007). The value of the psychological capital of immigrant entrepreneurs. *International Journal of Business & Globalisation* 1:161–75.

Lynn, M. (2006). Discourses of community: Challenges for social work. *International Journal of Social Welfare* 15:110–20.

Lyons, M., & S. Snoxell. (2005). Sustainable urban livelihoods and market place social capital: Crisis and strategy in petty trade. *Urban Studies* 42:1301–20.

McCarron, K. (2007, June 18). Marketing to Hispanics no longer just a niche opportunity: Tire firms noticing ethnic group's economic clout. *Business*, 1.

McClain, D., M. L. Lyle, N. M. Carter, V. M. Soto, G. F. Lackey, K. D. Cotton, S. C. Nunnally, T. J. Scotto, J. D. Grynaviski, & J. K. Kendrick. (2007). Black Americans and Latino Immigrants in a southern city: Friendly neighbors or economic competitors? *Du Bois Review: Social Science and Research on Race* 4:97–117.

McConnell, E. D. (2008). The U.S. destinations of contemporary Mexican immigrants. *International Migration Review* 42:767–802.

McDaniel, N., & A. I. Drever. (2009). Ethnic enclave or international corridor? Immigrant businesses in a New South city. *Southeastern Geography* 49:3–23.

Mcilwaine, C. (2005). *Coping practices among Colombian migrants in London.* London: University of London.

McKernan, S-M., & H. Chen. (2005). *Small business and microenterprise as an opportunity- and asset-building strategy.* Opportunity and Ownership Project. Urban Institute, 3, 1–7.

McQueen, K., J. Weiser, & B. W. Burns. (2007). *Small business development strategies: Practices to promote success among low-income entrepreneurs.* Branford, Conn.: Brody-Weiser-Burns.

McTaggart, J. (2004, October 15). Coast to coast, chains are vying to leave no Hispanic customer behind, but for the independents it's second nature. *Progressive Grocer*, 1.

Maine Center for Economic Policy. (2009). *The growing Latin American influence: Opportunities for Maine's economy.* Augusta: Maine Center for Economic Policy.

Maderazo, J. W. (2008). Latin@s forced to choose cremation. *Vivir Latino* 10:1.

Marcelli, E. A., & J. Granberry. (2006). Latino New England: An emerging demographic and economic portrait. In Torres 2006, 25–51.

Marcelo, P. (2009, May 18). Fast food the Latino way thrives on Providence's Broad Street. *Providence Journal*, 2.

Marcias, A. (2005). Latin holidays: Mexican Americans, Latin music, and cultural identity in postwar Los Angeles. *Aztlan: A Journal of Chicano Studies* 30:65–86.

Marks, E., M. D. Cargo, & M. Daniel. (2007). Constructing a health and social indicator for indigenous community health research. *Social Indicators Research* 82:93–110.

Marosi, R. (2009, November 27). At Mexican border, "churro man" walks a fine line. *Boston Globe*, A32.

Marquez, L. (2008, September 17). The state of South Los Angeles: Study released. *Urban Planning News.* University of California, Los Angeles.

Marquis, C., M. A. Glynn, & G. F. Davis. (2007). Community isomorphism and corporate social action. *Academy of Management Review* 32:925–45.

Marshall, C. (2007, June 15). Proposed ban on taco trucks stirs animosity in a California town. *New York Times*, A13.

Marske, S. L. (2008). Plaza Fiesta: A re-imagined homeland contributing to Latino identity and community. Master's thesis, Georgia State University, Atlanta.

Marte, A.C.B. (2004, November). The transnational institutions and ethnic entrepreneurship. Paper presented at the Business Association of Latin American Studies, Wellesley, Mass.

Martin, P. (2009). "No dogs or Mexicans allowed": Discourses of racism and ideology in Pahrump, Nevada. *Explorations in Anthropology* 9:91–105.

Martinelli, A. (2006). The social and institutional context of entrepreneurship. In *Crossroads of entrepreneurship*, ed. G. Corbetta, M. Huse, & D. Ravasi, 53–73. New York: Springer.

Martinez, J., & V. Garcia. (2004). *New Latino farmers in the Midwest: The case of Southwest, Michigan.* http://www.cambiodecolores.org/2004/Papers/Marinez-Garcia.htm (accessed July 27, 2009).

Martinez, A. (2004, September 22). *Hispanics in business: Small businesses boom, but little boardroom presence. Cable News Network*, transcript no. 092203cb.105. http://web.lexis-nexis.com (accessed June 8, 2005).

Marwell, N. (2004). Ethnic and postethnic politics in New York City: The Dominican second generation. In Kasinitz, Mollenkopf, & Waters 2004, 227–56.

Massey, D. S. (2008). *New faces in new places: The changing geography of American immigration.* New York: Russell Sage Foundation.

Massey, D. S., R. E. Zambrana, & S. A. Bell. (1995). Contemporary issues in Latino families: Future directions for research, policy, and practice. In *Understanding Latino families: Scholarship, policy, and practice*, ed. R. E. Zambrana, 190–204. Thousand Oaks, Calif.: Sage.

Mastro, D. E., & E. Behm-Morawitz. (2005). Latino representation on primetime television. *Journalism & Mass Communication Quarterly* 82:110–30.

Matasar, A. B., & D. D. Pavelka. (2004). Minority banks and minority communities: Are minority banks good neighbors? *International Advances in Economics Research* 10:43–57.

Mathie, A., & G. Cunningham. (2003). *Who is driving development? Reflections on the transformative potential of asset-based community development.* Antigonish, N.S., Canada: Coady International Institute.

Matza, M. (2008, November 16). As U.S. economy sours, immigrants head home. *Philadelphia Inquirer*, A1.

———. (2009, September 20). Soccer spoken here. *Philadelphia Inquirer*, B1.

Maul, K. (2009, April 27). Major brands buoy multicultural efforts despite ongoing recession. *PR Week (US)*, 1.

Maxwell, B., & M. Jacobson. (1989). *Marketing disease to Hispanics: The selling of alcohol, tobacco, and junk food*. Washington, D.C.: Center for Science in the Public Interest.

Mendes, (2008). Teaching community development to social work students: A critical reflection. *Community Development Journal* 44:248–62.

Mendez, M. (2005). Latino new urbanism: Building on cultural preferences. *Opolis: An International Journal of Suburban and Metropolitan Studies* 5:33–40.

Mendoza, C. M. (2008). Hispanic entrepreneur overcoming the odds of failure: A phenomenological study. *USASBE 2008 Conference Proceedings*.

Menzies, T. V., L. J. Filion, G. A. Brenner, & S. Elgie. (2003). A study of entrepreneurs' ethnic involvement utilizing personal and business characteristics. *Proceedings of the 20th Annual CCSBE Conference*, November 6–8, Victoria, B.C., Canada.

———. (2007). Measuring ethnic community involvement: Development and initial testing of an index. *Journal of Small Business Management* 45:267–82.

Mercer, C. (2006). Cultural planning for urban development and creative cities. http://www.culturalplanning.net/PDF_activities/maj06/shanghai_cultural_paper.pdf (accessed June 19, 2009).

Merritt, L. C. (2006, January 13). *The Hispanic market: Having an impact on San Diego's economy*. San Diego: 2006 Economic Roundtable.

Meyerson, H. (2007, May 2). Fires that still smolder in L.A. *Washington Post*, A15.

Miami Herald. (2009, August 10). Despite recession, companies target Latino market. http://www.miamiherald.com/business/story/1179072.html (accessed September 23, 2009).

Michael, Y. L., S. A. Farquhar, N. Wiggins, & M. K. Green. (2008). Findings from a community-based participatory prevention research intervention designed to increase social capital in Latino African American communities. *Journal of Immigrant & Minority Health* 10:281–89.

Michna, S., & L. M. Bednarz. (2006). Small business in the USA. *International Journal of Entrepreneurship and Innovation Management* 6:4–17.

Milam, D. (2008). Public library strategies for building strong economics and communities. *National Civic Review* 97:11–16.

Miley, M. (2009, February 2). Don't bypass African-Americans: Marketers make mistake by failing to target this nearly $1 trillion market. *Advertising Age*, 3.

Millard, A.V., & J. Chapa. (Eds.). (2001). *Apple pie & enchiladas: Latino newcomers in the rural Midwest*. Austin: University of Texas Press.

Miller, D. (1999). *Principles of social justice*. Cambridge: Harvard University Press.

Miller, G. W. (2008, June 27). Organizers of Black Latino Expo seek to raise urban fund. *Philadelphia Business Journal*, 1.

Min, G. (2007). Korean–Latino relations in Los Angeles and New York City. *Du Bois Review: Social Science Research on Race* 4:395–411.

Minich, L., S. Howe, D. Langmeyer, & K. Corcoran. (2006). Can community change be measured for an outcomes-based initiative? A comparative case study of the success 6 initiative. *American Journal of Community Psychology* 38:183–90.

Minority Business Atlas. (2005). *Hispanic/Latino businesses*. Los Angeles: Minority Business Atlas.

Mirabal, N. R. (2009). The politics of gentrification in San Francisco's Mission District. *Public Historian* 31:7–31.

Miraftab, F., & E. Diaz Mcconnell. (2008). Multicultural rural towns—insights for inclusive planning. *International Planning Studies* 13:343–60.

Misonzhnik, E. (2008, November 1). American melting pot. *Retail Traffic*, 33.

Mitchell, J. (2006). *Gallup Mainstreet community economic assessment*. University of New Mexico. http://hdl.handle.net/1928/1735 (accessed January 30, 2010).

Miyares, I. M. (2004). Changing Latinization of New York City. In Arreola 2004, 145–66.

Mock, B. (2007). Immigration backlash: Hate crimes against Latinos flourish. *Intelligence Report*, Winter, 1–3.

Model, S. (2008). *West Indian immigrants*. New York: Russell-Sage Foundation.

Momen, M. (2007). Remembering Laredo: Spatial reflections. *Space and Culture* 10:115–28.

Moncarz, R. (2007). Entrepreneurship, mobility, economic development, and stagnation of the South Florida economy. *Global Economy Journal* 7, 3, art. 5.

Monreal-Cameron, M. (2008, May 16). Wisconsin's growing Latino population provides wealth of opportunities for business. *BixTimes.com*.

Montemayor, R., & H. Mendoza. (2004). *Right before our eyes: Latinos, past, present and future*. Wheat Ridge, Colo.: Scholarly Publishing Group.

Montero-Sieburth, M. (2007). The "Si se puede" newcomers: Mexicans in New England. In Montero-Sieburth & Melendez 2007, 58–92.

Montero-Sieburth, M., & E. Melendez. (2007). *Latinos in a changing society*. Westport, CT: Praeger.

Monti, D. J., A. D. Ryan, C. Brush, & A. Gannon. (2007). Civic capitalism: Entrepreneurs, entrepreneurship, their ventures and communities. *Journal of Developmental Entrepreneurship* 12:353–75.

Moore, L. V., & A.A.D. Roux. (2006). Associations of neighborhood characteristics with the location and type of food stores. *American Journal of Public Health* 96:325–31.

Moore, M. T., & Overberg (2009, May 14). Gap between baby boomers, young minorities grow. *USA Today*, XA.

Mora, M., & D. Alberto. (2006). Mexican immigrant self-employment along the United States-Mexico border: An analysis of 2000 Census data. *Social Science Quarterly* 87:91–109.

Morawska, E. (2004). The immigrant transnational entrepreneurs in New York. *International Journal of Entrepreneurial Behavior and Research* 10:325–48.

Moreno, D. (2005). *Exile political power: Cubans in the United States political system.* Miami: Florida International University.

Moreno, J. (2009, September 21). Buying land fulfills a dream for many Hispanic immigrants. *Houston Chronicle*, 2.

Moreno, M. J. (2004). Art museums and socioeconomic forces: The case of a community museum. *Review of Radical Political Economics* 36:506–27.

Morgan, D. L. (2007). Paradigms lost and pragmatism regained. *Journal of Mixed Methods Research* 1:48–76.

Morrison, A. (2006). "New Generation Latino" in the crossfire: Urban Latino youth as a target market. Paper presented at the annual meeting of the American Studies Association, October 12, 2006. http://www.allacademic.com/meta/p113757_index.html (accessed April 19, 2009).

Murdock, S. H., & S. White. (2002). *A summary of the Texas challenge in the twenty-first century: Implications of population change for the future of Texas.* College Station: Center for Demographic and Socioeconomic Research and Education, Texas A & M University.

Murphy, D. E. (2003, February 17). New California identity predicted by researchers. *New York Times*, A13.

Myers, D. (1999). Demographic dynamism and metropolitan change: Comparing Los Angeles, New York, Chicago, and Washington, D.C. *Housing Policy Debate* 10:919–54.

Myers, D., J. Pitkin, & J. Park. (2005). *California demographic futures: Projections to 2030 by immigrant generation, nativity, and time of arrival in the U.S.* Los Angeles: School of Policy, Planning, and Development, University of Southern California.

Nagourney, A. (2010, April 28). Immigration: Complex test for 2 parties. *New York Times*, A1, A17.

Narrow, V. (2005). Impacting next wave organizing: Creative campaigning strategies of the Los Angeles' worker centers. *New York Law School Review* 50:465–515.

National and City Small Business Resources. (2007). *Hispanic entrepreneurs.* http://www.nationalcity.sbresources.com (accessed September 22, 2009).

National Council of La Raza. (2008). *Hate crimes against Latinos on the rise—2008.* Fact sheet, 1–9.

National Research Council. (2006). *Multiple origins, uncertain destines: Hispanics and the American future.* Washington, D.C.: National Academies Press.

Navarro, M. (2003, May 22). The media business: Advertising, advisers set targets on the Latino market that is urban, English-speaking and American-born. *New York Times*, A12.

Nelson, L., & N. Hiemstra. (2008). Latino immigrants and the renegotiation of place and belonging in small town America. *Social & Cultural Geography* 9:319–42.

Nembhard, J. G., & N. S. Chiteji, eds. (2006). *Wealth accumulation and communities of color in the United States: Current issues.* Ann Arbor: University of Michigan Press.

Newell, S. E., K. Banerji, R. Chandra, S. Chowdhury, R. Clarke, M. Endres, D. Stone, & F. Wagner-Marsh. (2008). Hispanic-American entrepreneurs: Research opportunities and challenges. *USASBE 2008 Conference Proceedings.*

New York Times. (1981, December 13). Sales lagging on streets of El Barrio. *New York Times*, 60.

Niehm, L. S., J. Swinney, & W. Miller. (2008). Community social responsibility and its consequences for family business performance. *Journal of Small Business Management* 46:331–50.

Niemi, G. J., & M. E. McDonald. (2004). Application of ecological indicators. *Annual Review of Ecology, Evolution, and Systematics* 35:89–111.

Nijman, J. (2007). Place-particularity and "deep analogies": A comparative essay on Miami's rise as a world city. *Urban Geography* 28:92–107.

Nolan, M. (2009, July 3). Latino market promotes health. *San Bernardino Sun*, 2.

Novak, L. (2007, June 23). For women, a recipe to create a successful business. *New York Times*, B4.

Nowak, J. (2007). *Creativity and neighborhood development: Strategies for community investment.* Philadelphia: TRF.

Nunez, E. (2007, October 12). Poultry, thread, and Whitewater. Paper presented at the Rethinking the Latin@ Intellectual Ecology Conference. Hartford: University of Connecticut.

Oberle, A. (2004). Si venden aqui: Commercial landscapes in Phoenix, Arizona. In Arreola 2004, 239–54.

Oberle, A. (2006). Latino business landscapes and the Hispanic economy. In Kaplan and Li 2006, 149–64.

Oberle, A., & W. Li. (2008). Diverging trajectories: Asian and Latino immigration in Metropolitan Phoenix. In Singer, Hardwick, & Brettell 2008, 87–104.

Ochoa, E. C., & G.K.L. Ochoa. (2005). *Latino Los Angeles: Transformations, communities, and activism.* Tucson: University of Arizona Press.

Odem, M. E, (2008). Unsettled in the suburbs: Latino immigration and ethnic diversity in metro Atlanta. In Singer, Hardwick, & Brettell 2008, 105–36.

Oh, J-H. (2008).The quest to understand self-employment in American metropolitan. *Urban Studies* 45:1769–90.

Ohmer, M. L., & W. S. Korr. (2006). The effectiveness of community practice interventions: A review of the literature. *Research on Social Work Practice* 16:132–45.

Oliveira, C. R. (2006). *Understanding the diversity of immigrant entrepreneurial strategies.* http://www.ceg.ul.pt (accessed April 13, 2009).

Olivo, A. (2008, August 12). Immigrant's death splits blue-collar town: White teens accused of targeting Latinos. *Chicago Tribune*, 24.

Ong, P. (2008). The state of South Los Angeles report. Los Angeles: University of California.

Ordonez, F. (2009, May 11). Latino business owners losing hope in NC. *Charlotte Observer*, 2.

Ordonez, J. (2006). How do banks spell "big profits"? Dinero. *Newsweek.* http://www.newsweek.com/2006/11/27/how-do-banks-spell-big-profits-dinero.html (accessed May 9, 2009).

Orfield, G., & E. Frankenberg. (2008). *The last have become first: Rural and small town America lead the way on desegregation. A Research Brief for the Civil Rights Project.* Los Angeles: University of California, Los Angeles.

Ormachea, P., and W. Langer. (2009). *Delivery of legal services to immigrant small business owners: The problem and a model to solve them.* http://works.bepress.com/cgi/viewcontent.cgi?article=1002&context=william_langer (accessed January 10, 2010).

Orum, A. M. (2005). Circles of influence and chains of command: The social processes whereby ethnic communities influence host societies. *Social Forces* 84:921–39.

Oxendine, J. (1999). Small business makes bug strides in New York. *Closing the Gap: The problem of accessing health care*, August/September, 1–2.

Pachon, H. (2008). Increasing Hispanic mobility into the middle-class: An overview. In Cisneros 2008, 57–69.

Padin, J. A. (2005). The normative mulattoes: The press, Latinos, and the racial climate on the moving immigration frontiers. *Sociological Perspectives* 48:49–75.

Pages, E. R. (2005). The changing demography of entrepreneurship. *Local Economy* 20:1–5.

Palumbo, F. A., & I. Teich. (2004). Market segmentation based on level of acculturation. *Marketing Intelligence & Planning* 22:472–84.

Pamaffy, T. (1998, July & August). El millonario next door: The untold story of Hispanic entrepreneurship. *Policy Review.* http://www.hoover.org/publications/policyreview/3564007.html (accessed May 3, 2009).

Pantoja, A. D. (2005). Transnational ties and immigrant political incorporation: The case of Dominicans in Washington Heights, New York. *International Migration* 43:123–46.

Park, E. J. W. (2001). Community divided: Korean American politics in post-civil unrest Los Angeles. In Lopez-Garza & Diaz 2001, 273–88.

Park, K. (1997). *Korean American dream: Immigrants and small businesses in New York City*. Ithaca: Cornell University Press.

———. (2004). Confronting the liquor industry in Los Angeles. *International Journal of Sociology and Social Policy* 24:103–36.

Parrado, E. A., & W. Kandel. (2008). New Hispanic migrant destinations: A tale of two industries. In Massey 2008, 99–123.

Passel, J. S. (2006). *The size and characteristics of the unauthorized migrant population in the U.S.: Estimates based on the March 2005 Current Population Survey*. Washington, D.C.: Pew Hispanic Center.

Passel, J. S., & Taylor (2009). *Who's Hispanic?* Washington, D.C.: Pew Hispanic Center.

Pastor, Jr., M. (2001). Economics and ethnicity: Poverty, race, and immigration in Los Angeles county. In Lopez-Garza & Diaz 2001, 102–38.

Patrick, H., A. Canvello, & C. R. Knee. (2008). The role of need fulfillment in relationship functioning and well-being: A self-determination theory perspective. *Journal of Personality and Self Psychology* 92:434–57.

Pearce, S. C. (2005). Today's immigrant woman entrepreneur. *The Diversity Factor* 13:23–29.

Pedraza, S. (2000). Beyond black and white: Latinos and social science research on immigration, race, and ethnicity in America. *Social Science History* 24:697–726.

Penaloza, L. (2007). Mainstreet revisited. *International Journal of Sociology and Social Policy* 27:234–49.

Peredo, A. M., & J. J. Chrisman. (2004). Toward a theory of community-based enterprise. *Academy Management Review* 31:309–28.

Perkins, J. (2004). *Beyond bodegas: Developing a retail relationship with Hispanic customers*. Ithaca: Paramount Market Publishing.

Petersen, D. A., & L. Assanie. (2005). *The face of Texas: Jobs, people, business, change*. Dallas: Federal Reserve Bank of Dallas.

Peterson, M. F., & J. Roquebert. (1993). Success patterns of Cuban-American enterprises: Implications for entrepreneurial communities. *Human Relations* 46:921–38.

Pethokoukis, J. (2005, October 15). Small biz watch: Get to know the Hispanic market. *U.S. News & World Report*, 29.

Pew Hispanic Center. (2002). *U.S. born Hispanic increasingly drives population development*. Washington, D.C.: Pew Hispanic Center.

———. (2008). *Latinos account for half of U.S. population growth since 2000.* Washington, D.C.: Pew Hispanic Center.

———. (2009a). *Mexican immigrants in the United States, 2008.* Washington, D.C.: Pew Hispanic Center.

———. (2009b). *Hispanics of Puerto Rican origin in the United States, 2007.* Washington, D.C.: Pew Hispanic Center.

———. (2009c). *Hispanics of Mexican origin in the United States, 2007.* Washington, D.C.: Pew Hispanic Center.

———. (2009d). *Hispanics of Cuban origin in the United States, 2007.* Washington, D.C.: Pew Hispanic Center.

———. (2009e). *Hispanics of Salvadoran origin in the United States, 2007.* Washington, D.C.: Pew Hispanic Center.

———. (2009f). *Hispanics of Dominican origin in the United States, 2007.* Washington, D.C.: Pew Hispanic Center.

———. (2009g). *Hispanics of Guatemalan origin in the United States, 2007.* Washington, D.C.: Pew Hispanic Center.

———. (2009h). *Hispanics of Colombian origin in the United States, 2007.* Washington, D.C.: Pew Hispanic Center.

———. (2009i). *Hispanics of Honduran origin in the United States, 2007.* Washington, D.C.: Pew Hispanic Center.

———. (2009j). *Hispanics of Ecuadorian origin in the United States, 2007.* Washington, D.C.: Pew Hispanic Center.

———. (2009k). *Hispanics of Peruvian origin in the United States, 2007.* Washington, D.C.: Pew Hispanic Center.

———. (2009l). *Latinos online, 2006–2008: Narrowing the gap.* Washington, D.C.: Pew Hispanic Center.

———. (2010). *Statistical portrait of Hispanics in the United States, 2008.* Washington, D.C.: Pew Hispanic Center.

Pfeffer, M. J., & A. Parra. (2009). Strong ties, weak ties, and human capital: Latino immigrant employment outside of the enclave. *Rural Sociology* 74:241–69.

Phelps, R., R. Adams, & J. Bessant. (2007). Life cycles of growing organizations: A review with implications for knowledge and learning. *International Journal of Management Reviews* 9, 1:1–30.

Phillips, R., & R. H. Pittman, eds. (2009). *An introduction to community development.* New York: Routledge.

Pina, T. (2004, March 30). Progresso Latino creates center to help small business owners in Rhode Island. *Providence Journal*, 1.

Pinal, J. del. (2008). Demographic patterns: Age, structure, fertility, mortality, and population growth. In Rodriguez, Saenz, & Menjivar 2008, 57–71.

Pinel, S. L. (2007). How two New Mexico pueblos combined culture and development. *Alternatives: Global, Local, Political* 32:9–39.

Pipes, F., & N. Rodriguez. (2007). *A research review of characteristics and contributions of foreign-born labor*. Houston: Texans for Sensible Immigration Policy.

Pittman, R. H., & R. T. Roberts. (2009). Retaining and expanding existing businesses in the community. In Phillips & Pittman 2009, 210–19.

Poole, D. L., & N. Negri. (2007). Transnational community enterprises for social welfare. *International Journal of Social Welfare* 17:243–46.

Popple, K., & M. Stepney. (2008). *Social work and the community: A critical context for practice*. Basingstoke, UK: Palgrave Macmillan.

Portes, A. (2007). The new Latin nation: Immigration and the Hispanic population of the United States. *DuBois Review: Social Science and Research on Race* 4:271–301.

Portes, A., & S. Shafer. (2007). Revisiting the enclave hypothesis: Miami twenty-five years later. In *The sociology of entrepreneurship*, ed. M. Ruef & M. Lounsbury, 157–90. New York: JAI Press.

Portes, A., & A. Stepick. (1993). *City on the edge: The transformation of Miami.* Berkeley: University of California Press.

Pothukuchi, K. (2005). Attracting supermarkets to inner-city neighborhoods: Economic development outside the box. *Economic Development Quarterly* 19: 232–44.

Powers, R. S. (2005). Working it out in North Carolina: Employers and Hispanic/Latino immigrants. *Sociation Today* 3:1–6.

Preston, J. (2009a, March 22). A slippery place in the U.S. work force. *New York Times*, 1, 18–19.

———. (2009b, April 15). Study sees more young citizens with parents in the U.S. illegally. *New York Times*, A12.

———. (2009c, May 15). Mexico data says migration to U.S. has plummeted: Recession stems a tide. *New York Times*, A1, A4.

Price, M., & C. Whitworth. (2004). Soccer and Latino cultural space: Metropolitan Washington futbol leagues. In Arreola 2004, 167–86.

Prieto, Y. (2009). *The Cubans of Union City: Immigrants and exiles in a New Jersey community*. Philadelphia: Temple University Press.

Purdum, T. S. (2000, July 4). Shift in the mix alters the face of California. *New York Times*, A1, A12.

Puryear, A. N., E. G. Rogoff, M-S. Lee, R. Z. Heck, et al. (2008). Sampling minority business owners and their families: The understudied entrepreneurial experience. *Journal of Small Business Management* 46:422–53.

Putnam, R. O. (2000). *Bowling alone*. New York: Simon & Schuster.

Queen, D. (2008, April 25). New venture pushes Hispanic business growth. *Denver Business Journal*, 1.

Qureshi, S., & A. S. York. (2008). Information technology adoption by small businesses in minority and ethnic communities. *Proceedings of the 41st Hawaii International Conference on Systems Sciences*.

Raijman, R. (2001). Mexican immigrants and informal self-employment in Chicago. *Human Organization* 60:47–55.

Raja, S., C. Ma, & P. Yadav (2008). Beyond food deserts: Measuring and meeting racial disparities in neighborhood food environments. *Journal of Planning Education and Research* 27:469–82.

Ramirez, A. (2007, April 13). A bodega's failure spawns a successful movement. *New York Times*, A16.

Ramirez, H., & P. Hondagneu-Soto (2009). Mexican immigrant gardeners: Entrepreneurs or exploited workers? *Social Problems* 56:70–88.

Ramirez, V. M. (2005). *Savings and wealth accumulation trends of the Hispanic/Latino U.S. population.* New York: Citibank Community Relations.

Ramos, C., & G. J. Gates. (2008). *California's Latino/Latina LGB population.* Los Angeles: Williams Institute, University of California.

Ramos, V. M. (2006, February 5). Puerto Ricans remember roots as they sink new ones. *Orlando Sentinel*, 18–19.

Rath, J. (2006). *The transformation of ethnic neighborhoods into places of leisure and consumption.* Amsterdam: Institute for Migration and Ethnic Studies, University of Amsterdam.

Ready, T., & A. Brown-Gort. (2005). *The state of Latino Chicago: This is home now.* Terre Haute: Institute of Latino Studies, University of Notre Dame.

Reamer, A. (2009, February 17). *Tempest over the census.* Washington, D.C.: Brookings Institution.

Reckard, E. S. (2006, July 23). Latino-owned banks seek to fill void in L.A. *Los Angeles Times*, 19.

Reed, A. M., & D. Reed. (2009). Partnerships for development: Four models of business involvement. *Journal of Business Ethnics* 90:3–27.

Reed, M. S., E.D.G. Fraser, & A. J. Dougill. (2006). An adaptive learning process for developing and applying sustainability indicators with local communities. *Ecological Economics* 59:406–18.

Reimers, C. (2006). Economic well-being. In Tienda & Mitchell 2006, 291–361.

Reinecke, G., & S. White, eds. (2004). *Policies for small enterprises: Creating the right environment for good jobs.* Geneva: International Labour Organization.

Renaud, J-P. (2008a, April 14). Putting the breaks on East LA's taco trucks. *Los Angeles Times.* http://www.latimes.com/news/local/la=me-tacotruck14apr14,0,4600263.story (accessed May 4, 2008).

———. (2008b, April 16). East L.A. taco truck owners say they'll stay put. *Los Angeles Times*. http://www.latimes.com/features/home/la-hm-moriarity1-2008 may01,1,1980024.story (accessed May 4, 2008).

ResearchWikis. (2008). Hispanic marketing research. http://www.researchwikis .com/Hispanics_Market_Research (accessed January 18, 2009).

Reyes-Ruiz, R. (2005a). Latino communities in the Tokyo-Yokohama metropolitan area. *Journal of Ethnic and Migration Studies* 31:151–69.

———. (2005b). The Latino culturescape in Japan. *Diaspora: A Journal of Transnational Studies* 14:137–55.

———. (2005c). Music and the (re)creation of Latino culture in Japan. *Journal of Latin American Cultural Studies: Travesia* 14:223–39.

Reynolds, D. (2007). *Entrepreneurship in the United States: The future is now*. New York: Springer Science/Business Media.

Reynoso, J. (2003). Dominican immigrants and social capital in New York City: A case study. *Encrucijada/Crossroads: An Online Academic Journal* 1:57–78.

Rhoden, W. C. (2009, July 4), For soccer to flourish in the U.S., its doors must open. *New York Times*, 3.

Rhodes, W. M., & C. Conly. (2008). Crime and mobility: An empirical study. In *Principles of geographical offenders*, ed. D. Cantor & D. Young, 127–48. Surrey, UK: Ashgate.

Richardson, H. W., & Gordon (2005). Globalization and Los Angeles. In *Globalization and urban development*, ed. H. W. Richardson & C-H. C. Bae, 197–210. New York: Springer.

Richtermeyer, G. (2004, March 10–12). Listening to Latino business owners. Paper presented at the Cambio de Colores Conference—Latinos in Missouri: Gateway to a New Community. St. Louis. http://www.cambiodecolores.org/2004/ Papers/GwenRichtermeyer.htm (accessed May 2, 2009).

Ricourt, M., & R. Danta. (2003). *Hispanas de Queens: Latino panethnicity in a New York City neighborhood*. Ithaca: Cornell University Press.

Rinehart, R. D. (2004). *Designing programmes to improve working and employment conditions in the informal economy: A literature review*. Geneva: International Labour Organization.

Rivera, A., J. Huezo, C. Kasica, & D. Muhammad. (2009). *The silent depression: State of the dream 2009*. Boston: United for a Fair Economy.

Rivera, G. (2008). *HisPanic: Why a fear of Hispanics in the U.S.* New York: Celebra Hardcover.

Robb, A. M., & R. W. Fairlie. (2009). Determinants of business success: An examination of Asian-owned businesses in the USA. *Journal of Population Economics* 22:827–58.

Roberson, P., & R. D. Smith. (2006). Gender differences in minority small business hiring practices and customer patronage: An exploratory study. In *Developmental entrepreneurship*, vol. 5: *Adversity, risk, and isolation*, ed. C. Stiles & C. S. Galbraith, 275–95. Oxford: JAI Press.

Roberts, S. (2008a, December 9). In biggest U.S. cities, minorities are 50%. *New York Times*, A27.

———. (2008b, December 9). Census shows a more diverse and prosperous New York. *New York Times*, A27.

———. (2009, May 14). Asian and Hispanic minorities growing, but more slowly. *New York Times*, A21.

Roberts, S., & S. D. Hamill. (2008, May 18). As deaths outpace births, cities adjust: A new phenomenon for some areas. *New York Times*, 16, 21.

Robertson, R. (2005, September 5). Latinos' economic power increasing. *Memphis Business Journal*, 2–3.

Robinson, W. I. (2006). "Aqui estamos y no nos vamos!" Global capital and immigrant rights. *Race & Class* 48:77–91.

Robles, B. J. (2006). Wealth creation in Latino communities: Latino families, community assets, and cultural capital. In Nembhard & Chiteji 2006, 241–66.

———. (2008). Latinos in greater Phoenix: A growing stakeholder community. *Greater Phoenix forward: Sustaining and enhancing the human-services infrastructure*. Phoenix: College of Public Programs, Arizona State University.

———. (2009). Exploring the wealth returns to Latino higher educational attainment: Estimates of work-life earnings profiles. *Journal of Hispanic Higher Education* 8:5–22.

Robles, B. J., & H. Cordero-Guzman. (2007). Latino self-employment and entrepreneurship in the United States: An overview of the literature and data sources. *Annals of the American Academy of Political and Social Sciences* 613:18–31.

Robles, M. (2007, June 11). By the numbers, a snapshot of Latinos' current financial standing. *La Presnsa de Minnesota*, 1–2.

Rodriguez, G. (1990). *The new civil rights movement: Economic empowerment*. Washington, D.C.: Heritage Foundation.

Rodriguez, H., R. Saenz, & C. Menjivar, eds. (2008). *Latinas/os in the United States: Changing the face of America*. New York: Springer.

Rodriguez, J. A. & W. Sava. (2006). *Images of America: Latinos in Milwaukee*. Chicago: Arcadia.

Rodriguez, P., C. S. Tuggle, & S. M. Hackett. (2009). An exploratory study of how potential "Family and Household Capital" impacts new venture start-up rates. *Family Business Review* 22, 3:259–72.

Rodriguez, Y. (2004, August 18). Bank on it: Latinos can count on being wooed as a red-hot, untapped market segment. *Atlanta Journal-Constitution*, 1F.

Rodriguez-Pose, A. & M. Storper. (2006). Better rules or stronger community? On the social foundations of institutional change and its economics effects. *Economic Geography* 82:1–25.

Rojas, J. (2006, February 27). Latino pedestrian safety. *Livable Places.* http://www.liveplaces.org/transportation/latinopedsafety (accessed May 12, 2009).

Romero, M. (1992). *Maid in the U.S.A.* New York: Routledge.

Romney, L. (1999, December 29). An inland empire for Latino success. *Los Angeles Times*, C-1.

Rosales, G. A. (2001). Labor behind the front door: Domestic workers in urban and suburban households. In Lopez-Garza & Diaz 2001, 169–87.

Rossin, J. E. (2003). *The pawnshop chronicles: Street wisdom for the business world.* Self-published.

Rubio, M., & L. M. Arteaga. (2000). *A new bottom line: Health insurance and minority owned small businesses in California.* Los Angeles: Latino Issues Forum.

Rueda, L. (2008). Hispanic community's new green card . . . economic strength. *Hispanic Trending*, November 30, 1–4.

Rumbaut, R. G. (2006). The making of a people. In Tienda & Mitchell 2006, 16–65.

Russakoff, D. (2006, July 17). U.S. border town, 1,200 miles from the border. *Washington Post*, A1.

Ryoo, H-K. (2005). Achieving friendly interactions: A study of service encounters between Korean shopkeepers and African-American customers. *Discourse & Society* 16:79–105.

Sabia, D. (2007). Migrant families in transition: A case study in the deep South. *Electronic Journal of Sociology.* http://www.sociology.org/content/2007/_sabia_migrant_families.pdf (accessed July 27, 2009).

Sacchetti, M. (2008, April 15). Beating the bank: Shops fill a void marketing money transfer services to immigrants. *Boston Globe*, A1, A12.

Saegert, S. (2006). Building civic capacity in urban neighborhoods: An empirically grounded anatomy. *Journal of Urban Affairs* 28:275–94.

Saenz, R., M. C. Morales, & M. I. Ayala. (2004). Immigration to the melting pot. In *Migration and immigration: A global view*, ed. M. I. Toro-Morn & M. Alicea, 211–32. Westport, Conn.: Greenwood Publishing.

Saenz, R., M. C. Morales, & J. Filoteo. (2004). The demography of Mexicans in the United States. In *Chicanos and Chicanas in contemporary society*, ed. R. De Anda, 3–20. Lanham, Md.: Rowman & Littlefield.

St. Clair, S. (2005, November 7). More Latinos live in suburbs: Drawn by opportunities, middle class leaves Chicago in droves. *Chicago Daily Herald*, 1.

Salaff, C. W., A. Greene, S-L. Wong, & L.X.L. Ping. (2002). In *Approaching transnationalism: Transnational societies, multicultural contacts, and imaging of home*, ed. B. Yeoh, T. C. Kiong, & M. W. Charney, 61–82. Norwell, Mass.: Kluwer.

Salazar, N. B. (2005). Tourism and glocalization "local" tour guiding. *Annals of Tourism Research* 32:628–46.

Salazar, Y. (2005). Latinas as entrepreneurs. *Journal of Chicana and Latina Studies at UW-Medison*, 1. http://www.chicla.wisc.edu/publiction/concientization/2005/journal14.html (accessed January 31, 2009).

Salcido, R. M. (2007). Latino population growth, characteristics, and language capacities: Implications for society, services and social justice. *Journal of Ethnic & Cultural Diversity in Social Work* 16:93–101.

Saldivar-Tanaka, L., & M. E. Krasny. (2004). Culturing community development, neighborhood open space, and civic agriculture: The case of Latino community gardens in New York City. *Agriculture and Human Values* 21:399–412.

Salinas, V. D. (2009, January 25). Latina tradition affected by economy hurts business. *Latino Business Review*. http://latinobusinessreview.blogsport.com/2009/01/latina-tradition-affected-by-economy.html (accessed September 19, 2009).

Samaad, M. (2009, August 11). Hispanic business owners helped by neighborhood trust. *Latino Business Review*. http://latinobusinessreview.blogsport.com/2009/08/hispanic-business-owners-helped-by-html (accessed September 19, 2009).

Sanchez-Jankowski, M. (2008). *Cracks in the pavement: Social change and resilience in poor neighborhoods.* Berkeley: University of California Press.

Sanchez-Korroll, V. E. (1983). *From colonia to community: The history of Puerto Ricans in New York City, 1917–1948.* Westport, Conn.: Greenwood Press.

Sanders, C. K. (2004). Employment options for low-income women: Microenterprises versus the labor market. *Social Work Research* 28:83–92.

Sandoval, S. (2007, March 15). Grocer rumor raises tension. *Dallas Morning News*, 1.

Santiago, J., & J. Jennings. (2004). *The Latino business community of Lawrence, Massachusetts: A profile and analysis.* Lawrence, Mass.: Northern Essex Community College.

Sarason, Y., & C. Koberg. (1994). Hispanic women small business owners. *Hispanic Journal of Behavioral Sciences* 16:353–60.

Sarathy, B. (2006). The Latinization of forest management work in southern Oregon: A case from the Rogue Valley. *Journal of Forestry* 104:359–65.

Sato, T. (2006). *Marketing to Hispanics: A strategic approach to assessing and planning your initiative.* New York: Kaplan.

Saunders, C., E. Zellman, & W. Kaye-Blake. (2007). *Applicability of performance indicators to farms and orchards.* ARGOS Research Report #07/04. Christchurch, N.Z.: Lincoln University.

Saunders, P. (2008). Measuring well-being using non-monetary indicators. *Family Matters* 78:8–17

Sava, W., & A. Vill. (2007). *Latinos in Waukesha (WI)*. Portsmouth, N.H.: Arcadia.

Schaller, S., & G. Modan. (2005). Contesting public space and citizenship: Implications for neighborhood business improvement districts. *Journal of Planning Education & Research* 24:394–407.

Schleef, D. J., & H. B. Cavalcanti. (2009). *Latinos in Dixie: Class and assimilation in Richmond, Virginia*. Albany: State University of New York Press.

Schneider, A. C. (2002, December 23). A changing America has changing tastes. *Kiplinger Business Forecasts*, 1.

Scommegna, P. (2004). *U.S. growing bigger, and more diverse*. Washington, D.C.: Population Reference Bureau.

Scott, J. (2001, June 27) A census query is said to skew data on Latinos. *New York Times*, B1.

Selig Center for Economic Growth. (2006). *Hispanics will top all U.S. minority groups for purchasing power by 2007*. Athens: University of Georgia.

Semenza, J. C., T. L. March, & B. D. Bontenpo. (2006). Community-initiated urban development. *Journal of Urban Health* 84:8–20.

Semple, K. (2010, January 4). At botanica, near year means renewal, and jinx removal. *New York Times*, A14.

Sequeira, J. M., & A. A. Rasheed. (2006). Startup and growth of immigrant small businesses: The impact of social and human capital. *Journal of Developmental Entrepreneurship* 11:357–75.

Shaw, S., S. Bagwell, & J. Karmowska. (2004). Ethnoscapes as spectacle: Reimagining multicultural districts as new destinations for leisure and tourism consumption. *Urban Studies* 41:1983–2000.

Shephard, D. A., J. Wiklund, & J. M. Haynie. (2007). Moving forward: Balancing the financial and emotional costs of business failure. *Journal of Business Venturing* 24:134–48.

Shim, S., & M. A. Eastlick. (1998). Characteristics of Hispanic female business owners: An exploratory study. *Journal of Small Business Management* 36: 18–34.

Shinew, K. J., T. D. Glover, & D. C. Parry. (2004). Leisure spaces as potential sites for interracial interactions: Community gardens in urban areas. *Journal of Leisure Research* 36:336–55.

Shinnar, R. S., & C. A. Young. (2008). Hispanic immigrant entrepreneurs in the Las Vegas metropolitan area: Motivation for entry into and outcomes of self-employment. *Journal of Small Business Management* 46:242–62.

Shrestha, L. B. (2006). *The changing demographic profile of the United States*. Washington, D.C.: Congressional Research Service.

Shuman, M. H. (2000). *Going local: Creating self-reliant communities in a global age.* New York: Routledge.

———. (2007). *The small-mart revolution: How local businesses are beating the global competition.* Second edition. San Francisco: Berrett-Koehler.

Shutika, D. L. (2005). Bridging the community: Nativism, activism, and the politics of inclusion in a Mexican settlement in Pennsylvania. In Zuniga & Hernandez-Leon 2005, 103–32.

Sichelman, L. (2007, April 8). Latino lending barriers fall slowly. *San Diego Union-Tribune,* 25.

Siles, M. E., I. Robison, C. G. Cuellar, & S. F. LaHousse. (2006). The impact of Latino immigrants in Grand Rapid's urban development: A social capital approach. *Julian Samura Research Institute Report* no. 37. East Lansing: Michigan State University.

Simon, W. (2001). *The community economic development movement: Law, business, and the new social policy.* Durham, N.C.: Duke University Press.

Singer, A., S. W. Hardwick, & C. B. Brettell, eds. (2008). *Twenty-first gateways: Immigrant incorporation in suburban America.* Washington, DC: Brookings Institution Press.

Singer, R. L., & E. Martinez, E. (2004). A South Bronx Latin music tale. *CENTRO Journal* 16:177–201.

Singh, N., D. W. Baack, S. K. Kundu, & C. Hurtado. (2008). U.S. Hispanic consumer e-commerce preferences: Expectations and attitudes toward web content. http://www.csulb.edu/web/journals/jecr/issues/20082/paper6.pdf (accessed July 28, 2009).

Siqueira, A.C.O. (2007). Entrepreneurship and ethnicity: The role of human capital and family social capital. *Journal of Developmental Entrepreneurship* 12:31–46.

Sisario, B. (2009, April 26). Out of the bodega and onto the scene. *New York Times* (Sunday Styles), 1, 7.

SITEL. (2003). Service, por favor: 10 reasons to better serve and woo the booming Hispanic market. http://www.sitel.com (accessed April 21, 2009).

Siu, L.C.D. (2007). Cuban Chinese in New York City. In *Cuba: Idea of a nation displaced,* ed. A. O'Reilly Herrera, 123–31. Albany: State University of New York Press.

Skelly, A. H., T. A. Arcury, W. M. Gesler, A. J. Cravey, M. C. Dougherty, S. A. Washburn, & S. Nash. (2002). Sociospatial knowledge networks: Appraising community as place. *Research in Nursing and Health* 25:159–70.

Skop, E. (2008). Emigres outside Miami: The Cuban experience in metropolitan Phoenix. In *Immigrants outside megalopolis: Ethnic transformation in the heartland,* ed. R. C. Jones, 43–64. Lanham, Md.: Lexington Books.

Skop, E., & T. Buentello. (2008). Austin: Immigration and transformation deep in the heart of Texas. In Singer, Hardwick, & Brettell 2008, 257–80.

Skop, E., B. Gratton, & M. Guttman. (2006). La frontera and beyond: Geography and demography in Mexican American history. *Professional Geographer* 58:78–98.

Smith, B. E., & J. Winders. (2007). "We're here to stay": Economic restructuring, Latino migration and place-making in the US. *Transactions of the Institute of British Geographers* 33:60–72.

Smith, H. A., & O. J. Furuseth. (2008). The "Nuevo South": Latino place making and community building in the middle-ring suburbs of Charlotte. In Singer, Hardwick, & Brettell 2008, 281–307.

Smith, J. S. (2004). The plaza in Las Vegas, New Mexico. In Arreola 2004, 39–54.

Smith, M. K. (2009). Hispanic market evolved in recession. *PR Week (US)*, 8.

Smith, R. C. (2001). Mexicans: Social, educational, economic, and political problems and prospects in New York. In *New immigrants in New York*, ed. N. Foner, 275–300. New York: Columbia University Press.

———. (2005). Racialization and Mexicans in New York City. In Zungia & Hernandez-Leon 2005, 220–43.

———. (2006). *Mexican New York: Transnational lives of new immigrants.* Berkeley: University of California Press.

Smith, S. K., J. Tayman, & D. A. Swanson. (2008). *State and local populations: Methodology and analysis.* New York: Springer.

Smith-Hunter, A. E. (2006). An initial look at the characteristics of Hispanic women business owners and their businesses. *Business Renaissance Quarterly*, Summer, 1–3.

Sonfield, M. C. (2008). Entrepreneurship and prisoner re-entry: The development of a concept. *Small Business Institute Research Review* 35, 4:193–200.

Song, M. (1999). *Helping out: Children's labor in ethnic businesses.* Philadelphia: Temple University Press.

Soro, R., & S. Tafoya. (2004). *Dispersal and concentration: Patterns of Latino residential settlement.* Washington, D.C.: Pew Hispanic Center.

Soto, H. (2008, July 24). Latino bank opens for business. *Union Tribune* (San Diego), 21.

South, S. J., K. Crowder, & E. Chavez. (2006). Geographical mobility and spatial assimilation among U.S. Latino immigrants. *International Migration Review* 39:577–607.

Spence, B. (2006, March 31). Lodi gauges Latino businesses. *Ricordnet.com.* http://www.recordnet.com (accessed May 14, 2009).

Sriram, V., T. Mersha, & L. Herron. (2007). The drivers of urban entrepreneurship: An integrative model. *International Journal of Entrepreneurship Behaviour & Research* 13:235–51.

State of Texas. (2008). *Texas in focus: A statewide view of opportunities.* Austin: State of Texas.

Stegman, M., et al., (2001). *Automated underwriting: Getting to "yes" for more low-income applicants.* Paper presented at the Conference on Housing Opportunity, Research Institute for Housing America Center for Community Capitalism, University of North Carolina, Chapel Hill.

Stein, J. (2005, September 18). Businesses here swing to Latin beat. *Wisconsin State Journal*, A1.

Steinhauer, J. (2008, May 3). In taco trick battle, mild Angelenos turn hot. *New York Times*, A1, A11.

Stephens, J. (2008, September 22). Out of the enclave: Latinos adapt, and adapt to, the American city. *Planetizen Interchange.* https://www.planetizen.com/node/3509/ (accessed April 20, 2009).

Stepick, A., G. Grenier, M. Castro, & M. Dunn. (2003). *Miami melting pot: This land is our land: Immigrants and power in Miami.* Berkeley: University of California Press.

Stern, M. J., & S. C. Seifert. (2007). *Culture and urban revitalization: A harvest document.* Philadelphia: School of Social Policy & Practice, University of Pennsylvania.

Stone, R. T., & J. McQuillan. (2007). Beyond Hispanic/Latino: The importance of gender/ethnicity-specific earnings analysis. *Social Science Research* 36:175–20.

Strom, R. D. (2007). Fostering research on minority entrepreneurship. *Annals of the American Academy of Political and Social Science* 613:6–9.

Stuart, J. V. (2005, May). Minority report: Hispanics in the region are committed to making central Florida a better place to live and work. *First Monday*, 6.

Stull, D., & M. Broadway. (2008). Meatpacking and Mexicans on the High Plains: From minority to majority in Garden City, Kansas. In *Immigrants outside of megalopolis: Ethnic transformation in the heartland*, ed. R. C. Jones, 115–32. Lanham, Md.: Lexington Books.

Su, J. A., & C. Martorell. (2001). Exploitation and abuse in the garment industries: The case of the Thai salve-labor compound in El Monte. In Lopez-Garza & Diaz 2001, 21–45.

Suarez-Orozco, M. M., & M. M. Paez, eds. (2002). *Latinos remaking America.* Berkeley: University of California Press.

Sullivan, R., & K. Lee. (2008). Organizing immigrant women in America's sweatshops: Lessons from the Los Angeles Garment Worker Center. *Signs: Journal of Economic Geography* 7:780–82.

Sunderland, L., E. G. Taylor, & R. M. Denny. (2004). Being Mexican and American: Negotiating ethnicity in the practice of market research. *Human Organization* 63:373–80.

Suro, R. (2002). *Metropolitan America: Changing patterns, new locations.* Washington, D.C.: Brookings Institution.

———. (2004). Known knowns and unknown knowns. In *The Hispanic challenge? We know about Latino immigrants*, ed. P. Strum & A. Selee, 4–6. Washington, D.C.: Woodrow Wilson International Center for Scholars.

Suro, R., & J. S. Passel. (2003). *The rise of the second generation: Changing patterns in Hispanic population growth.* Washington, D.C.: Pew Hispanic Center.

Sweeney, A. (2008, April 25). Miami students to team up with local Latino-owned businesses. *Miami Student* (Oxford, Ohio), 2–3.

Sweet, M. J. (2006). Minority business enterprise programmes in the United States: An empirical investigation. *Journal of Law and Society* 33:160–80.

Swinney, J., & R. Runyan. (2007). Native American entrepreneurs and strategic choice. *Journal of Developmental Entrepreneurship* 12:257–73.

Taylor, N. (2004). *The trails and tribulations of researching crime against ethnic small businesses.* Canberra: Australian Institute of Criminology.

Taylor, S. H., & R. W. Roberts, eds. (1985). *Theory and practice of community social work.* New York: Columbia.

TechWeb. (2009, April 18). U.S. Hispanics flocking to the Web. http://www .lexisnexis.com (accessed May 11, 2009).

Tellez-Giron, P. (2007). Providing culturally sensitive end-of-life care for the Latino/a community. *Wisconsin Medical Journal* 106:402–6.

Thelford, T., & E. Edgcomb, E. (2004). Microenterprises in the U.S. informal economy: Summary research findings. *Field Forum* 15:1–16.

Theodore, N., & N. Martin. (2007). Migrant civil society: New voices in the struggle over community development. *Journal of Urban Affairs* 29:269–97.

Theodore, N., A. Valenzuela, & E. Melendez. (2006). La esquina (the corner): Day laborers on the margins of New York's formal economy. *WorkingUSA* 9:407–23.

Thomas, J. V., & E. Deakin. (2001). *California demographic trends: Implications for transportation.* Berkeley: Transportation Center, University of California.

Thomas, N. D. (2001). The importance of culture throughout all of the life cycle. *Holistic Nursing Practice* 15:40–46.

Tienda, M. (2001). *Comparative perspectives on ethnic and immigrant entrepreneurship and business development in Chicago.* PrincetonPrinceton University Press.

Tienda, M., & F. Mitchell (2006a). *Hispanics and the future of America.* Washington, D.C.: National Academic Press.

———. (2006b). *Multiple origins, uncertain destines: Hispanics and the American future.* Washington, D.C.: National Research Council.

Tienda, M., & R. Raijman. (2004). Promoting Hispanic immigrant entrepreneurship in Chicago. *Journal of Developmental Entrepreneurship* 9:1–21.

Tierney, K. (2006). Social inequality, hazards, and disasters. In *On risk and disaster: Lessons from Hurricane Katrina*, ed. R. J. Daniels, D. F. Ketti, & H. Kunrenta, 109–28. Philadelphia: University of Pennsylvania Press.

Tipple, G. (2006). Employment and work conditions in home-based enterprises in four developing countries: Do they constitute "decent work"? *Work, Employment and Society* 20:167–79.

Tomas Rivera Policy Institute. (2009). *Majority/near-majority of first graders in top ten U.S. cities are Latino: The coming Latino revolution in our nation's largest urban school districts.* Los Angeles: University of Southern California.

Torres, A., ed. (2006). *Latinos in New England.* Philadelphia: Temple University Press.

Torres, C. F. (2007, June 11). Clout of Latina entrepreneurs—it's time for corporate America to say, En que la puedo server? *HispanicAd.com.* http://www.hispanicad.com/cgi-bin/news/newsarticle.cgi?article_id=22079 (accessed January 23, 2009).

Torres, D. L. (1990). Dynamics behind the formation of a business class: Tucson's Hispanic business elite. *Hispanic Journal of Behavioral Sciences* 12:25–47.

Torres-Gil, F. (2009, April 10). Latino boomers flying under radar. *USA Today,* 11A.

Toussaint-Comeau, M. (2008). Do ethnic enclaves and networks promote immigrant self-employment? *Economic Perspectives* 32:30–50.

Toussaint-Comeau, M., T. Smith, & L. Comeau. (2005). *Occupational attainment and mobility of Hispanics in a changing economy, a report to the Pew Foundation.* Washington, D.C.: Pew Foundation.

Tracey, P., N. Phillips, & H. Haugh. (2005). Beyond philanthropy: Community enterprise as a basis for corporate citizenship. *Journal of Business Ethics* 58, 4:327–44.

Trujillo-Pagan, N. (2007). From "Gateway to the Americas" to the "Chocolate City": The racialization of Latinos in New Orleans. In *Racing the story: Racial implications and lessons learned from Hurricane Katrina,* ed. H. Potter, 95–114. Lanham, Md.: Lexington Books.

Turcotte, D., & L. Sika. (2008). Reflections on the concept of social capital. In *Southeast Asian refugees and immigrants in the mill city: Changing families, communities, institutions thirty years afterward,* ed. T-C. Pho, J. N. Gerson, & S. Cowan, 49–68. Lebanon, N.H.: University of Vermont Press.

Turner, M., R. Varghese, & Walker (2007). *Recovery, renewal, and resiliency: Gulf Coast small businesses two years later.* Chapel Hill, N.C.: Political & Economic Research Council.

Turner, T., & S. Czekalinski. (2007, September 12). Spanish network signs on Nov. 1. *Columbus Dispatch* (Ohio), 3.

Turnovsky, C. (2004). *"Making the queue": Latino day laborers in New York's street corner labor markets.* San Diego: Center for US-Mexico Studies and the Center for Comparative Immigration Studies, University of California, San Diego.

Twelvetrees, A. (2008). *Community work*. Fourth edition. Basingstoke, UK: Palgrave Macmillan.

Underwood, T., & A. Ducker. (2007). Latinos in the spotlight. http://www.rclco .com/archivepdf/Apr262007337_Latinointhespotlight.pdf (accessed May 1, 2009).

United States Census Bureau. (2006). *Hispanic-owned firms: 2002*. Washington, D.C.: U.S. Department of Commerce.

United States Census Bureau. (2008a). Hispanic heritage month. Washington, D.C.: U.S. Census Bureau.

———. (2008b, May 1). U.S. Hispanic population surpasses 45 million, now 15 percent of total. *US Census Bureau News*. Washington, D.C.: U.S. Census Bureau.

———. (2008c, August 14). An older more diverse nation by mid-century. *US Census Bureau News*. Washington, D.C.: U.S. Census Bureau.

United States Department of Agriculture. (2007). *2007 Census of Agriculture: Hispanic farmers*. Washington, D.C.: U.S. Department of Agriculture.

United States Department of Commerce. (2000). *Minority purchasing power: 2000 to 2045*. Washington, D.C.: Minority Business Development Agency.

United States Department of Labor. (1989). The effects of immigrants on the US economy and labor market. *Immigration Policy and Research*, Report 1. Washington, D.C.: U.S. Department of Labor.

U.S. Fed News. (2007, May 22). Sen. Kerry issues statement on minority entrepreneurship hearing. http://web.lexis-nexis.com (accessed June 14, 2007).

United States Hispanic Chamber of Commerce. (2007). Statistics: Business and Entrepreneurship. http://www.ushcc.com/res-statistics.html (accessed April 15, 2007).

United States Hispanic Leadership. (2004). *Almanac of Latino politics*. Chicago: U.S. Hispanic Leadership.

United Way of Greater Los Angeles. (2003). *Latino scorecard 2003: Grading the American dream*. Los Angeles: United Way of Greater Los Angeles.

Uriarte, M. (2006). Growing into power in Rhode Island. In Torres 2006, 103–24.

Vaca, N. C. (2004). *The presumed alliance: The unspoken conflict between Latinos and Blacks and what it means for America*. New York: Harper Collins.

Valdes, I. (2008). *Hispanic customers for life: A fresh look at acculturation*. Ithaca: Paramount Market Publishing.

Valdez, Z. (2008). Latino/a entrepreneurship in the United States: A strategy of survival and economic mobility. In Rodriguez, Saenz, & Menjivar 2008, 168–80.

Valentine, B. E. (2005). *Uniting two cultures: Latino immigrants in the Wisconsin dairy industry*. San Diego: Center for Comparative Immigration Studies, University of California, San Diego.

Valenzuela, Jr., A. (2006). Economic development in Latino communities: Incorporating marginal and immigrant workers. In *Jobs and economic development in minority communities*, ed. M. Ong & A. Loukaitou-Sideris, 142–58. Philadelphia: Temple University Press.

Vallejo, J. A., & J. Lee. (2009). Brown picket fences. *Ethnicities* 9:5–31.

Varsany, N. W. (2008). Immigration policing through the backdoor: City ordinances, the "right to the city," and the exclusion of undocumented day laborers. *Urban Geography* 29:29–52.

Vasquez, M. A., C. E. Seales, & M. F. Marquardt. (2008). New Latino destinations. In Rodriguez, Saenz, & Menjivar 2008, 19–35.

Vaznis, J. (2009, April 19). City schools challenged by shifting ethnic mix. *Boston Globe*, A1, A18.

Vazquez, L. (2007). Bienvenidos. *Latinos and Planning Newsletter* 1:1–2.

Venkatesh, S. A. (2006). *Off the books: The underground economy of the urban poor*. Cambridge: Harvard University Press.

Verdaguer, M. (2009). *Class, ethnicity, gender and Latino entrepreneurship*. New York: Routledge.

Veronis, L. (2005). The Canadian Hispanic Day Parade, or how Latin America immigrants practice (sub) urban citizenship in Toronto. *Environment and Planning*, 38:1653–1671.

Vidal de Haymes, M., & K. M. Kilty. (2007). Latino population growth, characteristics and settlement trends. *Journal of Social Work Education* 43:101–16.

Viladrich, A. (2006). Botanicas in America's backyard: Uncovering the world of Latino healers' herb-healing practices in New York City. *Human Organization* 65:207–19.

Villa, R. H. (2000). *Barrio logos: Space and place in urban Chicano literature and culture*. Austin: University of Texas Press.

Vogel, R. (2006). Hardtimes: Undocumented workers and the U.S. informal economy. *Monthly Review*. http://www.monthlyreview.org/0706vogel.htm (accessed May 6, 2009).

Wahl, A. M. G. (2007). Southern (dis)comfort?: Latino population growth, economic integration and spatial assimilation in North Carolina micropolitian areas. *Sociation Today* 5:1–7.

Waldinger, R. (1984). Immigrant enterprises in the New York garment industry. *Social Problems* 32:60–71.

———. (2000). *Still the promised city? African-Americans and new immigrants in postindustrial New York*. Cambridge: Harvard University Press.

Waldinger, R., H. Aldrich, R. Ward, et al. (1990). *Ethnic entrepreneurs: Immigrant business in industrial societies*. Newbury Park, Calif.: Sage.

Walker, E., & A. Brown. (2004). What success factors are important to small business owners? *International Small Business Journal* 22:577–94.

Wang, Q., & W. Li. (2007). Entrepreneurship, ethnicity and local contexts: Hispanic entrepreneurs in three southern metropolitan areas. *GeoJournal* 68:167–82.

Warner, R., & J. Mandiberg. (2006). An update on affirmative businesses or social firms for people with mental illness. *Psychiatric Services* 57:1488–92.

Watanabe, T. (2008, January 9). Asian Americans form chamber of commerce. *Los Angeles Times*, 6.

Waters, M. C., & T. R. Jimenez. (2005). Assessing immigrant assimilation: New empirical and theoretical challenges. *Annual Review of Sociology* 31:105–25.

Waterson, A. (2008). Are Latinos becoming "white" folk? and what that still says about race in America. *Transforming Anthropology* 14:133–50.

Watson, A. (2005). Hispanic population and business trends in the Fifth District. *Marketwise Community Economic Development Magazine*2:16–19.

Wayne, T. (2009, May 4). The Hispanic audience grows online. *New York Times*, 3.

Weber, C. M. (2001). Latino street vendors in Los Angeles: Heterogeneous alliances, community-based activism, and the state. In Lopez-Garza & Diaz 2001, 217–40.

Weller, C. E. (2009). Credit access, the costs of credit and credit market discrimination. *Review of Black Political Economy* 36:7–28.

Westlund, H., & E. Nilsson. (2005). Measuring enterprises' investments in social capital: A pilot study. *Regional Studies* 39, 8:1079–94.

Wheary, J. (2006). *African Americans and Latinos and economic opportunity in the 21st century.* New York: Demos: A Network for Ideas and Action.

Whitehead, J., D. Landes, & J. G. Nembhard. (2005). Inner-city economic development and revitalization: A community-building approach. In Conrad et al. 2005, 341–56.

Wildflower Institute. (2003). *Cultural assets for Latino community building in East Palo Alto.* San Francisco: Wildflower Institute.

Wiklund, J., H. Patzelt, & D. A. Shepherd. (2009). Building an integrative model of small business growth. *Small Business Economics* 32:351–74.

Will, J. A., S. C. Cobb, & T. J. Cheney. (2008). Florida's changing rainbow: Identifying emerging markets through examination of racial composition and demographic change in Florida. *Population Research and Policy Review* 27:497–514.

Williams, C. C., J. Round, & P. Rodgers (2007). Beyond the formal/informal economy binary hierarchy. *International Journal of Social Economics* 34:402–14.

Williams, K., & C. Kang. (2006, March 22). The Latino small-business boom: Economy, demographics make surge even more pronounced here. *Washingtonpost.com*. http://www.washingtonpost.com (accessed April 14, 2007).

Willigen, J. van. (2005). Community assets and the community-building process. In *Community building in the twenty-first century*, ed. S. E. Hyland, 25–44. Santa Fe: School of American Research Press.

Winders, J. (2005). Changing politics of race and region: Latino migration to the US South. *Progress in Human Geography* 29:683–99.

———. (2008). An "incomplete picture? Race, Latino migration, and urban politics in Nashville, Tennessee. *Urban Geography* 29, 3:246–63.

Wingett, Y. (2006, November 1). Funeral homes tailoring services to Hispanics. *Arizona Republic*, 2.

Withers, L. (2008, October 19). Latino shoppers see a retail explosion. *North Carolina Piedmont Triad*, 1.

Wolf, K. L. (2005). Business district streetscapes, trees, and consumer response. *Journal of Forestry* 103:396–400.

Wood, D. B. (2008, December 9). East L.A., Latino heartland, revives its dream of cityhood. *Christian Science Monitor*, 1.

Woodward. D. (2006). *Mexican immigrants: The new face of the South Carolina labor force.* Columbia: University of South Carolina.

World Bank. (2008). *Local economic development.* Washington, D.C.: World Bank. http://web.worldbank.org (accessed April 7, 2008).

Wozniacka, G. (2009, August 20). Hispanic news: Helping Hispanics prosper. *Adelante Empresas*, 1–3.

Yago, G., B. Zeidman, & A. Abuyuan. (2007). A history of emerging domestic markets. *Community Development Review.* Federal Reserve Bank of San Francisco.

Yamamoto, S. (2006, August 10). Legitimizing informal economy: The role of intermediary in the case of Latino day laborers. Paper presented at the annual meeting of the Sociology Association of America, Montreal.

Yoder, M. S., & R. LaPerriere de Gutierrez. (2004). Social geography of Lorado, Texas, neighborhoods: Distinctiveness and diversity in a majority-Hispanic place. In Arreola 2004, 55–76.

Yoon, I-J. (1997). *On my own: Korean businesses and race relations in America.* Chicago: University of Chicago Press.

Young, R. D. (2005). *The growing Hispanic population in South Carolina: Trends and issues.* Columbia: University of South Carolina.

Yu, E-Y., Choe, S. Han, & K. Yu. (2004). Emerging diversity: Los Angeles' Koreatown, 1990–2000. *Amerasia Journal* 30:25–52.

Zabin, C., & L. E. Rabadan. (1998). *Mexican hometown associations and Mexican immigrant political empowerment in Los Angeles.* Washington, D.C.: Aspen Institute.

Zahra, S. A., E. Gedajlovic, D. O. Neubaum, & J. M. Shulman. (2009). A typology of social entrepreneurs: Motives, search process and ethical challenges. *Journal of Business Venturing* 24:519–32.

Zarrugh, L. H. (2007). From workers to owners: Latino entrepreneurs in Harrisonburg, Virginia. *Human Organization* 66:240–48.

Zavis, A., & C. Knoll. (2009, April 1). A spicy turf battle in Koreatown; campaign for a "Little Bangladesh" angers residents who say they have worked to create a cultural destination. *Los Angeles Times*, A8.

Zentgraf, K. M. (2001). Through economic restructuring, recession, and rebound: The continuing importance of Latina immigrant labor in the Los Angeles economy. In *Asian and Latino immigrants in a restructuring economy: The metamorphosis of Southern California*, ed. M. Lopez-Garza & D. R. Diaz, 46–74. Palo Alto: Stanford University Press.

Zhou, M. (2007). Revisiting ethnic entrepreneurship: Convergencies, controversies, and conceptual advances. In *Rethinking migration: New theoretical and empirical perspectives*, ed. A. Portes & J. DeWind, 219–56. New York: Berghahn Books.

———. (2008). The significance of ethnicity in immigrant enterprise. *Sociological Forum* 21:505–10.

Zhou, M., J. Lee, R. Tafoya-Estrada, & Y. S. Xiong. (2008). Success attained, deterred, and denied: Divergent pathways to social mobility in Los Angeles's new second generation. *Annals of the American Academy of Political and Social Science* 620:37–61.

Zlolniski, C. (2008). *Janitors, street vendors, and activists: The lives of Mexican immigrants in Silicon Valley*. Berkeley: University of California Press.

Zuniga, V., & R. Hernandez-Leon. (2005). *New destinations: Mexican immigrants in the United States.* New York: Russell Sage Foundation.

INDEX

acculturation: definitions of, 131–132; targeting markets based on levels of, 132

advertising, targeting Latinos, 133

affluence, and Latino culture, 128

African Americans, 66; business ownership of, 67; churches of, 7; income gap of, 124; Koreans and, 84; and Latino population increase, 32; in Los Angeles, 55; middle-class, 126–127; purchasing power of, 66; small businesses of, 80

agriculture sector, Latino small businesses in, 108–110

Alberto, D., 75

alcohol use, in low-income communities, 67

Aldrich, H. E., 185

Alonso, G., 140

Alonso, R., 120

Alstatt, K. E., 17

Alvarez, A. M., 113

Amigo's Deli and Groceries, 107–108

Amoruso, C., 83

analytical frameworks, asset- and needs-focused, 156

apparel retailing, 134

Arizona: Latino population in, 40; Latino population predictions for, 53

Arkansas, Latino population in, 47

Armington, M. M., 24, 71, 73

art, informal, 138

Asian Americans, 66; businesses of, 79; consumer market of, 66; small businesses of, 80

Asian enclaves, small businesses in, 19

assessment stage, in community en-
    hancement, 158
asset-focused conceptual paradigm,
    145
asset perspective, 52; newcomers in,
    115, 137–138; Spanish language in,
    197
Atlanta, Georgia, 42; Plaza Fiesta
    shopping center in, 12
auto loans, 100
auto repair and parts shops, 21

banking-related services: access to,
    102, 121–122; Latino-friendly, 102
Bank of America (BOA), 121
banks: black-owned, 99; ethnic, 85;
    focusing on niche, 101; "fringe,"
    21; mainstream, 101; "minority-
    owned," 101; non-Latino, 102;
    underuse of, 100
banks and banking, Latino, 99–102
Baraya, M. R., 77
Bares, S. L., 26
Barone, M., 52
barrios, businesses in, 71. see also
    communities; neighborhoods
Barth, J. R., 66
Bates, T., 64, 72, 74, 81, 116
Bauer, R. A., 164
Baycon-Levent, T., 73
Bean, F. D., 47
Bell, S. A., 131
Benioff, R., 16
Benitez, C., 23
Berger, P. L.
Bernard, A. B., 65, 91
Bernhardt, A., 56
Bhatia, R., 11
Bhattacharya, C. B., 28
Bibb, E., 29
big box retail development, 79

big business, dominance of, 4
birth-to-death ratio, Latino, 38–39, 38
    table
Bisman, C., 151
Blackburn, R., 80
Blackford, M. G., 23
Blackstock, K., 140
Blanchard, L., 85
Bletzer, K. V., 119
Block, D., 98
Blum, A. S., 106
Blumenthal, R., 139
boards, participation on, 177–178
bodegas, 88; disappearance of, 144
Bogan, V., 74
Bolin, T., 49
Borges-Mendez, R., 43, 97
Boston, Latino businesses in, 120–121
Boston, Latino businesses in, 16–17
Boston public school system, Latinos
    in, 39
botanica business, 97
Boyle Heights, Los Angeles, Latino
    artists in, 139
branding, and satisfied customers, 173
Brettell, C. B., 17
Brody, B. W., 190
brokering role, 187
Brown, A., 168
Brown-Gort, A., 54
Bryce, H. J., 26
Budden, M. C., 77
burials, Latino, 123. See also funerals
Burns, B. W., 154
Burthey, G. C., 80
business associations, 178; develop-
    ment of, 185–186; emergence of, 81
business creation: facilitating factors
    in, 80–82; hindering factors in,
    82–88
business districts, creating Latino, 11

businesses: home-based, 71; motivation for opening, 82

businesses, informal, for marginalized groups, 68. *see also* economy, informal

business ownership, and community well-being, 125. *see also* owners

business practices, 26

Café Bustelo brand, 141

California, xii; economy of, 140–141; and health care coverage, 142; Latina-owned businesses in, 105; Latino income in, 126; Latino population in, 40, 41, 53; Latino purchasing power in, 41, 131; Latino small businesses in, 99; Mexicans in, 114

Campbell, W. S., 114

Canadian Hispanic Day Parade (CHDP), 189

capital: access to, 128; for ethnic and racial small businesses, 85–87; startup, 85–86. *see also* social capital

capitalism, civic, 29

Capoccia, V., 157

Cargo, M. D., 165

Carley, M. J., 165

Carlson, J., 139

Carvagal, M. J., 59

case studies, 180

Caskey, J., 21

Castro, Fidel, 57

Cemex, 140

Census Bureau, U.S.: on children of color, 53; predictions of, 52

Center for Community Partnerships, UCLA's, 16

Central Americans, household income of, 128. *see also specific groups*

Cerrillo, Amalia, 51

Cervantes-Rodriguez, A. M., 77

Chaganti, R., 25

Chavez, E., 128

Chavez, L. R., 49

check cashing, 121. *see also* banking-related services

Chhabra, D., 138

Chicago: Hispanic merchandising in, 34; Latino demonstrations in, 49; Latino population of, 54; Latino purchasing power of, 54; urban underworld in, 5

chicharrines, 175

child labor, in Chinese small businesses, 68

children, Latino, born in U.S., 50

Chinchilla, N. S., 56, 86, 108

Chinese Americans, small business owned by, 15. *see also* Asian Americans

Chinese small businesses, child labor in, 68

Chrisman, J. J., 136

Churchill, N. C., 91

"Churro men," 143–144

Cisneros, H., 10

cities: in Connecticut, 43; Latinization of, 194; Latino businesses in, 3, 30; Latino concentration in, 131; and Latino population growth, 39; Latino population in, 17, 18, 32; public perceptions of, 21; shift in demographic composition in, 83–84; white non-Latinos in, 46. *see also* inner cities; *specific cities*

citizens, U.S., 114

"civil rights movement," new, 48–49

class resources, and small businesses, 74

coalitions, participation in, 177–178

Cobb, C. W., 164
Coen, S. E., 120
Coetzer, A., 95
Cohen-Cruz, J., 140
Cohn, I., 20
collaboration, in community social
    work practice, 155–156
college graduates, Latino, 127
Colombians, statistics for, 36
color, communities of: economic
    and social transformation in, 16;
    ethnic banks in, 99; ethnic small
    businesses in, 72; and informal
    economy, 69; research in, 180;
    small businesses in, 67, 90, 190;
    and social work theory, 92; urban,
    67, 190
color, people of: enterprises owned by,
    65; limited employment opportuni-
    ties for, 80–81; population predic-
    tions for, 53; purchasing power
    of, 129–131; in urban informal
    economy, 6; urban migration of, 3;
    use of term, 24
committees, participation on,
    177–178
communities: defining, 10; eco-
    nomically marginalized, 8; ethnic
    enclaves, 18; expertise of, 155;
    indigenous assets of, 149–150;
    informal art of, 138–139; Latiniza-
    tion of, 119; Latinos in, 21; and role
    of small businesses, 28; and social
    responsibility, 15; urban, 10–11. see
    also color, communities of; Latino
    communities
community assets, 151 fig., 153; iden-
    tification and mobilization of, 157;
    identification of, 154; manifestation
    of, 154
community context, 196

community development: assessment
    in, 158; defining, 11; evaluation
    in, 161; health promotion in, 10;
    indicators of success of, 166–167;
    intervention in, 160–161; mapping
    in, 159; perspectives on, 134–135;
    and social work practice, 182; so-
    lidification of support in, 159–160;
    tourism in, 138–139
community development centers, 8
community economic development,
    77–80; Latino small business as-
    sociations in, 185–186; life-cycle
    perspective on, 90–92; mentorship
    for, 178–179; support for, 178–179
community enhancement, 161–162,
    163
community gardens, 13
community interventions, effective-
    ness of, 169
community mapping, 159
community service: funerals, 122–124;
    of Latino small businesses, 122
community social work, 29, 182;
    barriers to, 199; challenge for, 195;
    and community economic develop-
    ment, 77–78, 135; and Latino small
    business expansion, 191; political
    considerations of, 157; research in,
    180; values of, 150–153, 151 fig.
community social workers: and public
    space, 198–199; role of, 200
community social work practice, 147;
    analytical framework for, 156; goals
    of, 183; in Latino economic devel-
    opment, 180
community social work practitioners,
    role of, 182
community social work support:
    "going green," 185; technology,
    183–185

community well-being, 151 *fig.*, 152–153

computers, 184

connectedness, transnational, 176–177

Connecticut, Puerto Ricans in, 42–43

construction sector: Latino small businesses in, 105; women-owned firms in, 105

consumer market, American, Latinos in, 46

Conte, C., 4

Cooke, D. K., 66

Corburn, J., 11

Cordero-Guzman, H., 127, 189

corporations, social responsibility of, 14–15, 28–30

credit, in Latino small businesses, 121–122

credit cards, 100

credit constraints, 144

credit history, 100

criminal justice, small business development and, 14

cross-sector collaboration, xii

Crowder, K., 128

Cruz, A. R., 118

Cuban Americans, 58

Cuban-Chinese restaurants, 97–98

Cuban-owned firms, 75

Cubans, 113, 145; in Florida, 58; median age of, 38, 38 *table*; in Miami, 57; statistics for, 36, 37

cultural capital success, measurement of, 173–177

cultural events, sponsorship of, 173–174

cultural traits, and small businesses, 73–74

Curran, W., 112, 169

customer base, and Latino business success, 172–173

customers, Latin origin of, 173

Dalton, Georgia, Latino immigration in, 42

Danes, S. M., 68

Daniel, M., 165

Danity, W., 74

Danta, R., 96

Datel, R., 111

Davila, A., 22, 132, 140

Davis, A. E., 185

Davis, D., 42

Davis, G. F., 14

Davis, H. L., 98

Davis, M., 12

death, in Latino communities, 123. *see also* funerals

decision making: community, 135; and self-determination, 154–155

Defilippis, J., 27

de Haan, L., 6

De la Isla, J., 126

Delapa, R. M., 9

DeLeon, A., 48

Delgado, M., 20, 150, 159, 171

democracy, participatory, 154

demographic dynamism, concept of, 34

demographic profiles: Los Angeles, 54–57; Miami, 57–59; New York, 59–62

demographics: interpretation of statistics, 31; Latino, 62; and public policy, 33; and small business development, 32, 33–34

Denhart, G., 28

DePalma, A., 49

DeRienzo, H., 135

Diaz, D. R., 71

Diaz-Briquets, S., 75
Dingemans, D., 111
disasters, collections for, 174–175
discrimination, against Latinos, 59
dispersal, of Latino population, 33, 40–44, 131, 134, 174, 194
Dolnick, S., 84
domestic sector, Latino small businesses in, 105–106
Dominicans: household income of, 128; median age of, 38, 38 *table*; in New York City, 60–61; statistics for, 36, 37
Dougill, A. J., 164
Dresser, L., 106
Drever, A. I., 76
Du, S., 28
Duneier, M., 68
duration of existence, in Latino business sucess, 171
Dymski, G. A., 99

earthquakes, collections for, 174
East Boston, Latino banking in, 101
East Coast, Mexican migration to, 48
East Los Angeles, 55
economic development: cultural assets in, 138; Latino, 136–138; small businesses in, 5
economic enclave, 58
economic justice, 150
economics, ethnic, 18
economic success, measurement of, 170–171
economy: cash-only, 100; and immigration, 194; Spanish language in, 195
economy, informal, 69–71; enterprise creation nurtured in, 70–71; in Latino community, 70; of Latino community in Los Angeles, 56; La-

tinos in, 70; Latino small businesses in, 97; negative consequences of, 69–70; small businesses in, 5–6; undocumented Latinos in, 115; in urban communities of color, 5; in U.S., 69; use of term, 24–25
Ecuadoreans, statistics for, 36
Edgecomb, E. L., 24, 71, 73
education: and business success, 74; of Latino small business owners, 116
educators, social work, 182
employees, number of, and Latino business success, 172
employment: of people with histories of criminal activity, 6; and small businesses, 17
"English as official language" policy, 43
English-as-the-official-language movement, 197
entrepreneurial process, and community well-being goals, 78
entrepreneurs, 4; Latina, 116; Latino, 94; nurturing new, 111
entrepreneurship: among Hispanic Americans, 3; concept of, 5; critical elements of, 110; hybrid forms of, 110; service-learning model of, 20; social implications of, 4; use of term, 23
"enviroclub," 185
environment, and small business survival, 112
Erick, P. C., 68
Escobar, L. M., 77
Estabrook, M., 6
Estrada, W. D., 12
ethnic, use of term, 24
ethnic businesses, 25–26, 72; characteristics of, 64; scholarly attention to, 67–69

ethnic enclaves, 18; Cuban, 58; and labor market, 75
ethnic groups, tension within, 87–88
Ethnic Inventory (EI) Index, 79
ethnicity, of Latino small business owners, 113–114
ethnic small businesses: class resources for, 74; and cultural traits, 73–74; importance of, 68; and labor market discrimination, 73; life-cycle developmental perspective on, 90–92; ownership of, 72; structural opportunities for, 75–77; theories on, 71–73
ethnoscapes, 139
European Americans, 66
evaluation, in community enhancement, 161
evidence-based practice, 169; and Latino small businesses, 196

Fainstein, S. S., 139
Fairlie, R. W., 65, 74, 78, 115
Falcon, Angelo, 114
family: budgets of, 144; impact of poor working conditions on, 70
family businesses, and ethnic collectivism, 69
family social capital theory, 69
Farhat, R., 179
Farmers Incubator Project, 186
farmers markets, 10, 108
farming, urban, 108
farms: Latino-owned, 110; small, 109
Farr, G. E., 186
federal government, large scale intervention of, 66
Fennelly, K., 48
Ferguson, K. M., 7
festivals, Latino, 111, 139, 188–189

financial advice, 86, 128
financial services, for Latino small businesses, 121–122
Fischer, M. J., 40
Fisher, R., 27
Florida: Cuban community of, 16; Cubans in, 114; Latina-owned businesses in, 105; Latino income in, 126; Latino purchasing power in, 41, 131; Mexicans in, 48; Puerto Ricans in, 114
Foner, N., 60
food, Latino, 175, 176
Food Lion, 133–134
food-related sector, Latino small businesses in, 106–108
food takeout delivery workers, 25
foster parents, 179
Fraser, E. D. G., 164, 167
Fried, B., 79
"fringe banking," 21
Fulfrost, B., 9
funeral homes, Latino-owned, 124
funerals: collections for, 174–175; in Latino communities, 122–124; and Latino small businesses, 17
Furuseth, O. J., 42, 98

Gabel, J. R., 142
Galbraith, C. S., 18
Galperin, B. L., 16
Gamboa, E., 7
Garcia, J. A., 18, 35
Garcia, J. L., 110
Garcia, O., 197
Garcia, V., 110
garment sector, Latino small businesses in, 108
Gates, G. J., 27, 40
Gawgy, K., 137

Gay, C., 83
gender: bias, 117; of Latino small business owners, 117–118
General Motors, 134
general stores, in Old West, 15. *See also* bodegas
gentrification, 140
Georgarakos, D., 17, 112
Georgia: Latinos in, 130; Mexicans in, 48
Getz, D., 139
ghetto firms, 65
Ghorm, K., 80
globalization, 135; and Spanish language, 195
Glynn, M. A., 14
Goldman Sachs, 133
Googins, B., 157
governmental programs, for business development, 137
green card, 114
Greene, P. C., 25
Greve, A., 18
Grey, M. A., 20
grocery stores: in community development, 9, 10; and social capital, 6. *See also* bodegas
Grossman, L. P., 94, 125
Gruidl, J., 77
Grupo Bimbo, 140
Guatemalans, statistics for, 36

Hackett, S. M., 69
Hagerty, M., 164, 166
Halkias, D., 75
Halter, M., 188
Hamilton, N., 56, 86, 108
Hammel, L., 28
Hanchett, Tom, 121
Hanson, S., 112

Hardcastle, D. A., 156
Harris, I. C., 68
Harris County, Texas, Latino small businesses in, 103
hate crimes, against Latinos, 88
Hayes-Bautista, D. E., 55
health care businesses, informal, 97
health insurance: brokering, 187; coverage, 141–143
health promotion, and role of small business, 9, 10
Heene, A., 15
helping professions, 7
Hernandez, S. A., 20
Hernandez-Leon, R., 47
Herron, L., 66
Hiemstra, N., 43
Hirschman, C., 31
Hispanic Federation, 122
Hispanics: business ownership of, 67; country origins of, 37 *table*; definition of, 35; household income of U.S.-born, 128; median age of, 38, 38 *table*; as nation's largest minority, 31–32
Hispanic Scholarship Foundation, 127
"Hispanic," use of term, 22–23
Hohn, M., 137
"holdout" type of small business, 89
Holguin, J., 7
Holyoke, Massachusetts, 176, 179; mural-painting enterprise in, 161
hometown associations, Mexican, 185
Hondagnu-Stelo, P., 110
Hondurans, statistics for, 36
households, Latino: purchasing power of, 129–130; wealth of, 125
Houston, Texas, Hispanic merchandising in, 34
Howard, P. H., 9

Hoy, F., 7
Huck, P., 85
Hudson, M., 67
Huerta, A., 104
Hum, T., 73
human capital: and business success, 74; and Latino small businesses, 116. *See also* social capital
Humm-Delgado, D., 159
Huppe, F., 185
hurricanes, collections for, 174
Hutchinson, B. O., 66
Hy-Vee grocery chain, 10

Iber, J., 48
Idaho, Latinos in, 130
identification, of Latino small businesses, 158
identity: cultural, 198; Latino, 119
Illinois, Latino purchasing power in, 41
immigrants: business ownership of, 78; demonization of, 50
immigrants, undocumented, 22. *See also* undocumented residents
immigration: influences on, 52; Latino, 34–35; Mexican, 44
immigration reform, demonstrations for, 1
"imperialist" type of small business, 89
Inagarni, S., 10
income, Latino, 124–129
indicators, building social, 163–164. *See also* social indicators
"indigenous" type of small business, 90
"informal knowledge," 155
information, connecting Latino businesses to, 187–188
information technology, 184
Inglessis, M., 132

inner cities: small businesses in, 4; U.S., 149
insurance industry, and Latino market, 142–143
interethnic tensions, and safety concerns, 83–85
Internet, Latinos on, 184
internships, 190
interracial tensions, and safety concerns, 83–85
intervention: in community enhancement, 160–161
Iowa, Latino businesses in, 130
Irazabal, C., 179
Iron Triangle, New York, 21
Irwin, M., 28
Isabela Project, 86
Islam, N., 7

Jackson, W. E., 72
janitorial services, 104
Jenkins, H., 14
Jennings, J., 97
Johnson, J. H., 72, 80
Johnston, D. F., 165
Johnstone, H., 28
joint ventures, 9
Jolly, L., 134
Jones, N., 5
Jones, R. C., 33
Jones, T., 73

Kaiser Family Foundation study, 142
Kasinitz, P., 45
Kauffman, N., 157
Kay, A., 7
Kaye-Blake, W., 167
Kerry, Sen. John, 86
Kilgannon, C., 21
Kim, H-Y., 134

Kim, Y-K., 134
Kirkpatrick, L. O., 135
Klass, G., 165, 166
Koberg, C., 117
Koehler, G., 41
Koehler-Jones, V., 41
Kollinger, P., 74
Koreans, and African Americans, 84
Koreatown, Los Angeles, 19, 76
Korr,W. S., 169
Korzenny, F., 132
Krauss, C., 140

labor market, and small businesses, 73
landscape companies, Latino-owned, 109
Langer, W., 188
Latina entrepreneurs, 116
Latin American businesses, in U. S., 140–141
Latinas, 96; challenges faced by, 118; in domestic service, 106; in garment sector, 108; in small business arena, 117–118
Latinidad, 98, 188
Latinization: defined, 22; of Miami, 57; of neighborhoods, 175–176; of United States, 196–197
Latino communities: age of, 37–38, 37 *table,* 38 *table*; birth-to-death ratio for, 38–39, 38 *table*; defining, 35–36; dispersal and concentration of, 46–48; economic side of life in, 144; informal economy in, 70; and national attention, 94; newcomers *vs.* native-born in, 17; and population increases, 44–46; population predictions for, 53; and small businesses, 14–22; transnational nature of, 176; ur-

ban, 29; in U.S., 44; youthfulness of, 39–40, 52
Latino economic development, and community social work practice, 180
Latino entrepreneurs, and social capital, 68
Latino Farmers Cooperative of Louisiana, 186
Latino Foundation (San Francisco), 86
Latino groups: differences between, 36; dispersal of, 47; undercounted by U.S. Census, 61; undocumented, 48–51
Latino Issue Forum, California, 142
Latino Plaza, 11–12
Latino population, increase in, 19
Latino residential patterns, 47
Latinos, 66; acculturation of, 131–132; adult market, 134; in business world, 93; concentration of, 131; consumer market of, 66; crime targeting, 88; definition of, 35; dispersal of, 33, 40–44, 131, 134, 194; economic empowerment of, 93; economic status of, 124; high-income, 127–129; life expectancy of, 130; marketing to, 132–134; media coverage of, 36; in Miami, 57; native-born, 17; and politics, 126; population growth of, 17, 18, 39, 45; population predictions for, 52–53; preference for walking of, 12; projected increases for, 51–53; purchasing power of, 40; second-generation, 45–46; transnational identity of, 111; undocumented, 49 (*see also* undocumented residents); urban, 194–195; in U.S. population, 14; use of term, 22–23, xiii

Latinos, undocumented: and economic crisis in 2008, 50; local efforts addressing, 115; scapegoating, 197. *see also* undocumented residents

Latino small business development, fostering, 199–200

Latino small businesses, 80, 94–99; accurate census of, 95; in agriculture sector, 108–110; categories of, 103–104; characteristics of, 102–104; as civic organizations, 29; community roles of, 122–124, 168; compared with African American businesses, 14; in construction sector, 105; development of, 8–9, 149; diversity of, 96; in domestic sector, 105–106; dynamic nature of, 98; economic impact of, 96; employees of, 95; failure rate of, 92; in food-related sector, 106–108; forced closure of, 198; in garment sector, 108; growth of, 95; increase in, 19–20; Latina-owned, 105, 117; and Latino identity, 98–99; life cycle of, 91–92; location of, 98, 103; motivation for, 21; naming process with, 118–119, 176; in New York City, 61–62; in post-Katrina New Orleans, 76–77; role for social work in, xiv; role in community, 30, xii; and role of *servidor,* 194; in service sector, 104–105; serving undocumented residents, 51; social indicators for success of, 163; as source of community leaders, 95; success indicators for, 167–169, 170 *fig.*; survival rates of, 112, 171; as topic of story, xi; women-owned, 96

Lavin, M., 10

Lawrence, Massachusetts: Latinization of, 97; Latino banking in, 101

Le, C. N., 72, 77, 83

Leach, M. A., 47

Lee, J., 132

Lee, Y., 76

legal advice, 86

Legalized Population Survey, 115

legal services, 188

legal status, of Latino small businesses owners, 114–116

lenders, discrimination of, 85

Lepoutre, J., 15

lesbian, gay, and bisexual community, Latino, 40

Levitt, P., 16

Lewis, V. L., 91

libraries, and small business development, 9

life-cycle developmental perspective, 90–92

Lionais, D., 28

Little Havana, 59

livelihoods, construct of, 7

local economic development (LED), purpose of, 7–8

"local knowledge," 155

Lofstrom, M., 14, 70, 116

Lopez, Bartolo, 115

Lopez-Garza, M., 56, 70

Los Angeles: Asian Americans in, 19; demographic profile for, 55; economic restructuring in, 77; historical demographic overview for, 54–55; Latino demonstrations in, 49; Latino purchasing power of, 54; Latino small businesses in, 103; Olvera Street Mexican marketplace in, 12; projected trends for, 56–57; riots of 1992, 83; small business profile in, 55–56; small contracting shops in, 108

Los Angeles, East, 55
Low, S. M., 11
Loza, J., 135

Ma, C., 10
magazines, Spanish-language editions of, 133
Maine, Latino population in, 43
Mandiberg, J., 27
mapping, of community assets, 159
Marcelo, 87
Marcias, A., 98
marginalized subgroups, in ethnic enclaves, 18
marketing, to Latinos, 132–134
market niche, and business creation, 81–82
Markley, D. M., 77
Marks, E., 165
Marquis, C., 14
Marske, S. L., 12
Marte, A. C. B., 74
Martin, P., 43
Martinelli, A., 179
Martinez, J., 110
Mason, L., 197
Massachusetts: Brazilian small businesses in, 74; Latino small businesses in, 103
Massey, D. S., 131
Masurel, E., 73
Matasar, A. B., 101
McClain, D., 84
McConnell, E. D., 47
McDonald, M. E., 164
McGavock, H., 132
McQueen, K., 154
McQueen,K., 190
McQuillan, J., 17
McTaggart, J., 33

media: Hispanic, 184; public opinion shaped by, 33
media coverage, of Hispanics, 36
Melendez, E., 9
mentoring programs, 190
mentorship, 178–179
Menzies, T. V., 79
"merchants of misery," 67
Mersha, T., 66
metropolitan areas: Chicago, 54; Latino population growth in, 45
Mexican Americans, in Los Angeles, 55
Mexican hometown associations, 185
Mexicans, 113, 145; destinations for, 47–48; household income of, 128; median age of, 38, 38 *table*; migration of, 34; in New York City, 61; self-employment rates for, 75–76; statistics for, 36; use of term, xiii
Mexico, formal retail market of, 129
Mexico-California border, 143–144
Miami, 197; demographic profile of, 58; historical demographic overview for, 57; Latino purchasing power in, 54; Little Havana of, 19; projected trends for, 59; race riots in, 84; small businesses in, 58–59
Miami-Dade County: Latino small businesses in, 103; Nicaraguans in, 77
Michelin Tire, 134
micro enterprises: assistance programs, 23–24; critics of, 24; use of term, 23
micro-level analysis, 33
Microsoft, 185
middle class: diminishing, 28; Latino, 125–127
middleman minority model, 75

migration, reverse, 50

Minneapolis Latino Development Economic Center, 136

Minniti, M., 74

minority, use of term, 24

"minority" businesses, targeting, 187

"minority-majority," concept of, 32

minority neighborhoods, business community of, 65

"minority-owned" businesses, category of, 20

Mirabal, N. R., 169

Mitchell, F., 39, 46

Miyares, I. M., 119

Model, S., 73

Mollenkopf, J. H., 45

Moller, V., 164, 166

"mom and pop" stores, 88–89

money laundering, effects on community of, 84–85

Montemayor, R., 132

Montero-Sieburth, M., 9, xiii

Monti, D. J., 29

Moore, L. V., 9

Mora, M., 75

Moreno, D., 58

Moreno, M. J., 139

Morrison, A., 130

mortgage loans, 100

murals, culturally influenced, 11

Museo Alameda, 139

music, Latino, 98

Myers, A., 34

Myers, D., 124

nail salons, 25

naming, Latino small business, 118–119, 176

Native Americans, small businesses of, 80

neighborhoods: beautification of, 175–176; immigrant, 111; Latinization of, 11, 175–176; low-income

Nelson, L., 43

networks, social, 177

Nevada: anti-immigrant climate of, 43; Latino population in, 40; Latino small businesses in, 103

newcomers, Latino: perspective on, 124; in self-employment, 65; and small businesses, 110–112

New England, and Latino migration, 42–43

"New Generation Latinos," 130

New Hampshire, Latino population in, 43

Newman, C. M., 20

New Mexico, Latino population in, 40

New Orleans: group tensions in, 87; Latinos in post-Katrina, 76–77; racialization of Latinos in post-Katrina, 36

New South, Latinization of, 42

New York: Hispanic merchandising in, 34; historical demographic overview for, 59–60; Latina-owned businesses in, 105; Latino businesses in, 103, 144; Latino income in, 126; Latino purchasing power in, 41, 54, 131; Mexicans in, 48; projected trends for, 62

New York City: demographic profile for, 60–61; group tensions in, 87–88; Latino demonstrations in, 49; Latino small businesses in, 103; restaurant industry of, 49; small businesses in, 61–62

Nicaraguans, in Miami-Dade County, 77

Niemi, G. J., 164

Nijkamp, P., 73
Nilsson, E., 7
nonprofit organizations, 26; in Latino small business development, 8
North Carolina: Latino businesses in, 112; Latinos in, 130
Nowak, J., 11, 67, 136, 138

Oberle, A., 15, 32
Oh, J-H., 75, 76
Ohmer, M.L., 169
"one-person operations," 142
operational success, measurement of, 170–171
oppression, and Latino small businesses, 194
oral health initiative, 28
Oregon, forest contracts in, 110
Orfield, M., 48
Ormachea, P., 188
Outgoing Rotation Group Files, 115
owners, Latino business: identifying potential, 190; Latin origin of, 173; and planning, 183; profile of, 113–118; and technological innovation, 184

Pacific Islanders, small businesses of, 80
Pages, E. R., 111, 137
Pamaffy, T., 115
paradigms: analytical-interactional dimension of, 157; capacity enhancements as, 162; developmental-stage perspective for, 157–161; mixed-method, 161; urban community-enhancement, 157–161
Park, K., 76, 83
partnerships, 9; collaborative, xii
Passel, J. S., 46

Pastor, M., Jr., 73
Pavelka, D. D., 101
pawnshops, 21
Pennsylvania, Latino businesses in, 130
Peredo, A. M., 136
Perez, D., 128
Perry, M., 95
personalization of customer, 120–121
Peruvians, 36, 103
Peterson, M. F., 16
Pethokoukis, J., 134
Pew Hispanic Center, 35, 47
Philadelphia: Latino groups in, 48; Spanish Merchant Association, 186
Phillips, R., 138
Phoenix, Latino community in, 32
Pickreign, J. D., 142
Pinal, J. Del., 52
Pittman, R. H., 90
place, sense of, 99
plaza: importance of, 13; in Latino culture, 11–12
politics, of evidence-based practice, 196
the poor, demonization of, 50
population growth: Hispanic, 45; Latino, 39; of Latino communities, 130
population size, determination of, 45
Pothukuchi, K., 9
Power, P. R., 156
Powers, J. C., 139
practice. see social work practice
Precita Eyes Mural Arts Center, 139
presidential campaign, 2008, 3, 4
Prieto, Y., 57
Proctor and Gamble, 133
profile statistics, 103

profitability, and Latino business sucess, 171–172
Progresso Latino social service agency, 8
Progresso Latino (social service agency), 8
"Project Salsa," 9
psychological capital, 29
public art, 13. *see also* murals
public markets, 16, 79
public spaces, 29; creating, 198–199
Puerto Ricans, 113, 145; in Florida, 58; household income of, 128; median age of, 38, 38 *table*; in New York City, 60, 88; statistics for, 36
Puerto Rico Business and Community Exchange program, 141
purchasing power, Latino, 20, 129–131
Purdum, T. S., 40–41
Puryear, A. N., 73
Putnam, R. D., 79

quinceañeras, 144
Qureshi, S., 184

Rabadan, L. E., 185
"race baiting," 22
racial, use of term, 24
racial groups, tension within, 87–88
racial small businesses, 25–26, 64; class resources for, 74; cultural traits and, 73–74; and labor market discrimination, 73; life-cycle developmental perspective on, 90–92; structural opportunities for, 75–77; theories on, 71–73
racism, and credit resources, 85
Raijman, R., 95
Raja, S., 10
Ram, M., 73, 80

Ramirez, H., 110
Ramirez, V. M., 129
Ramos, C., 40
Rath, J., 139
Ready, T., 54
recession, national, 40; and Latino small businesses, 143
Reed, M. S., 164
Reimers, C., 128
Reinecke, G., 23
religious associations, 74
Renzulli, L. A., 185
research: need for, 179–180; in support of Latino small businesses, 189–190
residency: length of, 103; stability, 171; status, 115
Reyes, Luis, 107
Reyes-Ruiz, R., 98
Rhode Island, 8; Latino small business association in, 16
Ricort, M., 96
Rinehart, R. D., 69
risk taking, 110–111
Rixford, C., 164
Robb, A., 81
Robb, A. M., 74
Roberson, P., 20
Roberts, R. T., 90
Roberts, R. W., 156
Roberts, S., 60
Robles, B. J., 8, 125, 127, 189
Rodgers, P., 70
Rodriguez, C. L., 18
Rodriguez, G., 93
Rodriguez, P., 69
Rojas, J., 12
role models, and business creation, 81
Romero, M., 106
Roquebert, J., 16
Rosales, G. A., 56

Ross, N. A., 120
Round, J., 70
Roux, A. A. D., 9
Rueda, L., 86
Rumbaut, R. G., 35
rural areas, Latino population growth in, 45
Ryoo, H-K., 84

safety concerns, and business creation, 83–85
Salaff, C. W., 76
Salaff, J. W., 18
Salazar, Y., 117, 118
Salcido, R. M., 182
Salinas, California, group tensions in, 87
Salvadorans, 103; median age of, 38, 38 *table*; statistics for, 36, 37
San Antonio, Texas, Latino immigrant residential patterns in, 33
Sanchez-Jankowski, M., 88–90
Sanchez-Korroll, V. E., 16
San Diego, Latino market in, 131
San Francisco, Latino purchasing power of, 54
Santiago, J., 97
Sarason, Y., 117
Saunders, C., 167
scholarship, Latino-focused, 179–180
scholarships, collections for, 174–175
second generation, rise of, 46
segregation, regional, 46
Seifert, S. C., 138
self-determination, 151–152, 151 *fig.*, 154–155
self-employment, 183; in communities of color, 71; individuals choosing, 72; Mexican, 75–76; use of term, 23

self-employment rate, among Latinos, 5
self-knowledge", 155
"Semana Laina," 174
Sen, S., 28
Senate Small Business and Entrepreneurship Committee, U.S., 86
service economy, in southern states, 42
service sector, Latino small businesses in, 104–105
service to community, of Latino small businesses, 122
Sharkova, I., 28
Shragge, E., 27
signs, Latino business, 119
Sika, L., 6
Silicon Valley, street vendors in, 71
Siqueira, A. C. O., 74
Siu, L. C. D., 97
Skelly, A. H., 119
Skop, E., 57
Slaughter, M. J., 65, 91
Small Business Administration, 9
small business development: and community assets, 150; role of, 78; sociocultural factors in, 93–94
small businesses, 65; as center of Latino universe, 197–198; as civic associations, 29; demographics of, 31; economic importance of, 4; ethnic, 24; Korean-owned, 83; Latino community and, 14–22; Latino-owned, 67; and population size, 64; racial, 24; role in communities of, 28; in service sector, 104; and social responsibility, 15; social work and, 6–10; study of, 15, 92; tensions related to, 25–26; typology of, 88–90; use of term, 23–24, 78. *See also* big business

small business owners: and health insurance coverage, 141–143; as role models, 94–95. *See also* owners, Latino

Smith, H. A., 42

Smith, M. K., 184

Smith, R. C., 48

Smith, R. D., 20

Smith, S. K., 51

Smith-Hunter, A. E., 105, 117

SMSAs, minority communities of, 64–65

social brokers, 29

social capital, 170 *fig.,* 177–179; construct of, 29; and farm ownership, 109; in informal economy, 6; language of, 6; of Latino community, 189; and small businesses, 26

social change, 27

social firm movement, 27

social indicators: building, 163–164; community development of success, 166–167; critique of, 165–166; defined, 164; in documentation of success, 180–181; Latino small businesses as, 169; principles of, 164; statistical fallacies found in, 165–166; use of, 165

social interactions, and Latino small businesses, 119–122

social justice, 150–151, 151 *fig.*

social research, 189–190

social services, cultural relevance of, 13

social work: and business sector, 26; community, 13–14, 30, xiv; redefinition of, 7; and small businesses, 6–10

social workers, bias of, 195

social work practice: business and economics in, 92; community, 5; and community assets, 151 *fig.,* 153; community well-being in, 151 *fig.,* 152–153; conflict-related tools in, 27; and Latino community events, 188–189; principles of, 153–156; self-determination in, 151–152, 151 *fig.*; small businesses in, 7; and social justice, 150–151, 151 *fig.*; targeting Latino communities in, 21; values and principles in, 149–150

social work schools, and Latino businesses, 188

Song, M., 68

Sosa, S., 132

South, S. J., 128

South Carolina: Latino businesses in, 112; Mexican immigrants in, 42; undocumented women in, 114–115

the Southeast, Latinos in, 134

Southern Hemisphere, 197

the Southwest, anti-Latino immigrant sentiments in, 43

Spanish language: as asset, 197; in economic framework, 195

Spanish Merchant Association, Philadelphia's, 186

sponsorship: of community events, 188–189; of cultural events, 173–174

sports teams, 111; support of, 175

Sriram, V., 66

stability, residential, 171

Staples, L., 150

startup costs, and business creation, 82

State Farm Insurance, 133
states: with fastest-growing Latino population, 41; with largest Latino market, 41; of New South, 42. *See also specific states*
Stephens, J., 12
stereotypes, of Latinos, 132
Stern, M. J., 138
Stiles. C. H., 18
Stone, R. T., 17
street corners, selling wares on, 68
street vendors, in Silicon Valley, 71
suburbs, Latinos in, 47
success, documentation of, 180–181
success indicators: for community development, 167–169; cultural capital, 170 *fig.*, 173–177; development of, 190; for Latino small businesses, 168, 170 *fig.*; measurement of domains for, 168–169; operational/economic, 170–173, 170 *fig.*; social capital, 170 *fig.*, 177–179
success measures, 163–164
supermarkets, departure of, 33–34
support: in community enhancement, 159–160; community social work, 183–190
Suro, R., 45, 46, 50
Swanson, D. A., 51
Sweeney, A., 95

taco trucks, 87
task forces, participation on, 177–178
TATs Cru, 97
Tatsiramos, K., 17, 112
Taylor, S. H., 156
Tayman, J., 51
technical advice, for ethnic and racial small businesses, 86–87

technical support: and business creation, 81; connecting Latino businesses to, 187–188
technology, and community social work, 184
telecommunication companies, 133
Tellez-Giron, P., 123
Tennessee, Latino small business owners in, 141
Texas: Latino income in, 126; Latino population in, 40; Latino population predictions for, 53; Latino purchasing power in, 41, 131; Mexicans in, 114
Tienda, M., 39, 40, 46
tiendas, 98, 120
tobacco, in low-income communities, 67
Torres, D. L., 113
tourism, 138–140; and Latino businesses, 58
Toussaint-Comeau, M., 18, 116
towns, small, Latino population growth in, 45
"trailblazer" type of small business, 89–90
transnational connectedness, 176–177
transnationalism, 76
Trujillo-Pagan, N., 36
Tuggle, C. S., 69
Turcotte, D., 6
Turner, S., 120

undervalued people, 182
undocumented residents, 50; contributions of, 49; geographical distribution of, 50–51; Latino small businesses serving, 51
unemployment, and small businesses, 17

United States: in global context, 63; Latin American companies in, 140; Latinization of, 196–197

universities, and Latino small businesses, 187–188

urban areas, communities of color in, 32–33

urban communities, 5; and Latino-owned businesses, 3

urban community-enhancement paradigm, stages of, 157–161

urbanism, Latino, 12–13

urban riots, 83

urban transformation, Latino-style, 10–14

Utah, Latinos in, 130

Valentine, B. E., 109

Valenzuela, A., Jr., 7, 18

Vallejo, J. A., 132

values: community assets, 151 *fig.*, 153; community well-being, 151 *fig.*, 152–153; convergence of Latino and American, 132; Latino, 55; self-determination, 151–152, 151 *fig.*; social justice, 150–151, 151 *fig.*

Venkatesh, S. A., 5

Verdaguer, M., 103

Veronis, L., 189

victimization rates, against Latino small businesses, 88

Vogel, J., 164, 166

volunteering, 179

Waldinger, R., 18

Walker, E., 168

Wang, C., 14, 70

Warner, R., 26

Washington, D.C., Latino small businesses in, 103

Waters, M. C., 45

wealth, defining, 129

wealth, Latino, 124–127; household, 127; net worth, 125; purchasing power, 129–131

Weber, C. M., 56

Weems, R. E., 99

Weiser, J., 154

Weiser, J.., 190

well-being: and community development, 13; construct of, 152; of country, 25

Wenocur, S., 156

Westlund, H., 7

White, S., 23

Williams, C. C., 70

Wingett, Y., 123

women: in self-employment, 65; undocumented Mexican, 114–115. *see also* Latinas

women of color, businesses owned by, 117

women-owned enterprises, 117

Woodruff, C., 115

workforce, Latinos in, 41

World Bank, 7

Xie, B., 7

Yadav, P., 10

Yago, G., 66

Yankee Stadium, Latino food concession stand at, 20

Ybor City neighborhood, Tampa, 16

Yinger, J., 85

York, A. S., 184

young Latinos, as national resource, 40

youthfulness, of Latino community, 20, 127

Zabin, C., 185

Zambrana, R. E., 131

Zarrugh, L. H., 19

Zeidman, B., 66

Zellman, E., 167

Zentgraf, K. M., 77

Zhao, B., 85

Zhou, M., 72

Zlolniski, C., 71, 97

Zoomers, A., 6

Zuniga, V., 47